The Future of Piagetian Theory

The Neo-Piagetians

The Future of Piagetian Theory

The Neo-Piagetians

Edited by

VALERIE L. SHULMAN

Director, Special Projects
Fordham University
New York, New York

LILLIAN C. R. RESTAINO-BAUMANN

School of Education
Fordham University
New York, New York

and

LORETTA BUTLER

School of Education
Fordham University
New York, New York

PLENUM PRESS • NEW YORK AND LONDON

Library of Congress Cataloging in Publication Data

Main entry under title:

The Future of Piagetian theory.

Includes bibliographies and index.
1. Child psychology – Philosophy. 2. Cognition in children. 3. Piaget, Jean, 1896– .
I. Shulman, Valerie L. II. Restaino-Baumann, Lillian C. R. III. Butler, Loretta. [DNLM:
1. Piaget, Jean, 1896– . 2. Child Psychology. 3. Cognition – in infancy & childhood.
4. Psychological Theory. WS 105.5.C7 F996]
BF722.F87   1985   155.4'13   85-6303
ISBN 0-306-41940-8

© 1985 Plenum Press, New York
A Division of Plenum Publishing Corporation
233 Spring Street, New York, N.Y. 10013

Printed in the United States of America

Contributors

Loretta Butler, School of Education, Fordham University, New York, New York

André Bullinger, Faculty of Psychology and the Educational Sciences, University of Geneva, Geneva, Switzerland

Harold Chipman, Faculty of Psychology and the Educational Sciences, University of Geneva, Geneva, Switzerland

Anik de Ribaupierre, Faculty of Psychology and the Educational Sciences, University of Geneva, Geneva, Switzerland

Willem Doise, Faculty of Psychology and the Educational Sciences, University of Geneva, Geneva, Switzerland

Jacques Lautrey, Laboratory of Differential Psychology, University of Paris V, Paris, France

Pierre Mounoud, Faculty of Psychology and the Educational Sciences, University of Geneva, Geneva, Switzerland

Alberto Munari, Faculty of Psychology and the Educational Sciences, University of Geneva, Geneva, Switzerland

Lillian C. R. Restaino-Baumann, School of Education, Fordham University, New York, New York

Laurence Rieben, Faculty of Psychology and the Educational Sciences, University of Geneva, Geneva, Switzerland

Elsa Schmid-Kitsikis, Faculty of Psychology and the Educational Sciences, University of Geneva, Geneva, Switzerland

Hermine Sinclair, Psycholinguistic Center, Department of Applied Genetic Psychology, University of Geneva, Geneva, Switzerland

Valerie L. Shulman, Director of Special Projects, Fordham University, New York, New York

Annie Vinter, Faculty of Psychology and the Educational Sciences, University of Geneva, Geneva, Switzerland

Foreword

Until recently, most books and articles on Piaget's theory, whether laudatory or critical, were written by psychologists or, more rarely, epistemologists, who had had no direct contact with the research that provided the basis for the theoretical constructs, nor with the ongoing work on the theory itself. These authors, who looked into the theory, so to speak, from the outside, often noted aspects that were less visible to those working "inside" the theory and in this way raised a number of important questions. However, because most of these authors were psychologists, they often overlooked the main thrust of Piaget's work, which is epistemological. Many complained about a gap between the theory and the experimental data as reported. Such criticism may be justified, at least in part, if the theory is taken to be a psychological theory. But Piaget himself always emphasized his epistemological orientation; with this in view, the methodology of the research and its links to the conceptual framework of the theory appear in a different guise. The value of a given methodology depends on its contribution to the theory for which it was designed. The gap between theory and experiment that was frequently criticized is, in fact, the gap between the psychological and the epistemic subject.

The present volume brings together a number of studies by authors who were all at the University of Geneva during Piaget's later years and who continue to work there. They are psychologists who look at Piaget's theory from the inside and who, within the theory, have found ways and means of bridging the gap. Often, such a change from the epistemic to the individual subject implies a change in methodology, and rightly so, as a different aim calls for different means. Piaget once said that he hoped this theory of knowledge had laid bare a more-or-less general skeleton, of which the main features would remain unchanged, but whose articulations might well be altered. The authors of the present volume are not concerned with changing the general outlines; they have succeeded in putting flesh on the bones and show how alive the theory is in their various fields of psychological endeavor.

HERMINE SINCLAIR

Preface

Piagetian developmental theory has gained considerable acclaim since its introduction in the United States approximately 25 years ago. During that period, it has attained the status of one of the preeminent theories guiding research and program development in education, psychology, sociology, and health care services. However, its transition from experimental, small-group settings, to practical, large-group applications has been difficult. Interest began to wane as practitioners became disenchanted with its purely theoretical, rather than practical, focus and, hence, with the difficulties involved in translating theory into practice. However, in recent years, more practical interpretations of the theory have been made because the theory itself has begun to take on new form and added dimensions, often described in terms of applications, through the efforts of the "neo-Piagetians," many of whom are included in this volume.

This book is the culmination of more than five years of collaboration between the University of Geneva and Fordham University, initiated by Alberto Munari and Loretta Butler, respectively. Several of the chapters are based on presentations made by the contributors during four international seminars (1978–1981) under the guidance of the editors.

The primary purpose of the seminars, and hence of this book, was two fold. First, it was designed for both the "Piagetian" as well as the "non-Piagetian" practitioner, scholar, or student. For the former, it merely highlights the pertinent elements addressed by the presenters, whereas for the latter, familiar with only the popularized aspects of the theory, it provides an organized theoretical overview of traditional theory. Second, building on the theoretical rationale, we had as our purpose providing insights into the *ongoing* theory development and research pursued by the Genevans, specifically in terms of potential applications in a variety of settings.

The concept on which this book has been compiled—and hence the title of the book, *The Future of Piagetian Theory: The Neo-Piagetians*—immediately suggests a distinction between "traditional Piagetian" and "neo-Piagetian" theory. However, if one accepts the concept that Piagetian theory consists of the same or similar characteristics as those inherent in knowledge (or man), then Piagetian theory is dynamic, active, and open and thus amenable to change. In other words, Piagetian theory is analogous to or isomorphic with an open system that is responsive to systemic and/or environmental changes over time. From that perspective, it would be redundant to speak in terms of "neo-Piagetian" theory. Thus, in this book, the term *neo-Piagetian* refers to the new directions that the theory has taken under those who are currently pursuing their research and theoretical development in Geneva.

The individuals who have contributed to this book are, in our opinion, representative of those who have used traditional Piagetian concepts, structures, tenets, and/or methods as a means of explaining unique aspects of development. Each has endeavored to expand the theory to include elements that had been given cursory attention or had been neglected during Piaget's more than six decades of research. Further, a large part of this volume is devoted to the explication of the Piagetian model in terms of the *individual* rather than the *epistemic* system.

Each of the principal authors included in this book is currently working in the Faculty of Psychology and the Educational Sciences at the University of Geneva, Switzerland. Although there are many other renowned scholars, in the United States as well as in other countries, who are considered among the neo-Piagetians, this book is limited to those who worked with Piaget in Geneva during his later years and who have remained at the university to continue his work.

During his tenure at the University of Geneva and the Center for Genetic Epistemology, Piaget encouraged his students and colleagues to pursue their own research interests with the epistemological framework. As director of the center, he fostered a climate that provide an opportunity to go beyond the orthodoxy of his epistemology into related areas that would enhance and enrich the overall model. Indeed, on the number of occasions, Piaget himself reevaluated elements of the theory and reinterpreted their relationships within the overall model, often going off in new directions. Thus, whereas Piaget conceptualized a global epistemological theory, providing an armature on which to build, permitting his students and colleagues to pursue their own research interests that would contribute to the explication of the larger theory, that does not appear to be the case with the neo-Piagetians. As the reader will soon discover, the neo-Piagetians have continued to pursue of their own interests, tending to expand the theory into new areas, rather than explicating areas already enunciated by the traditionalists.

As we will attempt to illustrate in this book, many neo-Piagetians have taken divergent paths: whereas some have refuted elements of the basic theory (Mounoud), others have supported it with new data (Munari, de Ribaupierre *et al.*, Chipman), still others have generated new components (Doise, Schmid-Kitsikis, and Bullinger). The resulting collection of material will, we hope, provide the reader with some insight into the dynamic character of Piagetian developmental theory as it exists today, and as it is evolving, reflective of Piaget's view of the dynamic characteristics of man and knowledge.

We thank our colleagues who have read this manuscript for their valuable suggestions and encouragement, particularly Max Pusin, M.D., and Gita Kedar-Voivodas, who diligently read and reread the material. We are grateful to Joyce Anne Shulman for having typed the entire manuscript and to Carolyn Shulman and Edward Baumann for preparing the figures for publication.

Peter Coles of the University of Geneva translated a large part of Chapter 3 (Mounoud). Valerie Shulman translated a large part of Chapter 5 (Doise).

Finally, masculine pronouns are used throughout this book for grammatical clarity and simplicity. They are not meant to be exclusionary.

VALERIE L. SHULMAN
LILLIAN C. R. RESTAINO-BAUMANN
LORETTA BUTLER

Contents

Introduction

VALERIE L. SHULMAN

The work of Jean Piaget and his colleagues has become internationally renowned as an important, comprehensive undertaking of the study of knowledge and its systematic development in man. Piaget devoted more than 60 years of his career to research on the origins, development, mechanisms, limits, and applications of knowledge. Throughout those investigations, he and his colleagues, informally referred to as the Genevan School, elaborated a theory of genetic epistemology conceived of as organized, open, and dynamic, reflective of their conceptualization of the functions of intelligent behavior.

From his orientation as a biologist, Piaget endeavored to bridge the gap from the classic historical-critical epistemologies of the era that attempted to explain a static state of knowledge to a genetic epistemology that would explain its dynamic properties, and thus its development, through scientific investigations. Piaget (1971) described the status of classic epistemologies:

> Classic theories of knowledge first asked the question "How is knowledge possible?" which soon differentiated into many problems dealing with the nature of previous conditions of logico-mathematical knowledge,

VALERIE L. SHULMAN • Director of Special Projects, Fordham University, New York, New York 10023.

experimental knowledge of the physical type, and so forth. The common
postulate of various traditional epistemologies, however, is that knowledge is a fact and not a process and that, if our various forms of knowledge
are always incomplete and our various sciences still imperfect, that which
is acquired and therefore can be studied statically. Hence the absolute
position of the problems "What is knowledge?" or "How are the various
types of knowledge possible?" (p. 1)

Certainly, that conceptualization could not lead to the uncov-
ering of the evolutionary properties of the mechanisms of knowledge
but could merely describe its current contents. The transformation
of knowledge as a static state to knowledge as a process required a
rephrasing of the question to permit an explanation of its elaboration
and, hence, the mechanisms of its development on an ongoing basis.
Piaget (1971) conjectured:

In fact, if all knowledge is always in a state of development and consists
in proceeding from one state to a more complete and efficient one, evidently it is a question of knowing this development and analyzing it
with the greatest possible accuracy. (p. 6)

Thus, Piaget formulated his problem by questioning the means
by which the human mind is capable of progressing from a state of
less sufficient knowledge to a higher state. He hypothesized that the
elaboration of knowledge is a continuing, developmental process,
rather than a static state, conceived as a progression that proceeds
in a series of stages throughout the life of the individual. He attempted
to determine how the process proceeds from one stage to the next,
becoming increasing complete, complex, and efficient. In so doing,
he undertook to study the stages of development as they occur, at
their source, in maturing children. Continuing interest in analyzing
specific details of that elaboration permitted the Geneva school to
determine various milestones of behavior, which were corroborated
in other cultures. Piaget and his colleagues are best known, perhaps,
particularly in the United States, through those investigations into
development and the analysis of the elaboration of the structures of
knowledge that are the bases of the developmental theory.

Any discussion of neo-Piagetian theory, research, or practice
is, naturally, based on comparisons with the traditional model. Thus,
in the next section, we briefly present the elements of the traditional
theory that are effected in this volume.

Elements of the Theory

Piagetian developmental theory is predicated on two functional invariant characteristics: organization and adaptation. It is based on the premise that coordinated actions, as those exhibited by human beings, cannot occur in a chaotic state. Piaget (1952) discussed the functional invariants on two levels: the epistemological (generic) and the biological (individual). This approach tends to be confusing because he referred to the *generic* as all people and the *biological* as *a* person, rather than *a specific person*. This point will become clearer as we begin to discuss the evolution of the theory.

Briefly, the concept of *organization* refers to the underlying, internal coordinations of the human system. In the epistemological sense, it refers to the unique organization within man that enables him to develop on an intellectual plane. Biologically, it refers to the human physical structure—that is, the nervous system and sensory organs, which permit the intake of sensory data—and, consequently, to the development of mental structures that are the basis of intellectual development. In other words, epistemological organization provides the function, whereas biological organization provides the structure of intellectual development.

The concept of *adaptation* refers to the adjustment of a system to its environment. Two simultaneous processes comprise the function of adaptation: assimilation and accommodation. Epistemologically, *adaptation* refers to man's unique manner of dealing with his environment through increasingly adequate processes of developmental intelligence. Biologically, the concept refers to the developing structures of intelligence, that is, the dynamic process through which the individual becomes increasingly capable of dealing with the environment.

The complementary processes of assimilation and accommodation comprise the dynamic external aspects of the adaptive function. Assimilation is the process through which the individual integrates new data into existing behavioral patterns. It is the means by which he is able to adapt to and organize the environment by altering that environmental data in such a way that he is able to incorporate it into his organizational structure. As information is assimilated, the individual simultaneously changes in response to those data, a process that is the companion of accommodation.

Accommodation requires an alteration of the current organizational structure. Either the individual modifies a current cognitive structure, or a new one is created to incorporate that information, a process that causes the development and expansion of cognitive structures. In other words, the individual reacts to environmental information on the basis of what is currently possessed or known. New data are thus altered to conform to existing structures, or new structures are formed; conversely, existing structures are altered to provide for the incorporation of new data. Thus, the human system accommodates its functioning to the environment as it alters the environmental data to that system, through the process of assimilation.

Each assimilation requires the reciprocal process of accommodation; however, in reality, the two cannot be divorced from one another. As the individual develops, through continuous interactions with the environment his responses became increasingly complex and efficient, and thus, capable of adapting to more varied situations.

The human system attempts to maintain a balance between assimmilation and accommodation. The self-regulating mechanism is referred to as *equilibrium*; the process as *equilibration*. Piaget explained that equilibration is an active process of regulating a balance between internal and external factors. Equilibration is thus a factor within the organizational function; hence, it is internal to the system. Therefore, even through the system is in constant interaction with its environment (i.e., in a constant state of flux), the mental structures within the individual are capable of achieving progressive states of equilibrium. Thus, equilibration is a process of selection, an active process of choice between and/or among alternatives within a specific field.

The primary example of the *adaptive function* in man, is the development of intelligence. Piaget and his colleagues analyzed the structures of developmental intelligence, that is, those properties that permit the development of intelligent behavior. They determined that there are four broad stages of cognitive development, which tend to emerge in a constant order. The ages at which they appear are affected by numerous variables, including heredity, motivation, experience, and culture. That evolution depends on the native endowment of the child as well as on the quality of the physical and social environment. Although traditionalists did not determine in what manner or to what extent those variables affected development; they were accepted as "givens."

Stages are hierarchical in nature. Each represents the formation of a total structure that includes its predecessors as substructures. The structures characterizing any stage represent the integration of the preceding stages, whereas achievement of each stage is the necessary preparation for successive stages. Thus, earlier structures are incorporated into later ones. The structural properties that define a particular stage are the integrating elements of the entire cognitive structure or stage.

Each stage is divided into two major segments: the period of initial awareness and the period of mastery or achievement. During the initial period, earlier structures are used regularly; newer ones that are in a process of evolution are used sporadically. As the structure is exercised, it becomes increasingly organized and stable, forming an integrated whole (Piaget, 1960).

Transition from period to period, from stage to stage, is not discrete but tends to flow along a continuum. Development is cumulative, although not linear, even though clusters of behavior appear as milestones.

Intelligence adult behavior is rooted in the earliest stage. It is during the sensorimotor period, from birth to the acquisition of language, that the structures of intelligence begin to evolve.

Each of these concepts is a necessary element of the traditional model and hence of Piagetian developmental theory. The reader will note that even when a neo-Piagetian does not agree with one of the elements, it is reconceptualized in another form, and then the new element is reintegrated into the model so that it maintains its overall integrity.

Elements of Change

As a group, the neo-Piagetians accept the basic conceptualization of the theory and, hence, the model of development, or they would not consider themselves Piagetians in the first place. However, each tends to refute selected elements of the model. In general, there are three major points that distinguish the neo-Piagetians from the traditionalists.

First, they are concerned with the individual as opposed to, or as well as, the epistemic subject. As mentioned earlier, Piaget described development in terms of the *epistemic subject*, that is, all individuals at a given level of development, or the universal subject. However, as research has indicated, when data are generalized in that manner, the extremes tend to disappear. Nevertheless, the neo-Piagetians have attempted to explicate the theory on the individual level, seeking to determine just those extremes of behavior that can be anticipated at a given period of development under defined conditions. Thus, whereas Piaget sought to define the overall system of development, the neo-Piagetians have attempted to discover the differences between and among individuals and groups at the same level of development in order to more fully describe the process of development.

Second, they are concerned with the total individual rather than solely with cognitive development. Whereas Piaget acknowledged differences in development due to heredity, culture, motivation, and experience, among other factors, he did not explore them. On the other hand, the neo-Piagetians have sought to explicate those elements as primary variables in relation to cognitive development. They have extended the theory to include interactions of the subject that go beyond the traditional interactions with knowledge, be they physical or intellectual. Specifically, the neo-Piagetians have again added the individual dimension in order to more fully understand the aggregate and, hence, the mechanisms of development. Thus, they have investigated the interactions between developing cognition and social relationships, cultural influences, personality, and selected biological factors.

Third, they have sought to relate the theory to reality, the reality of the maturing child, often suggesting appropriate applications for their research data. Further, they have attempted to create experimental settings that demand the interaction of a variety of elements. Whereas Piaget isolated one particular variable for investigation in a variety of experiences, the neo-Piagetians more often select interactive variables to investigate, an approach that tends to provide data that are more readily adapted to practical applications.

Taken together, these three points appear to reorient the overall theory. Further, they underscore the nature of Piaget's work, which was "to uncover the mechanisms of cognitive development," as well as the nature of the work of the neo-Piagetians, which in the absence of any definitive group statement may be stated as "to discern the parameters of behavior within the developmental model as well as the variables that foster or impede it."

Thus, as in Piaget's conceptualization of development (1973), it would appear that Piagetian developmental theory is "proceeding from one state to a more complete and efficient one" (p. 6). The theory has begun to reorganize, placing greater emphasis on noncognitive variables, in the strict sense, and has begun to adapt to environmental change. As a final point, it is interesting to note that the theoretical orientation of the theory has come almost full circle since Piaget began his research at the University of Geneva more than 60 years ago.

Organization of the Book

This book is organized conceptually, based on the three major points discussed earlier. It is organized in such a way as to afford a progression of concepts that reflect the traditional theory as well as the overall characteristics of the neo-Piagetians, while highlighting the specific areas of research of the contributing authors. Thus, in addition to this introduction, which sets the stage for the "development" of Piagetian developmental theory, there are three major sections. The first concerns the individual's awareness of and personal relations with the environment; the second concerns the individual in relation to the larger group (society), as well as his means of communicating within that group. The third section consists of three models for assessment and teaching within the Piagetian framework.

The first chapter, by Alberto Munari, former chairman of the Faculty of Psychology and the Educational Sciences at the University of Geneva, traces the 90-year history of this division of the university. From the perspective of a former student as well as an administrator, Munari guides us through the various "stages of development" of the famous Genevan school, from a small, intimate school to an international center. We become aware of Piaget's interest and involvement in education and of the unique working relationships between Genevans and the public school system of the Canton of Geneva.

If we are surprised to learn of Piaget's involvement in education, we are less so to learn that, in time, that interest waned and that he turned inward, devoting increased attention to the study of cognitive processes and genetic epistemology. It is interesting that the neo-Piagetians have reverted to practical applications and have again become involved in "environmental interactions."

The following three chapters present various aspects of the individual in relation to the environment. Chapter 2, by André Bullinger, "The Sensorimotor Nature of the Infant Visual System: Cognitive Problems," discusses the infant's first interactions with the environment, his first visual encounters with the external world. Bullinger states that "the eye is an instrument that allows cognitive understanding of the world"; we would hasten to add that the eye is only one of many biological tools of exploration. He speaks in terms of four elements of oculomotor activity, which, as we shall see in later chapters, are the basis for a range of activities. The four elements presented are

1. The biomechanical potentialities of the system being used
2. Its sensory potentialities
3. The properties of the object to be explored
4. The orientation imposed on, or determined by, the subject

We learn that the dynamic properties of the environment include the subject's body, and that his own functions become objects of the same systematic coordinations and interiorizations as do experiences; hence, cognition may be turned inward. Thus, Bullinger has gone beyond the actual physical to the relationships between these mechanisms and the cognitive processes of knowing and the individual.

Chapter 3, by Pierre Mounoud and Annie Vinter, "A Theoretical Developmental Model: Self-Image in Children," utilizes many of these same concepts to discuss the development of self-image. However, self-image in this case is merely one example of a variety of objects, or persons, including the subject himself. Mounoud and Vinter illustrate how environmental variables—in this instance, two distorting mirrors—affect one's perception of an object. The purpose, of course, is to note the steps and processes involved in constructing new representations of the object, the person, and so on.

Chapter 4, by Elsa Schmid-Kitsikis, "Some Epistemological Aspects of Mental Functioning," illustrates another dimension of the individual's interactions with the external world: the affective. Schmid-Kitsikis attempts to determine the role of the individual's inner world in relation to the development of his cognitive processes. Here we note that the inner world (unconscious) may be perceived as an orientation imposed on, as well as determined by, the individual from his earliest internal and external interactions. In her investigations, she seeks to determine the degree of flexibility/rigidity, fantasy/realism, and so on utilized in problem solving that reveal the dynamics of the individual's mental functioning.

The next two chapters shift from a concern for the individual in relation to his immediate environment, to a considerations of the individual in interaction with the larger environment, society. Chapter 5, by Willem Doise, "On the Social Development of the Intellect," continues to build on the concepts presented earlier. Here we see the added dimension of the social environment as a means of fostering cognitive development. In his research, Doise has demonstrated how the social milieu provides the context for interindividual exchange, within which the individual coordinates his actions with those of others, a process that, in turn, facilitates his own internal coordinations of cognitive structures.

Chapter 6, by Harold Chipman, "Aspects of Language Acquisition: Developmental Strategies," discusses the societal system of interaction: the development of language skills. Language is perceived as a highly structured system of representations dependent on intricate rules that have been established within society as well as transmitted by it. Thus, language is a system within a system, which is manipulated in response to demands imposed on and determined by the larger subject, society. However, as Chipman points out, language is dependent on cognitive development and, hence, responds to the demands imposed on the individual and determined by his inner and outer interactions with the environment.

The final section of this book consists of three chapters that, in our opinion, illustrate the neo-Piagetian concern for assessment and subsequent applications. Chapter 7, by Elsa Schmid-Kitsikis,

"Clinical Investigation and Piagetian Experimentation," presents an integrated theory of both cognitive and affective development that highlights the importance of each as well as the interaction between the two. The chapter then provides a two-phase technique, based on the theory, that is applicable to a variety of assessment settings. The information derived from the use of the technique provides insights into the ways in which the individual processes particular types of information and thus, the most appropriate means of presenting new information, including problems, in order for the individual to respond at his most effective level.

Chapter 8, "Horizontal Decalages and Individual Differences in the Development of Concrete Operations," by Anik de Ribaupierre, Laurence Rieben, and Jacques Lautrey, presents a model for the assessment of inter- and intraindividual differences, specifically in the area of horizontal decalages. These authors seek to determine the ways in which individuals process figurative and operative aspects of knowledge, postulating that there are complex relationships between the two. They provide a means of determining the ways in which individuals process difference types of information, as well as the ways in which different individuals process the same information, providing insight into the myriad means of presenting and reinforcing similar information.

In the final chapter, "The Piagetian Approach to the Scientific Method: Implications for Teaching," Alberto Munari offers a model for teaching that is based on six major elements derived from both traditional as well as neo-Piagetian theory. Among the six points, the foremost is the presentation of material within a context that permits the student to draw relationships between and among selected data. Further, Munari suggests that an array of alternative methods and materials be presented whenever possible. In addition, models and samples should be provided, as well as an opportunity for the individual to experiment with the problems and solutions. It should be noted that this model is as appropriate to assessment as to active teaching, as it permits the instructor to observe the ways in which the individual confronts and organizes the problem.

The work of this group of neo-Piagetians is, in our opinion, reflective of the ways in which Piagetian developmental theory has indeed changed and grown in response to environmental demands.

We hope that the reader will see many applications to his own professional pursuits and thus will continue the tradition of enriching, expanding, and questioning the model.

References

Piaget, J. *The origins of intelligence in children.* New York: International Universities Press, 1952.

Piaget, J. *The language and thought of the child.* New York: World Publishing, 1955.

Piaget, J. *The child's conception of the world.* Totowa, N.J.: Littlefield Adams, 1960.

Piaget, J. *Psychology and epistemology: Towards a theory of knowledge.* New York: Viking Press, 1971.

Piaget, J. *Biology and knowledge.* Chicago: University of Chicago Press, 1973.

Introduction to Chapter 1

LORETTA BUTLER

Alberto Munari has fulfilled many roles at the University of Geneva, including student, faculty member, and university administrator. Beginning in 1960, he has come to know the faculty, the research, and the university structure.

In this chapter, Munari presents the current status of the Genevan neo-Piagetians from a historical perspective. He points to the historical roots of the Faculté de Psychologie et des Sciences de l'Éducation in the laboratory of Theodore Flournoy in 1892. The relationship of Flournoy's laboratory at the University of Geneva with the Institut Jean-Jacques Rousseau is characteristic of the public-private ambience in which Piaget and his colleagues conducted their research.

For many years, the relationship between genetic psychology and education were of central concern to Piaget and his colleagues. Later, Piaget lessened his interests in pedagogy as he became involved in sociological and political concerns. With Piaget's growing international reputation, the institute attracted students and scholars from around the world, and much of the informal character of the school, which Munari and the early students had enjoyed, disappeared. The focus now emphasized psychological research on the cognitive processes and the study of epistemology. Today, the more orthodox Piagetians continue Piaget's epistemological genetic research, while the neo-Piagetians orient their research in the direction of cultural, social, emotional, and personal dimensions within the Piagetian model.

Alberto Munari had a long personal acquaintance with Piaget, and observed the development of the theory over a comparatively long period of time. Munari was numbered among the small nucleus of scholars who were early involved with Piaget at the University of Geneva. From this vantage point, he was able not only to perceive the institutional changes of the world in which Piaget worked, but to be a firsthand observer of the various emphases and directions through which Piaget evolved as a genetic epistemologist, a logician, and a psychologist.

CHAPTER 1

Mise en Scène

ALBERTO MUNARI

Pretending to write about the future directions of the Genevan neo-Piagetians is without doubt outrageously arrogant. No one but an inspired seer could attempt such a dangerous task. But as Marshall McLuhan has observed "nothing is inevitable if we understand the dynamics of the process that produces it." So, with this authoritative encouragement, as well as my incorrigible inclination toward risk, I will try this risky exercise. After all, it does not seem impossible to pick out some political, sociological, epistemological, or psychological factors that may influence the dynamics of the process that probably produces neo-Piagetian ideas.

As usual, a good way to look toward the future is to begin by looking at the past. As most of the Genevan neo-Piagetians are working within the framework of the Faculty of Psychology and Educational Sciences of the University of Geneva, a good start may be to look at the history of this institution. It is undoubtedly true that ideas arise in people's minds, although the institutions in which these people work are not usually considered with regard to this emerging process. Using socioanalysis, one can say that the institution's unconscious is as influential as the individual's impact. Most likely Piaget's concepts would not have grown elsewhere to the degree that

ALBERTO MUNARI • Faculty of Psychology and the Educational Sciences, University of Geneva, CH-1211 Geneva 4, Switzerland.

they have in an internationally tempered country like Switzerland, in the euphoria of the post–World War I period, and among illuminated ex-Protestant academicians seduced by Anglo-American positivism but still in love with Franco-German rationalism. Of course, most of the neo-Piagetians still work and live in Geneva, but in a deeply modified institution, in a very different time, and in changed political and cultural surroundings. But let us return to history.

The Past

Like psychology itself, the Faculty of Psychology and the Educational Sciences (FPSE) of the University of Geneva has a long past indeed, although it has a short history.

The seed of the FPSE was sown by Theodore Fournoy in 1892 when he founded his Laboratoire de Psychologie Expérimentale of the Faculty of Sciences of the University of Geneva. After Wilhelm Wundt's, this was the second European laboratory to be founded in the history of experimental psychology. It is interesting to note the institutional location of Flournoy's laboratory: at the Faculty of *Sciences*, not Arts or Humanities. Like Wundt, and Piaget himself during his entire life, Flournoy's main preoccupation was to give the newborn discipline the status of a science, and to extirpate it from the field of philosophy. The book *Sagesse et Illusions de la Philosophie* (1971) by Piaget is particularly interesting in relation to this problem, and clearly shows how much Piaget was still concerned some 70 years later with the same struggle against the philosopher's "imperialism"— that no longer existed at the time. This kind of defensive reflex has almost disappeared among the neo-Piagetians. Some years later, in 1901, Flournoy founded the *Archives de Psychologie*, a well-known scientific journal still published by the FPSE. A glance at early volumes of the *Archives* shows that despite Flournoy's scientific position, his interests spanned a broad spectrum of psychology: articles on parapsychology, dream analysis, clinical observations, and extrasensory perception coexist with reports of more "classical" psychophysical experiments.

This somewhat ambivalent position toward the epistemological and sociopolitical status of psychology is probably one of the important factors that influenced the dynamics of the process we are discussing here. Flournoy's laboratory was located in the Faculty of Sciences, as noted before; nevertheless, its articles were published not in the proceedings of this faculty, but in a *private* journal. It is true that the *Archives* still is, strictly speaking, a private foundation, but at Flournoy's time, it received no official recognition or support from the university, although it is now considered an official publication of the Section of Psychology of the FPSE. Delving further into this issue, one can also note that Piaget was appointed professor at the Faculty of Sciences, although the most important part of his work was carried out in the Institut Jean-Jacques Rousseau, formerly a *private* institution that only later became attached to the university. Further, we can ask ourselves if the *scientific* preoccupation of Piaget was not in some way responsible for his deliberate choice of not attempting to study motivation, emotion, and affectivity. But if that was the case, why was Flournoy not reluctant to study such topics—and even more unorthodox ones—although he shared the same interest. Further still, what are the respective parts that epistemological considerations, political account, and private personality preferences played in Piaget's construction of Piagetian psychology and epistemology? Some neo-Piagetians are extremely concerned with these questions. But let us return to history.

In 1912, Edouard Claparède, a well-known Genevan physicist, psychologist, and pedagogist, founded the Institut Jean-Jacques Rousseau, a private school for the professional training of elementary-school teachers. He named as its first director Pierre Bovet from Neuchâtel, who had a doctorate in philosophy and was teaching psychology at the Faculty of Arts of the University of Geneva. One year later, Claparède, Bovet, and Aldophe Ferrière— the promoter of the *école active* movement—founded the Maison des Petits, a preprimary experimental school, that, as a demonstration school, was directly dependent on the Rousseau Institute. The reputation of this little private school rapidly spread all over the world, contributing to the international notoriety of the institute, which was already well known when Piaget started his work. The Maison des Petits is still attached to the FPSE, but now with an official public status.

A young biologist, Jean Piaget, who also came from Neuchâtel to Geneva, was summoned by Claparède and Bovet who appointed him as a research assistant to the institute in 1921. During that same period, Claparède obtained official recognition from the University for his institute, which was attached to the university under the supervision of the Faculties of Sciences, Medicine, Arts, and Socioeconomics. At that point, Flournoy's experimental laboratory of psychology that was still formally attached to the Faculty of Sciences, was transferred to the institute and became a laboratory for Flournoy and Claparède. Meanwhile, Piaget's work was highly regarded by his colleagues, and four years later, at the age of 29, he was appointed professor at the Faculty of Sciences.

Note again the extremely intricate institutional network: in a semipublic institute emerging from four different faculties of the official state university, a full professor of the Faculty of Sciences performed fundamental research in psychology, even though the explicit principal aim of the founder of the institution—another full professor, but from the Faculty of Medicine—was the development of educational techniques, all under the formal direction of a full professor from the Faculty of Arts. Was this, then, interdisciplinary academic liberalism, or was it a political arrangement for placing the newborn nondiscipline? Probably both intentions were present. And probably, both the university and the concerned professors were aware of this machination, which allowed the university not to disturb the traditional academic order, and the professors to develop their somewhat disturbing research. Remember, also, that the University of Geneva was founded in 1559 by Calvin himself as a theological academy, and that, for him, the human mind was the province of the Eternal.

The particularly euphoric period after World War I encouraged innovations. In 1929, Claparède, Bovet, Piaget, and Pedro Rossello founded the *International Bureau of Education* (I.B.E.). The I.B.E. was created as a neutral entity designed to foster the goals of education and research. Jean Piaget, who at the time still adhered to the pedagogical implications of his psychology, was the first director. The first subscribers to this new international organization were the governments of Poland and Ecuador, and the cantonial government of Geneva.

The I.B.E. was apolitical and remained independent of any political body until its absorption by U.N.E.S.C.O. in the 1970s. It was unconcerned with the political environment or with the political complexities surrounding education. The fact that Piaget himself seemed to be undisturbed by political subtleties may be another important point that differentiates orthodox Piagetians from neo-Piagetians.

The relationships between genetic psychology and education were of major interest to Piaget and his collaborators for many years. But during the last decades of his life, Piaget's interest in this question lessened, and he declared that he was not competent enough in education to make pronouncements regarding it. It has been said that the reason was, more probably, a growing mistrust in the competence of pedagogists, but of course, Piaget never confirmed that supposition. Another possible factor for this change in Piaget's personal position regarding educational problems was the growing consciousness in Europe, after the 1960s, of the political dimensions of education. As just mentioned, throughout his life Piaget was a strong defender of the political neutrality of science, and that position was probably the reason for his unwillingness to enter into the new political debate on education, and consequently on science. But this debate on the ideological dimensions of science—and particularly of the human sciences—had in many respects an influence on the emergence of some neo-Piagetian currents.

In the 1930s, the Institut Jean-Jacques Rousseau changed its name to Institut des Sciences de l'Éducation (note the term *sciences*). Among the numerous students who attended the institute during that period were some who rapidly became Piaget's first well-known collaborators, such as Alina Szeminska, now a professor at Warsaw University, and Barbel Inhelder, now a professor on the Genevan faculty. Among the students of subsequent generations, let us mention the pedagogists Samuel Roller, Laurent Pauli, and Germaine Duparc and the psychologists Édouard Lambercier, Andre Rey, and Vinh-Bang, who all eventually became professors at the institute. At that point, there were some 20 or 30 of us attending the lectures of these scholars. The informal atmosphere of the institute, the direct involvement of each student in experimental research, the many occasions for informal scientific discussion between students and teachers (Piaget included), and the high level of teaching were a powerful incentive to real learning.

In order to acknowledge the growing importance and international fame of the Genevan psychologists, the name of the institute was changed once again, in about 1964, and became École de Psychologie et des Sciences de l'Éducation. Note the two major changes:

the change from *institute* to *école* and the addition of the term *psychologie*. The first change implied a tighter relationship with the university and the lesser—but always present—dependence on the four guardian faculties. The addition of the term *psychologie* meant a more radical change in the organization, and therefore in the objectives, of the institution. It was divided into two sections: a section of psychology and a section of educational sciences, each having its own director, professors, students, and degrees. Thus, the divorce between psychology and education became official. Piaget was the permanent director of the section of psychology; the directors of the other section were successively Robert Dottrens, Samuel Roller, Laurent Pauli, and Michael Huberman.

Some further discussion about the relations between psychology and education, as they appeared in the historical development of the Genevan institutions concerned, merit consideration here. In founding the Institut Jean-Jacques Rousseau, Claparède, Bovet and Ferrière were mainly concerned with pedagogy and education. Their institute, as well as the associated Maison des Petits, worked essentially with these two concerns. The example of this little experimental school had a serious influence on the primary and preprimary schools of the state of Geneva. Claparède and Bovet were highly regarded by the Genevan political authorities responsible for the school. The situation was enhanced by the founding of the IBE, and by the international reputation of the research of young Piaget. Robert Dottrens was appointed by the Genevan government to a key post in the primary education system. Piaget and Dottrens obtained permission from the government of Geneva to conduct research in all of the public schools of the republic. All teachers were invited to open their classrooms to students and assistants from the institute, with the promise that modern psychological research would furnish them with innovative pedagogical prescriptions. Many teachers responded to the invitation with enthusiasm and cooperation; some have not lost their interest.

Piaget's growing interational reputation attracted many people to Geneva who were interested more in Piagetian psychology than in its educational implications. Piaget's adherents continued to grow. The pedagogists of the initial period of the institute retired, some from the battle for progressive education, some from work, some from life. From the 1940s onward, the institute became internationally known as "Piaget's institute"—even though its official name remained Institut des Sciences de l'Éducation. The later "institute " period and the entire "école" period were characterized by an overwhelming increase in the psychology section, whereas the educational sciences section gradually declined.

Pedagogy and education were put aside, and the main concern became the study of the development of cognitive processes: intelligence, perception, and their epistemological counterparts. The mainstream of research focused on the experimental genetic psychology of Piaget and Inhelder, a trend that was further emphasized by the work of a team of outstanding scholars whom Piaget invited to collaborate at the Centre International d'Épistemologie Génétique. This center was, and still is, a private foundation, supported by several American, European, and Swiss grants. Officially there are no links between the center and the university, although many of its collaborators are teachers or assistants on the university's faculty. Its private status allowed Piaget to continue working at the center even after his official retirement as a university professor. Note once again, the politics of linkage among private and public stuctures. An important question arises: Is it really necessary to set up private reserves for carrying on new ideas?

Besides this mainstream of fundamental research, some other Piagetians tried—with equal involvement, though with less success—to develop parallel directions. André Rey worked on clinical applications of genetic psychology and Vinh-Bang, with Samuel Roller and Laurent Pauli, on the implications of genetic psychology for teaching. But besides the dominance of psychology over education, there was also one of fundamental research over applied research in psychology. In his struggle against philosophical speculation, and in defense of the scientific (i.e., "serious") status of psychology, Piaget always had in mind a unique model that could attain what he considered a more pure and "serious" experimental science: physics. Physicists were his favorite interlocutors at the Center of Epistemology. His attempts to describe his views of psychology in logico-mathematical terms were—not only, of course, but also—supposed to demonstrate that fundamental psychology can be as serious as fundamental physics. Thus, it is not surprising that Piaget looked to his colleagues for research applications in the same way that physicists look to their engineering colleagues.

Fundamental and applied research have always been very different, especially in the minds of academicians. This is perceived as being much more important by the neo-Piagetians than is the old argument about the scientific value of psychology; this concern is another important characteristic that differentiates the neo-Piagetian movement from the position of the orthodox Piagetians.

The dominance of psychology over the educational sciences continued until the early 1970s when the rector of the University of Geneva invited the American professor from U.N.E.S.C.O., Michael Huberman, to become the head of the Educational Sciences Section in an attempt to end its downward evolution. Huberman, who is still on the faculty, managed to revive this section within an astonishingly short period of time. He restored the weakened links with the political authorities responsible for the state educational system, reorganized the curricula in order to offer permanent training to primary teachers, improved pedagogical research, and opened up new directions in adult education, educational innovation, and the sociopolitics of education systems, among other things.

Finally, in December 1973, the Geneva Grand Conseil (i.e., the legislative body of the Canton of Geneva Republic) granted to the École de Psychologie et des Sciences de l'Éducation the status of seventh faculty of the University of Geneva, on equal footing with the other six. Thus the Genevan Faculty of Psychology and Educational Sciences, the only faculty of this kind throughout Switzerland, was born. Simultaneously, the admininstrative staff changed: Hermine Sinclair became the president of the psychology section, Michael Huberman became the president of the educational sciences section, and I was appointed dean of the faculty. This fundamental institutional change occurred during a period of general economic expansion and was accompanied by two other major changes: the retirement of Jean Piaget from the university and the removal of the faculty from the old Palais Wilson building (the original home of the Sociétés des Nations) to a modern new building in the center of town, near the principal seat of Calvin's university. Both events signaled a break with the past, and most of the faculty understood that a new era was beginning.

The number of students tripled. The number of teachers and assistants doubled, and many of them came from other universities and from other countries. New directions in research and teaching were introduced: social psychology, ethology, formal logic, artificial intelligence, psychobiology, and psychoanalysis. The educational sciences section, now more established, began new research and teaching orientations and summoned many new collaborators from abroad. The equilibrium reached between the psychology section and the educational sciences section during this period resulted in better collaboration between psychology and pedagogy. Moreover, the trends of the "école" period were almost inverted because of the political, cultural, and scientific work of Huberman and his colleagues, who continued to collaborate actively with other public schools and government institutions. A good illustration of this inversion appears in the following events during the Grand Conseil discussions about the promotion of the "école" to the status of a faculty: Some deputies suggested that the official appellation must be "Faculty of Educational Sciences"; others suggested the name "Faculty of Educational Sciences and Psychology," which appeared to be acceptable to the assembly until the Minister of Education, a former disciple and good friend of Piaget, gave a dynamic speech recalling the outstanding role that Piaget had played in contributing to the international fame of the University of Geneva. For this reason, he suggested placing the term *psychology* before *educational sciences*. The recognition of history was favored over the acknowledgement of the emerging present, and this latter version was finally passed by a majority vote.

Becoming a faculty also implied more rigid structures, more precise regulations, more organization, and more hierarchy. The "big-family" climate of the *école* and of the Palais Wilson period disappeared. More offices and more laboratories implied more distances, and thus fewer occasions to meet each other and to engage in informal conversations. Students who met the old Piaget on the elevator did not know him. We became a "typical" faculty.

The Present

The FPSE is still divided into two major sections: educational sciences and psychology. The former is organized into four departments. The Department of Pedagogical Research is centered on the various problems—psychological, pedagogical, sociological, and didactical—of teaching, especially in elementary school; innovation and change in school practice is also a main interest of this department. The Department of Adult Education is mainly concerned with the so-called life-long education, particularly with "special" audiences like women, migrant workers, and linguistic minorities. The Department of Development and Planning of Educational Systems concentrates on a comparative approach, such as the management of whole educational systems in different countries, especially in the developing ones. The Department of Special Education is concerned with the problems and issues in the education of physically, mentally, or socially handicapped children and adolescents. The Department of Methodology is interested in the development of new methodologies in educational research. A Center for the Philosophy of Education also functions within the framework of the educational sciences section and organizes frequent public debates on the fundamental aims of modern education.

The psychology section is also divided into four departments. The Department of Genetic Psychology is comprised of the more orthodox of Piaget's disciples, whose work focuses on several specific areas: Barbel Inhelder and her group carry out research on learning strategies; Guy Cellerier works on artificial intelligence and epistemology; Ariane Etienne on ethology; Vinh-Bang on methodology and didactics; Henry Wermus and Gil Henriques on formal logic; and Pierre Dasen on intercultural psychology. The Department of General and Social Psychology includes three professors with their collaborators: Willem Doise working on social psychology; Jacques de Lannoy on general psychology; and Jacques Voneche on child psychology. The Department of Genetic Psychobiology is more "hardware" oriented: André Bullinger carries on research on sensorimotor development, and Pierre Mounoud on personality development, both working with very young subjects of a few weeks old; Michelangelo Fluckiger researches the development of visual and acoustic perception, and Jean-Daniel Stucki works in the field of personality disorders. This department collaborates with the physiology department of the Faculty of Medicine and offers an important technical infrastructure for developing computer-assisted experiments. Finally, the Department of Applied Genetic Psychology is organized into four subunits. The psycholinguistic unit, with Hermine Sinclair and her group, is involved in the well-known research on the development of language; the clinical psychology unit, with Elsa Schmid-Kitsikis and her collaborators, is studying the relations between affectivity and intelligence and their pathologies in childhood and adolescence; the educational psychology unit is where I work with my team on the psychological and epistemological problems of educational intervention, inside and outside the school systems, particularly with the use of modern media; and the audiovisiual communication unit, with Paolo Frignani and his assistants, has built a sophisticated TV studio, a rich media library, and an audiovisual laboratory servicing all the faculties of the University of Geneva.

The Center of Genetic Epistemology is still functioning after Piaget's death. Although it is a private foundation, as mentioned before, it is, in fact, closely united with the psychology section. Its principal supporters are professors of this section, such as Barbel Inhelder, Guy Cellerier, and Gil Henriques, as well as many invited scholars from foreign universities, such as Rolando Garcia, Maurice Halbwachs, and François Bresson among others.

Who are the Genevan neo-Piagetians? Most of them are faculty members in the departments of genetic psychobiology and applied genetic psychology, as the reader may already have noticed, and this is not accidental. In fact, what differentiates neo-Piagetians from orthodox Piagetians is essentially a special concern about those aspects of psychological research that were somewhat neglected by Piaget and his early collaborators: the role played in cognitive development by social relationship, cultural influences, affectivity factors, and biological infrastucture; the relations between normal and pathological cognitive development; and the implications of the Piagetian approach for teaching, for education, and for psychoeducative intervention in general. But some neo-Piagetians may be found in other departments, such as Willem Doise, or in other sections, like Jean-Paul Bronckart, who is well known for his work on the process of learning languages; Laurence Rieben-Lamouille, who is especially concerned with early childhood education; and Jean Brun, who is working on mathematical learning.

From the institutional point of view, the FPSE is now a large enterprise—from a Swiss perspective of course! About 2,000 students attend its classes, almost equally distributed over the two sections.

The teaching staff goes beyond one's personal contact span. Admin-
istrative power has increased, and informal procedures have disappeared. As the economy drops, inflation and unemployment, much
more than university life, preoccupy the government and its deputies. Whether one is an orthodox, a neo- or a non-Piagetian is a debate
that preoccupies only the long-time scholars. The more immediate
problems consist of finding funds and collaborators and of improving
conditions of employment at the university.

The Future

Piagetian genetic psychology is a European product emanating
from the mid-twentieth century. Its roots may be recognized in the
progressive lay as opposed to religious culture movement of that
period, in the debate on evolution, in the dialectic positivism current,
and in the struggle for the independence of human sciences made
popular by Jean Piaget. Many authors have already compared Piaget
with Freud, Einstein, Bergson, Marx, Darwin, and Russell—all outstanding people who shared a similar network of ideas, although
each had its unique orientation. But old controversies agitated the
scientific and philosophical debate of that period: subject versus
object, body versus mind, perception versus intelligence, determin-
ism versus free choice, the analytical versus the holistic approach,
and so forth. Piaget was naturally engaged in these debates, and his
epistemology was in many respects influenced by this kind of questioning ambience.

Neo-Piagetian genetic psychology is primarily a European product, although it emerged from very different times. It came out of an
era begun in May 1968 and blurred barriers between the academy
and the city, between scientific and political debate, and between
public and private spheres. In an emphasis on human values, the
old body-versus-mind debate has been replaced by a holistic body-
mind perspective that perceives the body and the mind as one dynamic
system, an energy field embedded within other energy fields. This
is an age in which quantifiable data and rational cognitive thinking
are no longer recognized as the sole sources of knowing. A new thrust

has appeared in the additional values of subjective, intuitive, qualitative, metaphoric, and holistic knowledge. It is an age in which
education has begun to regard learning not only as a social necessity
(i.e., as training for a particular role), but as a life-long process (only
partly related to school) that enhances one's own personal development. Science is no longer equated with knowledge, and the
fragmentation between scientific and cultural knowledge is now
rejected.

Most of the Genevan neo-Piagetians were and still are influenced by this change in the view of education. It is, therefore, normal
for them to orient their investigations toward cultural, social, emotional, and personal dimensions, and to attempt to integrate these
dimensions into their primary cognitive approach. It is not surprising, moreover, that they are concerned with concrete applications, and that they try to bypass the anachronistic oppositions of
fundamental and applied research, engaging themselves in "action research" on other theoretical grounds. Also, the "hardware-
oriented" scholars, who develop sophisticated computer-assisted
experiments on psychobiological behavior, tend to leave their laboratories, and—thanks to microprocessors—to develop research
studies in actual human environments.

The neo-Piagetian position represents not only a desire to add
new dimensions to the original Piagetian approach, but a tendency
to explore, with the aid of modern technology, ages or conditions of
life that were technologically out of reach for Piaget and his early
collaborators.

In addition, the term *neo-Piagetian* implies the deliberate intention of questioning some assumptions of Piagetian psychology and
epistemology, in the light of current scientific and cultural trends,
by using advanced experimental techniques. Some of the questions
posited, for instance, may be the following: Is it true that affectivity
is the only motor of cognitive development, and that it does not
interfere structurally with cognitive development? Is it true that social
relations may enhance cognitive development? Is it true that sociocultural representations do not affect logical functioning or thinking?
Is it true that the physical characteristics of concrete reality do not
interfere with the development of cognitive structures? Can we continue to accept, in view of recent experiments on very young babies,

the basic constructivistic assumption in which the subject constructs the concept of himself at the same time that he constructs the concept of the external world? Are the cognitive structures in some way biologically preformed?

Trying to answer these questions, and similar ones, is the main concern of the Genevan Neo-Piagetians. Answering these questions is surely not easy nor within immediate reach. This is an ambitious long-range program of extensive research.

Some Points of History

1559   Founding of the University of Geneva by J. Calvin
1892   Founding of Flournoy's Laboratoire de Psychologie Experimentale at the Faculty of Sciences of the University of Geneva.
1896   Birth of Jean Piaget in Neuchâtel.
1901   T. Flournoy founded the journal *Archives de Psychologie*
1907   First scientific publication by J. Piaget
1912   E. Claparède founded the Institut Jean-Jacques Rousseau
1913   E. Claparède, P. Bovet and A. Ferrière founded the "Maison des Petits"
1918   J. Piaget received Ph.D. from the University of Neuchâtel
1921   J. Piaget appointed research assistant at the Institut Jean-Jacques Rousseau
1923   Publication of *The Language and Thought of the Child*, by J. Piaget; the official beginning of Piagetian psychology
1925   J. Piaget appointed professor at the Faculty of Sciences at the University of Geneva
1929   E. Claparède, P. Bovet, J. Piaget and P. Rossello founded the International Bureau of Education
1933   Institut Jean-Jacques Rousseau became the Institut des Sciences de l'Éducation, attached to the University of Geneva
1955   J. Piaget founded the Centre International d'Épistemologie Génétique
1964   The Institut des Sciences de l'Éducation became the École de Psychologie et des Sciences de l'Éducation (EPSE).
1973   The Geneva Grand Conseil granted to the EPSE the status of Faculté de Psychologie et des Sciences de l'Éducation of

the University of Geneva. A. Munari appointed Dean of the Faculty.

1976   Publication of *Les Révolutions Psychologiques de l'Enfant* by P. Mounoud; the first step toward the neo-Piagetian movement.

1978   First Fordham University–University of Geneva institute on Piagetian and neo-Piagetian research.

1980   Death of J. Piaget.

1985   Publication of *The Future of Piagetian Theory: The Neo-Piagetians*, first collection by Genevan neo-Piagetians as a group.

References

Piaget, J. *Sagesse et illusions de la philosophie.* New York: World, 1972. (Published in English as *Insights and illusions of philosophy.*)

Introduction to Chapter 2

LILLIAN C. R. RESTAINO-BAUMANN

André Bullinger may be described as the major visual perceptual theorist in the neo-Piagetian group. He has not only engaged in extensive work in this field in Geneva but has also collaborated with Lipsitt and Bower in the United States.

His interest is in infant perception, but his work goes beyond the typical focus of those dealing with the early development of visual processes. He is certainly concerned about describing the complex visual mechanisms manifested by the infant, but his concern goes beyond the mechanisms to the attempt to determine the relationship between those mechanisms and the cognitive processes of knowing, as they are defined in Piagetian theory.

Bullinger's research and theory concentrate on subject–object relationships as these are represented by mechanisms and processes of visual perception. Bullinger describes two levels of learning as the outcome of the processes of visual orientation manifested by the infant: the first level is mastering the systematic coordinations between objects in the environment; the second level is learning how one's own eyes work. In other words, the visual sensorimotor activities of the infant function to coordinate the objects of the outside environment; in addition, their functioning provides the child with the opportunity to learn about the working of his own eyes as "objects"

19

for consideration. Thus, his own body functions, as well as outside objects, become objects of knowing for the infant.

Bullinger extended the Piagetian definition of the interiorization of systematic coordinations of exterior objects in the world to cover the interiorization of systematic coordinations of the body functions; that is, the subject's own functions become objects of systematic coordinations and interiorizations. His work examines the level of acquisition by subjects of the objective properties of their own sensorimotor systems.

Bullinger's research focuses on two ideas novel to traditional Piagetian theory:

1. The extension of the initial state of subject–object interaction to in utero activity; specifically, the adaptation of ocular activity in the absence of light
2. The development of the subject's awareness of how his own bodily instruments of knowing function

Bullinger's description of the infant's growing differentiation between subject and object, in terms of the functional processes of the subject's body as environmental object, as well as the functional properties of exterior objects as environmental object, presents us with a description of levels of self-awareness unique in the literature of infant development.

It is not unreasonable, however, to interpret such manifestations of self-awareness as the precursor to the metacognitive processes of self-awareness defined by Brown (1977) and by Flavell and Wellman (1981).

Brown (1977) described the essential characteristic of the metacognitive process of the subject as the capacity for "performing intelligent evaluation of its own operations, for some form of self-awareness, or explicit knowledge of its own workings, is essential for any efficient problem-solving" (p. 242).

Flavell and Wellman (1981) used the label metamemory to define the same set of processes. According to these authors, the essential property of the subject's metamemory is the awareness of "himself as a mnemonic organism." The growing child "may gradually learn how to read his own memory states and status with fair accuracy, and also to understand the behavioral implications of being in this as opposed to that state" (p.11).

As a matter of fact, Flavell and Wellman actually interpreted metamemory development in terms of "something analogous to reflective abstraction."

Thus, Bullinger's hypotheses must be interpreted as being very much in the tradition of Piagetian theory but nevertheless as being equally appropriate to the mainstream of the information-processing movement in American cognitive psychology.

References

Brown, A. Development, schooling and the acquisition of knowledge about knowledge: Comments on Chapter 7 by Nelson 1977. In R. C. Anderson, R. J. Spiro, & W. E. Montague (Eds.), *Schooling and the acquisition of knowledge.* Hillsdale, N.J.: Erlbaum, 1977.

Flavell, J. F., & Wellman, H. M. Metamemory. In E. V. Kail & J. W. Hagen (Eds.), *Perspectives on the development of memory and cognition.* Hillsdale, N.J.: Erlbaum, 1981.

CHAPTER 2

The Sensorimotor Nature of the Infant Visual System
Cognitive Problems

ANDRÉ BULLINGER

For almost a century, oculomotor activity has been a privileged area of experimentation for the psychologist. Technical advances over the past few decades have alleviated many of the previous constraints, allowing access to younger and younger subjects in much less uncomfortable situations. The technology surrounding the recording and analysis of eye movements has often been the primary motivation for much of this research, and the theoretical framework within which these studies are carried out, and which allows the results to be interpreted, may often be deceptive. We will attempt, in this discussion, to identify some of the cognitive problems underlying oculomotor activity.

ANDRÉ BULLINGER • Faculty of Psychology and the Educational Sciences, University of Geneva, CH-1211 Geneva 4, Switzerland.

The Meaning of Oculomotor Activity

The recording of eye movements allows us to gather a number of parameters of one kind of motor activity (motricite). The sensorimotor character of oculomotor activity is often reduced solely to its motor component in which the movement is an expression of the activity "necessary" for operating the sense organ, as if that activity did not possess a certain number of properties in its own right. For us, the recording of eye movements implies both the sensory and the motor sides, and eye movements must be interpreted as sensorimotor (Mayer, Bullinger, & Kaufmann, 1979).

A trivial example will perhaps clarify this point of view: Imagine a person walking around a town. Looking only at his itinerary, we might see elements related to the *biomechanical properties* of the locomotor system (e.g., the size of his footsteps), just as we might also see elements related to the *properties of the sense receptors* (e.g., orienting them or placing them at the appropriate distance for detection of certain properties of surrounding objects) and the goals that the person has set himself (e.g., going from one point to another).

In this example, it is easy to dissociate the sensory and the motor components. At the level of oculomotor activity, this distinction becomes less clear. Often, it seems as if the oculomotor system is divorced from the biomechanical contingencies and directly reveals the goals or sensory capacities of the subject.

It seems to us to be important to put forward an approach to oculomotor activity that takes account of the following elements:

- The biomechanical potentialities of the systems being used
- The sensory potentialities
- The properties of the object to be explored
- The orientations imposed on, or determined by, the subject

Recordings of eye movements may be considered as a record of what a subject can achieve within a space; according to the frame of reference of the investigator and the nature of the experimental situation, the interpretation of results may be biased in favor of one or another of various parameters, but it is not possible to ignore the others altogether.

The Analysis of Eye Movements within a Cognitive Framework

We do not endorse those theories that treat oculomotor activities as a privileged indicator giving direct access to activities such as the determination of relationships or the search for information. From the cognitive point of view, oculomotor activity is an index permitting *inferences* about underlying cognitive activity, but the underlying cognitive activity could be dominated either by a discovery of the properties of the eye as an instrument or by activity leading to a relative stability of interiorizations. In the first case, the subject's task is to forge new tools for understanding; *cognition may equally well be turned toward the subject's body as toward the experimental situation*. It seems to us that, in many experimental situations with very young infants, the first type of activity predominates, or at the very least, that the cognitive elaborations about the oculomotor system are different *from those of the adult* (Bullinger, 1977, 1979; Bullinger & Jouen 1983).

We use the term *interiorization* here in the sense defined by Galpérine (1966). The general idea is drawn from the work of Vygotsky (1977), who hypothesized that higher mental processes are formed taking root from the exterior towards the interior. This passage from the exterior to the interior is the central theme of the "theory of reflection." The work of the Russian school, presented by A. Leontiev (1976), shows that this concept is applied particularly to psychopedagogical problems. For us, the concept is applied at the level of the subject's acquisition of the objective properties of his sensorimotor systems. This approach is not radically different from the Piagetian approach: activity plays a major role, the emphasis there being mainly on the individual's elaboration of the physical and social properties of objects (Bullinger & Pailhous, 1980).

In the context of oculomotor activity, the notion of interiorization seems to restate the problem in a more coherent form. It links together the sensory and the motor apparatus in a manner that reminds us that all of the properties of a particular system are not used by the subject from the beginning by the subject and that it *is always possible for the subject to turn his attention to those properties of his sensory system still unknown to him*.

This point of view leads one to recognize that the subject, in the psychological sense, exists only as a function of his interiorizations. The eye, like the hand, is an instrument (in the sense of being a tool) that allows cognitive understanding of the world only to the extent to which certain properties of that instrument have been interiorized.

Genetic Aspects of Ocular Sensorimotor Activity

The Problem of "Initial State"

A theoretical and experimental approach to the oculomotor activity of the infant cannot avoid an attempt at a description of the "initial state" of the newborn. The idea of *initial state* should not be taken to mean an absolute beginning. The actions that the fetus develops *in utero* are important and constitute a sensorimotor activity adapted to that milieu. Féré, in his book *Sensation et Mouvement*, (1887) wrote a striking chapter entitled "On the Psychology of the Fetus." In this chapter, he analyzed among other things, the so-called voluntary movements of the fetus and said:

> The maternal organism reduces excitations due to light, sound, touch, etc., to a common form for the fetus, this form being movement, which under these conditions obviously becomes the common unit of sensation.

The mother's body is described as an interface, a sensorimotor artificial aid, or a prothesis for an active subject. We also know that reactions at the biochemical level are capable of influencing the motor behavior of the fetus. Féré cited the case of a young woman, addicted to morphine, "in whom the side effects of withdrawal from morphine were manifested first of all as spasmodic movements of the fetus, movements which made further consumption of the narcotic exigent." Féré suggested that "all of the so-called voluntary movements of the fetus are in reality reflexive movements contingent on stimulation of which the mother may be unaware."

Consequently, the notion of *initial state* has meaning only when regarded as the moment of change in the physical milieu—the suppression of an interface indispensable for survival of the organism in favor of a reorganization of other behaviors that have developed under other constraints *in utero*. The radical separation occurring at the birth of what could be considered as one part of the baby *qua* subject leads us to assert again a radical separation of the *body of the subject* (the physical object) and the *subjectivity that is constructed*. This clear-cut separation clarifies the whole of human sensorimotor development by regarding the body of the subject as an object that is capable of being discovered through the activity employed.

The First Stages of Development

At birth, the organism supports certain reflex schemes; the totality interacts with material objects in the environment. For this reason, the situation may be described as being that of a functioning totality (Bullinger, 1981).

This functioning causes the emergence of a number of regularities in the unfolding of the schemes of action, regularities that are "written into" the body of the subject and the surrounding objects. These regularities exist only when the totality is functioning and go on to be the "aliments" of assimilation and accommodation—in Piaget's terms (1936)— of action schemes. We can suppose that certain dynamic configurations at the physiological level are the material bases for the auguring interiorizations. These indices, when organized in representation, constitute what Piaget termed "tableaux perceptifs"; we would like to add that, for us, these representations exist only when sensorimotor activity is engaged by something that mobilizes and orients it totally. One could say that the baby is "all vision" or "all sucking," in as much as other sources of peripheral stimulation cause an increase of the ongoing activity (e.g., the stimulation of the grasping reflex during nutritive sucking augments this sucking activity).

The process of interiorization to which we appeal is a process, manifested through functioning, whereby indices are organized into representations, and representations are organized among themselves. The state of interiorizations at a given moment is a *subjectivity*, that is to say, a subject in the Piagetian sense of the term, where a subject is not to be confused with his body (Piaget,1936, chap. 1, para. 2).

So, at this level of functioning totality, regularities emerge through a reflex scheme. These regularities, organized into representations, are stable at the time that the sensorimotor scheme is functioning. The activations of the various sensorimotor loops go on to create universes that are predominantly visual, tactile-kinesthetic, oral, and so on. Succeeding this first phase, where activity creates the universes, is a phase of progressive stabilization that assures their permanence. So it is that we could speak, for example, of the visual world, the tactile-kinesthetic world, or the oral world of the infant. At this level, the various subjectivities that are formed are oriented by the pecularities of the sensorimotor schemes that initially organized them. There is no dissociation of subject from object (no object relation); rather, there are diverse totalities oriented by sensorimotor loops. Their parallel and simultaneous existence is one of the conditions for the occurrence, at a third level, of coordinations between these different subjectivities. The other conditions relate to contingencies existing at the level of physical properties, of the subject's body and of objects. A cube placed before a baby contains within itself in the *same place in physical space* its visual, tactile, and sound properties. The next interiorization coordinating visual and tactile-kinesthetic space simultaneously creates a visuo-tactile subject (subjectivity) and an object embodying visual and tactile properties in a coordinated space.

At this level, there is an inversion; there is a movement away from separate universes functioning in parallel and engulfing both subject and object toward a coordination of these universes, creating a subject and an object, and at the same time an elementary object relation.

The Oculomotor System

It is probably useful at this point to summarize some properties of the oculomotor system. At the sensory level, the retina has a central zone and peripheral zones (or a distribution gradient of receptors permitting a more-or-less arbitrary division into different zones). The covariations between "fovealization" and "peripheralization," which the movements of this receptor surface give rise to, are *anatomically* laid down within these zones (the fovea occupies a defined place on this retina). This is probably one of the most powerful contingencies to be imposed, permitting the interiorization of properties through motor activity.

The reflex scheme for ocular fixation (present at birth) puts the sensory aspects (seeking to fovealize) and the motor aspects (execution of the action that manifests the anatomical dependence of fovea and periphery) into a reciprocal dependence.

The extraocular musculature is functional from birth: Haith (1980) has shown that the newborn (a few hours old) develops well-organized oculomotor patterns in the dark. The distribution of saccadic amplitudes and the apportionment of fixations over the field are capable of being biased by lateral sound stimulation: the sound source and the pattern of exploration are focalized. But the same babies, presented with a dim homogeneous field of light, show quite "disorganized" patterns of eye movements: the rate of nystagmus increases and the infant, in order to escape this activity, closes his eyes; when he opens his eyes again, the eyeballs are recentered and the nystagmus has disappeared. The source of the disturbance was detected and the reaction was an adaptive one.

So, oculomotor activity is operational at the effector level; the control of this activity, on the other hand, operates on a set of bases that are not suited to the physical environment into which the baby has just been plunged. Light arriving on the retina causes a transitory disruption of oculomotor activity; later on, it becomes an important source of regulation. The physical properties of the retina and of the environment, as yet not interiorized, will provide the link through which oculomotor activity may be made use of in a new way on a new set of bases. We have seen that oculomotor activity functions in the dark by being divorced from what will become its principal retroactive sensory loop, and as soon as light arrives, there is a disruption and reorganization of this loop. For this reason, it is necessary to speak of the "reflex scheme" in the sense of Piaget (1936); after this level, the reflex is transcended (Bullinger & Chatillon, 1983).

To illustrate this point, we will discuss an experiment that we have carried out. Babies 10 weeks old were presented with a three-dimensional object that could be held in a constant position and then be moved so that it ended up either at a new location or at the original position. Recordings of the eye movements in these situations showed, among other things, that when the object changes its location, the line of regard follows it perfectly and then continues to explore it in its new location. But the eye makes short back-and-forth excursions from the actual location of the object to that position occupied prior to movement. We interpreted these results as showing a dissociation of the systems for inspecting objects in motion and those for inspecting stationary objects, which are then reflected back on the properties attributed to the objects. At this level, each object at rest in a given place may be considered as unique; in other words, the location of an object is one of its properties. As soon as the properties of the oculomotor system are integrated with the behavioral contingencies of objects (violated in some of Bower's experiments, 1976), the object is assured of continuing identity during its displacements.

If our hypothesis about the simultaneous interiorization of properties of the subject's body and of objects in relation to it is sound, we should find similar phenomena in other modalities. We have already seen the interdependence maintained between the ocular fixation reflex and the auditory system. Oculomotor activity is certainly not isolated, the links with the vestibular system having been well demonstrated in a large number of psychophysiological studies.

Traditionally, ocular fixations are differentiated into two types, one static and the other dynamic. This dichotomy corresponds to the two types of motor activity known as the *saccadic system* and the *smooth pursuit system*. These two systems bring into play similar but distinct reflex schemes and address themselves, respectively, to static and dynamic properties of the environment (including the subject's body). One could hypothesize that the interiorizations formed through the use of the two systems may also be separable. The work of Bower (1976) shows that infants react differently to substitutions when an object is in motion. Bower quite rightly discussed these differences in terms of the movement or lack of movement of the objects concerned, but he neglected something that seems to us to be fundamental, namely, a necessary reference to the properties of the oculomotor system. For us, the cognitive constitution of the properties of the object is *cotemporal* with and *correlated* with that of the properties of the sensorimotor systems involved. Cognitive elaborations bear on the liaisons between the properties of the object and those of the sensorimotor systems; there is "solicitation" through this relationship and that will be the properties that go on to constitute the raw material of interiorizations.

We mean by this that, out of the set of physical properties of the sensorimotor systems, only some are brought into play through a dialogue with the object which will give rise to interiorizations.

The visuopostural link, which involves the vestibular apparatus, is less apparent. However, we feel that this link is fundamental during the first month of life. Orientation of the head toward a visible object is possible from birth (Bullinger, 1977), and a number of as-yet-unpublished observations seem to show fluctuation in the links between eye movements and the dynamics of posture in the infant.

References

Bower, T. G. R. *Development in infancy.* San Francisco: Freeman Press, 1976.

Bullinger, A. Orientation de la tête du nouveau-né en présence d'un stimulus visuel. *L'Année Psychologique,* 1977, *2,* 357–364.

Bullinger, A. La réponse cardiaque comme indice de la sensibilité du nouveau-né à un spectacle visuel. *Cahiers de Psychologie,* 1979, *22,* 195–208.

Bullinger, A. Cognitive elaboration of sensorimotor behavior. In G. Butterworth (Ed.), *Infancy and epistemology: An evaluation of Piaget's theory.* New York: Harvester Press, 1981.

Bullinger, A., & Chatillon, J.-F. Recent theory and research of the Genevan School. In P. H. Mussen (Ed.), *Handbook of child psychology* (Vol. 3), J. H. Flavell & E. M. Markman, *Cognitive development.* New York: Wiley, 1983.

Bullinger, A. & Jouen, F. Sensibilité du champ de détection péripherique aux variations posturales chez le bébé. *Archives de Psychologie,* 1983, *51,* 41–48.

Bullinger, A. & Pailhous, J. The influence of two sensorimotor modalities on the construction of spatial relations. *Communication and Cognition,* 1980, *13*(1), 25–36.

Féré, C. *Sensation et mouvement.* Paris: Alcan, 1887.

Galpérine, P. Essai sur la formation par étapes des actions et des concepts. In *Recherches psychologiques en URSS.* Moscow: Éditions du Progrès, 1966.

Haith, M. M. *Rules that babies look by.* Hillsdale, N.J.: Erlbaum, 1980.

Leontiev, A. *Le développement du psychisme.* Paris: Éditions Sociales, 1976.

Mayer, E., Bullinger, A., & Kaufman J. L. Motricité oculaire et cognition dans une tâche spatiale. *Archives de Psychologie,* 1979, *183,* 309–320.

Piaget, J. *La naissance de l'intelligence.* Neuchâtel: Delachaux et Niestlé, 1936.

Vygotsky, L. S. The development of higher psychological functions. *Soviet Psychology,* 1977, *15*(3), 60–73.

Introduction to Chapter 3

VALERIE L. SHULMAN

Pierre Mounoud is, perhaps, the most controversial of those who have contributed to this volume. The large chapter that follows, "A Theoretical Developmental Model: Self-Image in Children," embodies three major transitions in Mounoud's work over the past 15 years. Each of these transitions has served to clarify and/or expand a specific aspect of traditional Piagetian theory, from its methodology to its core.

The first of these transformations concerned methodology and can be seen in "Structuration de l'Instrument chez l'Enfant" (Mounoud, 1968), as well as in other research of that period. Mounoud conjectured that traditional theory placed too great an emphasis on the role of the experimenter who presented a noninteractive situation to the subject. The subject was presented with a situation that was simplified to the extent that only one aspect, property, or transformation was isolated for his response. Mounoud, on the other hand, perceived the importance of the content as well as the methodology; he attempted to create an experimental situation that demanded the interaction of several elements, rather than a single isolated experience. He hypothesized that, in order to appropriately investigate the child's "structures," the child must be presented with an opportunity to isolate, extract, or identify the properties of the objects or events that are relevant to the situation. Thus, the onus was shifted from the experimenter to the subject, a process that expanded the potential specificity of the results, rather than limiting them to "presence" or "absence."

The second major transition (from about 1976 through 1978 or 1979) involved a more controversial divergence from traditional theory while rekindling the debate in psychology about preformed structures. Central to Mounoud's rationale was a refutation of a new major Piagetian principle, that of the construction of new structures as formal instruments of knowledge. Further, and at the core of traditional Piagetian theory, Mounoud refuted the concept of equilibrium. Rather, he hypothesized that the basic apparatus of intelligent behavior exists at birth in the form of an information-processing program, an internal system of organization that changes over time through a series of "revolutions." Thus, we begin to see the processes inherent within development as progressively built and as offering the child new capacities for representations. As new organizations evolve, information is redefined in those terms; dynamic development is based on the discrepancies between the prior and the evolving systems, and on the regulations that must be performed by the child. The three major models of organization that have been defined are the sensorimotor organization, which is defined in terms of reflex responses to given information; perceptivo-motor organization, which is defined in terms of coordinated actions in response to given stimuli; and conceptuomotor organization, which includes symbolic and verbal responses. In each instance, it is the period of partial programming, or partial organization, that is most important for understanding the structures. Thus, in Mounoud's conceptualization, a preformed apparatus provides the basis for the evolution of successive organizations of processing information that permit increasingly complex sampling, analyses, and organizations of reality. In other words, for Mounoud, the evolution of increasingly complex systems of organization, based on a preformed apparatus, replaces the Piagetian theoretical construct of the construction of formal structures of knowledge that are common to all. Further, the mechanism of development is, then, the discrepancy between the models— that is, the period of partial reorganization—rather than a disequilibrium.

One can see a continuing refinement of the first, methodological transformation, in Mounoud's creation of purposeful experimental situations. These experiments provide a setting in which the subject must attain a goal by isolating and then composing an objective; his selection of a variety of behaviors at varying points in time, which can be explained as the creation and recreation of the same reality several times, through the application of different systems of organization.

It is the third transformation, or transition, that is the most interesting and most exciting. Here, Mounoud and his collaborator Annie Vinter have enunciated a theoretical model based on a stage theory that is reminiscent of traditional Piagetian theory. Although the vocabulary is different, the essence of many of the elements is familiar, creating a convergence between traditional and neo-Piagetian theory. Mounoud and Vinter have woven a theoretical rationale based on Mounoud's redefinitions of traditional theory and methodology. Each aspect is clearly stated and explicit. Here, they have applied the theoretical hypotheses to a new treatment, self-image. In this research, they state that "the aim of the research is to show how children reconstruct new representations of themselves and to identify the steps of these constructions." Again, they have called into play the individual's ability to isolate and analyze specific elements and then to reconstruct them or reconcile them with their perceived reality. The individual was confronted with a manipulative (or manipulatable) situation where it was incumbent on him to reflect the reality of the situation. The fact that Mounoud and Vinter are currently working in the area of self-image, or the relation of the individual to his objective reality, places their work clearly within the mainstream of current psychological investigations both in the United States and elsewhere.

References

Mounoud, P. *Structuration de l'instrument chez l'enfant.* Geneva, Switzerland: Delachaux et Niestlé; 1968.

CHAPTER 3

A Theoretical Developmental Model
Self-Image in Children

PIERRE MOUNOUD AND ANNIE VINTER

Theoretical Background

In this chapter, we present a model of psychological development that may be considered "paradoxical" when compared with the usual conceptualizations. This conceptualization is presented in terms of Piagetian theory, from which it derives, but from which it diverges considerably on numerous points.

Initially, our position focused on the mechanism of development, those processes that permit the passage from one organization of behavior to another within each of the broad stages of development (infancy, childhood, and adolescence). In other words, we have attempted to show how the infant comes to infer new meanings from the objects or people with whom he interacts, or how new determinants of behavior are defined (reflexive abstraction).

PIERRE MOUNOUD AND ANNIE VINTER • Faculty of Psychology and the Educational Sciences, University of Geneva, CH-1211 Geneva 4, Switzerland.

More recently, we have attempted to define (a) what the child constructs in the course of development and (b) what makes these constructions possible.

With regard to knowing what is constructed by the child, during the last few years our position has become more radical, in that we have criticized the Piagetian position that states that the child constructs structures or new forms of action or of thought. By way of an alternative hypothesis, we now contend that the child does not construct new *structures* (i.e., new ways for processing information) in the course of development. Nor does he construct, as Piaget believed, either general coordinations of his actions or the logico-mathematical operations of thought. In our view, formal structures of action and reasoning are not constructed but are preformed. Instead of constructing structures, or processing abilities, the child, in the course of development, elaborates on internal *representations* (models or memories) conceived of as structurations or organizations of content. These representations are elaborated by means of the formal structures that the child possesses. It is by the application of these structures that new representations are constructed. The constructed representations reveal or manifest, more-or-less completely, the structural capacities of the child.

The first point leads automatically to the second point, that is to say, to what makes possible the elaboration of new representations, what gives the child the ability to redefine and redetermine behavior differently at the different stages in the course of his development. In this respect, we propose that *new coding capacities* appear successively in the course of development. The appearance of these new capacities is subject to a *genetic regulation*; it thus shows very little dependence on particular interactions that the child engages in with his environment, unless in a broad, nonspecific sense. It should be recalled that for Piaget the construction of new structures is explained by an interactive process between preexisting structures and different environments or different aspects of the environment. For Piaget, the passage from one stage to the next is due to the achievement (or closing) of new structures, and these new structures then reveal new aspects of the environment, with new dimensions engendering new interactions; this process can be endlessly repeated.

We will attempt to schematize our position with the following propositions or postulates:

1. The forms or general structures of our actions (their coordinations) and of our reasoning (their logical operations) are preformed.

2. There exists in the roots of representations, particularly of the body, what we call *sensory representations*. These representations, coupled with preformed structures, determine the initial forms of behavior, that is to say, the initial exchanges with the environment, the sensorimotor organization.

3. Development consists of the construction of new representations (models or memories) of objects, of self and of others, and consequently of new programs.

4. New representations are constructed because new coding capacities appear successively in the course of development. We propose to call *perceptual* those that appear at birth, and *conceptual* those that appear around 18 months, formal or semiotic those that appear at approximately age 10. Table 1 illustrates the progression of the constructions of new forms of representation through adolescence based on the preformed structures existent at birth.

5. The appearance of these new coding capacities is generated by a maturational process that depends only very indirectly on the interactions of the child with the environment (the nonspecific role of the milieu).

6. The construction of new representations occurs according to a succession of periods or of phases (which we have previously described in terms of revolutions) whose occurrence is equally strongly determined by maturational regulation (phase of dissociation, integration, decomposition, and syntheses). Table 2 provides an overview of the elaboration of new representations from birth through adolescence indicating the steps and processes utilized at each stage.

7. The constructed representations are directly dependent on the experiences in which the child is involved; the environment plays a specific role in this construction.

8. These new representations intervene in the functional exchanges that the subject engages in with his environment and that permit their organization (patterns, programs, procedures, and schemes): preformed sensorimotor organization at birth, perceptivomotor organization at around 18 months, conceptuomotor organization at around 10 years, and semioticomotor organization at around

Table 1. Constructions of Systems of Organization

Birth	Sensory representations (preformed) linked with preformed structures + new coding capacities, the perceptual code : Construction of perceptual representations	Sensorimotor organization (preformed)
18–24 months	Perceptual representations (constructed) + new coding capacities, the conceptual code → Construction of conceptual representations	Perceptivomotor organization (constructed)
9–11 years	Conceptual representations (constructed) + new coding capacities, the semiotic code → Construction of semiotic representations	Conceptuomotor organization (constructed)
16–18 years	Semiotic representations (constructed)	Semioticomotor organization (constructed)

Table 2. Elaboration of New Representations

1st Stage	2nd Stage	3rd Stage	Steps	Process
0–1 month	1½–3 years	10–11 years	Initial global representation syncretic	
1–4 months	3–5 years	11–13 years	New elementary representations, separate and juxtaposed	Sampling of object and action properties by means of new code
4–8 months	5–7 years	13–15 years	New total representations nondecomposable, rigid with global relationship between them	Coordination-integration of elementary representations and establishment of correspondence with objects and situations
8–14 months	7–9 years	15–16 years	New total representations partly decomposable, with partial relationship between them and with their components	Decomposition-analysis of new total representations in their components and establishment of correspondence with objects dimensions
14–18 months	9–10 years	16–18 years	New complete representations fully decomposable, with complete relationship between them and their components	Composition-synthesis of the components of new total representations

Table 3. Identity Forms Taken by Objects and Subject

1st Stage	2nd Stage	3rd Stage	Identity Forms	G. H. Mead
At birth	2 years	10 years	Syncretic	Experienced role
3 months	3 years	12 years	Multiple	Conceptualized role
8 months	6 years	14 years	Unique	
18 months	9 years	16–18 years	Typical	Generalized role

16–18 years. Table 3 illustrates the identity forms taken by objects and subject during the first, second, and third stages.

The principal consequences of these propositions are the following: (a) The existence of stages and of periods is determined by maturation; (b) The passage from one stage to another occurs independently of the degree of achievement of preexisting constructions (within certain limits); and (c) The constructed representations are directly dependent on the contents of particular experiences in which the child engages and even on the nature of previous exchanges. For this reason, the constructed representations reveal, more-or-less accurately, the structural capacities or processing capacities of the organism.

In conclusion, it is possible to say that, in the Piagetian conception, the environment plays a nonspecific role despite the interactionist aspects of the model. We are taking the contrary position that, although the environment plays a nonspecific role in the appearance of new coding capacities in steps more-or-less fixed in the course of development, the role of the environment becomes specific in the elaboration of new representations. We have progressively developed this point of view over the past years in various articles (Mounoud, 1976, 1978, 1979; Mounoud & Hauert, 1982a,b; Mounoud & Vinter, 1981).

The Problem

One of the guidelines for our research is related to the nature of the development of self-image in children. Thus, we posed the question: Within development, can a progressive evolution be described from the absence to the presence of self-recognition, or does one witness turn-off points that suggest levels of reconstruction, through new means of previously acquired knowledge?

According to our point of view, during development the child proceeds to successive elaborations of self-image, each of which gives evidence of a new kind of relationship established between the world and himself. The varied images built are always related to his representations of himself and of objects belonging to his physical or social environment. These representations are determined by the kind of cognitive means at the child's disposal. The newly emerging capabilities of coding and translating reality oblige the child to reelaborate the previously built representations (Mounoud, 1979; Mounoud & Vinter, 1981). Indeed, the understanding of reality, achieved first through conceptual and then through formal means, leads the child and the adolescent to new definitions of himself and his environment.

The complexity of the problem of self-recognition is closely related to the concepts of awareness and representation. The very term *recognition* seems to us ambiguous. There is an immediate temptation to pose the problem in terms of the presence or the absence of recognition, and indeed, the majority of studies on this question have initially adopted that orientation. They have attempted to define an age after which the child is able to recognize his own image(s). Every problem dealing with recognition—or, in more general terms, memory or knowledge—raises the question of the accuracy of that recognition, which, itself, can be more-or-less general (I recognize a face of a child's face) or more-or-less specific (I recognize the face of a 5-year-old boy or the face of my child or my face 18 years ago). Consequently, we feel that it is necessary to refer to different kinds of recognition of self or others, with all the intermediaries possible from a *singular* or individual recognition to *schematizing* recognition (Mounoud, 1978).

In a discussion of faces, we may speak of recognition as the identification of a global configuration (nose, eyes, forehead, mouth) or the identification of a particular face. In the first case, recognition is schematizing or categorical; in the second, it is singular or specific. These are, of course, two forms of recognition usually regarded as developmentally distinct and, more often than not, are linked to the two first organizers described by Spitz (1957): the smile at 3 months and anxiety at 8 months. The two kinds of recognition correspond to different degrees of perceptual organization.

In other words, recognition refers to a repeated confrontation with a given situation or object. This is the empiricist point of view, where knowledge arises essentially from the object. From this point of view, it is possible to speak of objects or realities as being novel (i.e., never before encountered), of which there can, consequently, be no question of recognition. In contrast, from a cognitivist point of view, where knowledge arises mainly from the categories possessed by the subject, it is never possible to talk of absolutely novel realities or objects: a given object is always recognizable through those aspects or dimensions that it shares with other objects. All knowledge is thus partially based on recognition. This is the fundamental principle of assimilation, which renders every object recognizable to a certain degree. From this standpoint, recognition does not necessarily presuppose previous contact with the recognized object. It is in this second line of argument that we suggest placing the recognition of one's image. The individual is always capable of recognition, but it is necessary to distinguish the different kinds: more-or-less general or more-or-less specific. The categories of representation providing the basis for recognition may correspond to different levels of elaboration, such as the perceptual level or the conceptual level.

We would like to emphasize that for most authors the child's recognition of his own image is fundamentally a problem of representation. From this point of view, it is possible to reformulate the problem as follows: Of what kind of recognition is the child capable, and to what level do the categories of representations that he is using belong? From this point of view, one would ask about the degree of elaboration of the child's representations of himself at a given moment in his life.

Within psychology, there are many orientations, both theoretical and experimental, for research on the self-image. L'Ecuyer (1975) summarized various conceptions of the organization of self in the child and the adolescent. The majority of these conceptions (Allport, 1961; Symonds, 1951) introduce a division between two modes of self-understanding: one mode is based on perpetual apprehending—deriving essentially from the physical aspects of self—which is usually referred to as the *perception of self;* the other mode is based more on the subject's conceptualizations about the social or affective aspects of self, which is usually referred to as *self-image.* A perceptual apprehending of reality is taken to be the result of a direct and immediate contact, not mediated by representations. The development of the "self-structure" is translated, within these conceptualizations, as a passage from the perceptual to the conceptual.

We are opposed to such a distinction between self-perception and self-image. At every level of development, the child's perceptions are mediated by representations, which, alone, enable the perceived objects to be given meaning; in the same way, at every level of development, the subject's actions are controlled by the representations of the objects to which they are applied (Hauert, 1980; Mounoud & Hauert, 1982b). Furthermore, we do not think that the child's preoccupations concerning himself pass from a physical to a social self during development. These aspects of the self exist at every age and are elaborated simultaneously by the child.

Each of the various dimensions distinguishable within the self will necessarily be reconstructed by the child in the course of development. It is thus not possible to distinguish, in development, a period of nonrecognition of the self (even in the sensorimotor period) and a period of self-recognition. Nevertheless, Amsterdam (1972) and Zazzo (1973) expressed their research in these terms. In their studies on mirror image, they attempted to set a date for the age of self-recognition in the child. Amsterdam's research led him to propose that the period from 21 to 24 months is decisive for the recognition of self (using Gallup's task as a criterion). Zazzo suggested 27 months, using a criterion based on the child's reactions to a mark placed on his forehead and a flashing light behind him. To say that the recognition of self arrived at by the 2-year-old child constitutes the final result in a process of construction beginning with the absence of self-recognition does not seem to us to be an acceptable theoretical approach.

For us, different forms of self-recognition may be demonstrated at every age of development, just as it is possible to characterize different forms of recognition of people and situations at every age (Widmer-Robert-Tissot, 1980). The relative precocity of one form with respect to another must refer to the criterion used to determine the appearance of self-recognition.

Zazzo (1978) has modified his position with research on the nonreversed (video) image. This research has led him to a belief that the form of self-recognition in the 5- to 6-year-old child is less stable than that of the 3- to 4-year-old. This belief implies that the younger child's self-image is subjected to upheavels and reelaborations.

Authors differ in their ideas about the determinants of the development of self-image. Certain of them, such as Gottschaldt (1954) and Zazzo (1966), invoke external factors. To account for the evolution of the self-image that he noticed in adolescence, Gottschaldt resorted to roles in the social milieu, to which the adolescent is becoming sensitive, and to the ideal self (the development of the "persona"). Zazzo suggested that the models of growing up presented by the adult serve to modify the child's self-image. For other authors, such as Erikson (1968), the principal determinant of the reconstructions of self-image is internal factors. According to Erikson, body growth and the maturation of the genitalia necessitate a reevaluation of the identity achieved in childhood.

From our point of view, neither social nor constitutional factors are sufficient to explain the reelaborations of self-image throughout the course of the child's development. As we have already stated, these reconstructions follow the appearance of new cognitive instruments (*instruments de connaissance*), which are perceptual at birth, conceptual at around age 2, and formal at about age 10–11. But if these modifications in the representations of the self reflect the appearance of new cognitive instruments, the content of these representations is closely dependent on the nature of the interactions that the child experiences with his environment. Relevant aspects of the social milieu constitute the formative factors (e.g., body growth), and social factors thus take on an identical status, within this perspective, regarding their importance in reelaborating the self-image.

Certain authors, notably Wallon (1959) and Mead (1934), have insisted on the interdependence between constructions of the self and constructions of others. For Wallon, the "me" and the "other," which are not initially differentiated, are constructed through a double process of appropriations and exclusions. For Mead, the self is constructed progressively by the interiorization of the roles of each of the partners in a social situation. We would simply like to point out the empiricist tendency of such a position, in which the self is entirely determined by the characteristics of others.

There are some studies in ethology that illustrate the close interdependence of the self-image and the image of the other. These studies concern the influence of the first social experiences of the animal on its behavior in relation to its mirror image (Gallup & McClure, 1971; Schulman & Anderson, 1972).

For us, the interdependence of the perception of others and the perception of the self signifies that the child simultaneously constructs representations of others (or more generally of objects) and representations of himself. This amounts to making oneself, one's body, an object to be known in the same way that the child must learn to know his parents and his various partners; which allows us to draw hypotheses about the development of the self-image from a model of the construction of representations of objects (Mounoud & Vinter, 1981).

Studies of the genesis of the construction of the object or of object relations have led to the attribution of a different status to the object throughout a given developmental period or state (Mounoud, 1977). We put forward the idea that to each object status there corresponds a different status of the self-identity, each one defining a distinct mode of self-image.

Generally, the first level of organization in the exchanges between child and environment is described in terms of nondifferentiation (Wallon, Piaget). The initial status of self-identity would thus correspond to a *syncretic* and nondifferentiated identity, where the self and the other are not distinguished.

Throughout a second phase, the child moves on to partial reelaborations of internal and external realities, in the form of elementary representations and by means of new cognitive instruments. These, in turn, lead to partial objectifications of objects, in the sense that the objects do not exist complete, with a simultaneous set of properties, as seen from the subject's point of view. This "multiple" object will mean that there is a corresponding "multiple" identity, the subject having various partial representations of himself that are not intercoordinated.

The third phase is characterized by coordinations between the different piecemeal elaborations of the object carried out previously. These coordinations bring into being a "total" object (Klein et al., 1966), "unique" and identifiable because it possesses simultaneously the set of characteristics that the subject has been able to discover in it. In the same way, one may envision the child in this phase constructing a total representation of himself, integrating, within a coordinated ensemble, several dimensions of himself. The identity thus elaborated by the child we will qualify as *unique*, the child himself being constituted as a subject differentiated from others.

In the fourth phase, the child constructs a network of inter- and intraobject relations enabling the construction of classes of equivalence between objects ("typical" objects). One could hypothesize a parallel integration of his own identity in a diversified causal and social complex. The child recognizes being similar to others because of certain dimensions of himself. Thus, we may refer to a *typical identity.*

We feel that it is worthwhile to compare the genesis of self-identity, as we have conceived of it, to the evaluation of role as proposed by Mead (1934). According to Mead, the individual initially activates each of his roles ("lived roles") by means of behavior without being able to refer them to any other role in particular. In the elaboration of self, Mead also distinguished a phase of partial self-constitution, where the child is successively able to adopt the roles of partners in a social situation, without being able to fit them into an organized system of rules as a multiple form of definition of role or self. Next, the individual proceeds to a conceptualization of roles, that is, a "conceptualized role," thus elaborating a unique definition of each one. Finally, the individual arrives at a generalization of roles through which each role is fitted into a socioaffective system or *système relationnel* that enables confrontation with other roles. For Mead, this phase constitutes the "whole self." It is reached when the individual comes to a simultaneous interiorization of the various roles of his partners and of their relationships, which Mead translated as the notion of "generalized others," typical form of definition of the role of self. However, from our point of view, these various phases are repeated several times throughout development, whereas for Mead they characterize development as a whole.

The Method

The experimental population consisted of two samples.[1] One sample of children between the ages of 2.6 and 6.5 was made up of 80 children (40 girls and 40 boys) divided into four age groups. The

---

[1]We also carried out a pilot study by using a sample of adolescents between the ages of 12 and 15. The results of this study may be found elsewhere (Mounoud & Vinter, 1984) and so will not be presented here.

second sample consisted of 140 children between the ages of 6.6 and 11.5 (70 boys and 70 girls) divided into five age groups.

The subjects were confronted with a distorting mirror made of a sheet of flexible chromed plastic, 23.5 cm × 24 cm, held in an adjustable metal frame.[2] A handle at the base of the frame turned a screw that moved a vertical metal rod flush with the rear surface of the mirror. Rotations of the handle bent the metal frame and thus engendered convex or concave distortions in the vertical axis of the mirror. Each rotation of the handle caused a linear displacement of a marker placed behind the mirror, thus providing a measure of distortion on a scale graduated in centimeters. The nondistorted image of the face corresponded to a scale value of 0. The range of variation used for the distortions was 10 mm on either side of zero point.

It should be stated that the 7- to 11-year olds were confronted with a mirror of a higher quality and precison than that used for the 3- to 6-year-olds. The two mirrors functioned, however, in exactly the same manner.

Experimental Method

Experimental Hypotheses. On the basis of our theoretical hypotheses, it was possible to formulate essentially three experimental hypotheses. If the child has a unique form of identity, he shows concern for accuracy in his choice of image; to do this, he would have to have a clearly defined internal representation. *Accuracy* should be understood in the dual sense of accuracy of the objective image (no distortion) and/or in terms of the stability of the chosen image regardless of the experimental conditions. If, on the other hand, the child has elaborated diverse images of himself (i.e., multiple identity), each one taking into consideration only certain dimensions, then the different experimental conditions should lead to different choices, each revealing particular aspects of his face.

Finally, if the child may be characterized by a typical form of identity, his choices should reflect the establishment of categories

[2]We are grateful to Mr. Christian Husler and Mr. Lucien Pitetti for their ingenuity in constructing this apparatus.

based on the relationships between the various images of himself
without a definition of any unique category.

Experimental Design

We employed a factorial design with 3 crossed factors (age,
order, and sex), matching on a fourth factor (mirror curvature).

The four age groups in the sample of 3- to 6-year-old children
(Sample A) were as follows: 2.6–3.5 years, 3.6–4.5 years, 4.6–5.5
years, and 5.6–6.5 years. Each group was made up of 20 subjects, 10
girls and 10 boys. The five age groups for 7–to 11–year-old children
(Sample B) were divided as follows: 6.6–7.5 years, 7.6–8.5 years,
8.6–9.5 years, 9.6–10.5 years, and 10.6—11.5 years. Each group consisted of 28 subjects, 14 girls, and 14 boys.

Two measures were taken for each subject in Sample A, one
with an initial concave distortion and the other with an initial convex
distortion of the mirror image. Each age group was made up of two
independent subgroups, randomly assigned to one of the two orders
of intervention (concave-convex or convex-concave).

A procedure based on a repetition of the measures was used
with Sample B. Five consecutive measures were first recorded for
each subject; the initial distortion of the mirror image was either
concave or convex depending on the subgroup to which the child
was assigned. We then proceeded to a new measurement after modifying the initial curvature of the mirror (convex or concave).

The measures recorded were expressed as the difference in the
number of centimeters between the marker position corresponding
to the image selected by the child and its position for the nondistorted
image.

Experimental Procedure

The subject was seated facing the mirror at a distance of 30 cm.
The experimenter first showed the subject the range of possible distortions. The mirror was then set to either its maximum convex or
its maximum concave position.

For Sample A children, each measure was taken under the
following conditions: The experimenter produced the deformations
in the mirror (passive method). For each step of mirror distortion,

the child had to say if the resulting image corresponded to his "objective" image. He was thus confronted with discrete distortions of his image.

Sample B children, however, were confronted with continuous modifications of their image: they themselves manipulated the handle to bend the mirror (active method) and were allowed to make to-and-fro movements.

Results

Three- to Six-Year-Olds

A repeated-measures analysis of variance was carried out on the data; this analysis essentially involved intragroup comparisons on the curvature factor (within-subjects design) and intergroup comparisons of the effects of age, order, and sex (between-subjects design).

This analysis enabled us to look at, among other things, the effect of the curvature on age and the effect of order on age. As sex did not emerge as a significant differentiating factor for these children (neither alone nor in interaction with other factors), we collapsed the data for boys and girls in the following analyses.

Effect of Curvature to Age. The curvature factor ($p = .001$) and the age × curvature interaction ($p = .001$) seemed to significantly differentiate the children's choices.[3]

Figure 1 illustrates the effect of curvature plotted against age; the values of the points on the graph are the result of summing the two concave measures, on the one hand (concave in the first position and concave in the second position), and summing the two convex measures, on the other hand.

For all ages, the direction of distortion of the selected image was determined by the initial position of the same kind of initial distortion.

By individual age group, the influence of the initial mirror position affected the performance of the 4- and 5-year-olds to a significantly greater extent than that of the 3- and 6-year-olds. The images selected by the 3- and 6-year-olds following initial concave or convex

---

[3]The age × order × curvature interaction was not significant at the chosen .05 level.

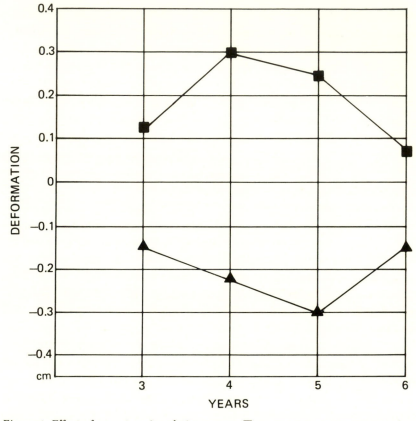

Figure 1. Effect of curvature in relation to age; ■ = concave measurements; ▲ = convex measurements.

distortion were much closer together than were those chosen by the 4- and 5-year-olds.

We verified that this effect of the curvature with respect to age had an equal effect on the performance of the children on an intra-group level. What emerged was that, regardless of the order of taking the measures, the initial curvature of the mirror had a greater influence on the 4- and 5-year-olds' choices than on those of the 3- and 6-year-olds. However, this effect was more clearly evident for those children passing from concave to convex. Apart from that, the 3- and 6-year olds distorted themselves, on average, less than the 4- and 5-year-olds.

The influence of the initial mirror position on the choice of mirror image showed that this choice appeared to depend on the external conditions at the time. The 4- and 5-year-olds were more sensitive to the initial values of distortion than were the 3- and 6-year-olds. The chief characteristic of the self-image elaborated by these children thus seemed to be its inaccuracy, in the sense of instability. This image did not reflect a stable definition of facial traits but resulted from a choice that took different facial aspects into account according to context. A concave distortion (fattening) of the face probably revealed certain facial dimensions that were sufficiently recognizable to enable these children to identify themselves with the image reflected in the mirror, and a convex distortion (thinning) created others that were equally pertinent.

In contrast, the image elaborated by the 3- and 6-year-olds was accurate inasmuch as their choice altered little with the experimental conditions. Their choice was thus made on the basis of a stable set of facial dimensions, apprehended globally.

Order Effects with Respect to Age. Only the order factor was significant (p = .0007). None of the interactions involving this factor was significant. If concave and convex measures are separated, order was significant only for the concave (p = .0029).

The values of the points in Figure 2 were the result of the sum of the two measures for the subjects: concave and convex or convex and concave, depending on the order of measurements. Regardless of age, the two orders, concave-convex and convex-concave, led the children to make different choices. The order effect was the same in both cases: the means of the children's choices corresponded to the kind of distortions initially encountered (concave for the first order, convex for the second). Although the age x order interaction was not significant, the 3- and 6-year-olds' choices nonetheless tended once again to appear more stable than those of the 4- to 5-year-olds. An asymmetry may be observed between the effects of an initial concave and an initial convex distortion of the mirror: starting with convex seemed to have a greater effect on the second measure than starting with concave. The order effect was therefore greater for the concave than for the convex measures.

The same kind of interpretation carried out for the effect of the curvature may be extended to the effect of the order: the more the individual referred his choices to an accurate and stable image, the less he was affected by the order of taking the measures.

Overall, the children's choices were partially determined by the order of the measures: the nature of the first measure (concave

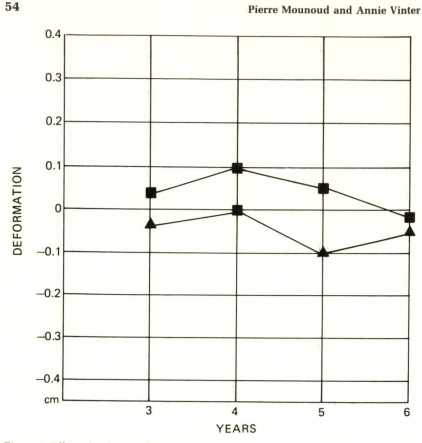

Figure 2. Effect of order in relation to age; ■ = concave-convex order; ▲ = convex-concave order.

or convex) oriented the direction of distortion of the chosen images. The 3- and 6-year-olds nevertheless tended to show a more consistent stability in their choices than the 4- and 5-year-olds.

Seven- to Eleven-Year-Olds

Effect of Taking Repeated Measures with Respect to Age. It will be recalled that five measures were initially taken for each subject, concave or convex, according to the order in which the mirror curvatures were produced. The analysis of potential tendencies in these repeated measures was carried out by comparing, for each subject, the first measurement with either the last measure or the mean of measurements. A statistical analysis of these data for each age group (analysis of variance with polynomial correction) revealed no significant tendencies at the chosen .05 level, which means that statistically the five measures may be treated as equivalent to a single measure. Nevertheless, we feel that a qualitative analysis of the tendencies arising from taking repeated measures is of interest.

At age 7, a general decrease in the distortion of the chosen images could be perceived. At age 8, there is a tendency toward stability (i.e., each time choosing images that were equally distorted). At age 9, we see as much constancy as diminution (especially for the convex measures) or indeed augmentation (especially for the concave measures). It is worth noting that to diminish the distortion of the chosen image for the convex curvature is to move toward the territory of concave curvatures. At age 10, the children hardly modified their choices, which were images as distorted for the first trial as for the successive trials. Finally, at age 11, the modifications that arose over the five measurements primarily consisted of a decrease in the distortion and, secondarily, of a constancy of distortion for the concave measurements and an augmentation of distortion for the convex measurements.

There was an analytic aspect to the behavior (fonctionnement) of the 7-year-olds: over the five measurements, they extracted more and more subtle cues from the mirror image, which enabled them to approach their objective image. This behavior was possible only when the internal image to which the children referred in making their choices was not too rigidly defined. Between ages 8 and 9, a coherence or consistency appeared in the way in which the children were affected by the initial curvatures of the mirror: essentially, a decrease in distortion for the convex measures and an increase for the concave. These children seemed able to establish relationships between the different images with which they were confronted, leading to coherent modifications of their choice, always tending toward a fattening of the image. The stability of the 10-year-olds' choices was evidence of the existence of a fairly precise internal reference.

At age 11, a progressive inversion of the 9-year-olds' tendency emerged: the choices began to veer toward a thinning of the face. One might feel that, after age 10, the children proceeded to the construction of new images of themselves.

For the following analyses, the five consecutive measures taken for a given subject have been averaged; these are the means that were

compared to the measures obtained after changing the mirror curvature.[4] The statistical analysis of this set of data was identical to
that carried out for the 3- to 6-year-olds' data. The results are as
follows:

The curvature factor (p = .0001) and the order factor (p =
.001), on the one hand and the order $\times$ curvature (p = .0022) and
age $\times$ order $\times$ curvature (p = .0094) interactions, on the other hand,
significantly differentiate the data. In addition, the age factor (p =
.0047) and the age $\times$ order interaction (p = .437) are significant if
a quadratic distribution of the data with respect to age is hypothesized. First of all, we will analyze the effect of curvature with respect
to age; then the effect of order with respect to age; and finally the
simultaneous effects of order and curvature with respect to age (the
only interaction interpretable from a statistical point of view).

Effect of Curvature with Respect to Age. Regardless of age, these
children chose much more distorted images when the initial mirror
curvature was concave rather than convex (see Figure 3).

Compared to the 6-year-old children, the 7- to 9-year-olds
appeared to be much more influenced by the initial mirror position,
whereas at ages 10 and 11 the children's choices tended to be quite
similar. Furthermore, the 8-year-olds and especially the 9-year-olds
opted specifically for concave distortions of their images, which distinguished them from every other age group in the study.

Order Effects with Respect to Age. At each age, the children
passing from concave to convex chose more distorted images than
those going from convex to concave, for whom the mean of the chosen
images were symmetrical with respect to the abscissa (see Figure 4).
The 7- to 11-year-olds chose more distorted images for the concave
than for the convex condition; this was particularly characteristic of
the 8- to 9-year-olds and the 10-year-olds, an effect that is shown
statistically by the fact that the age $\times$ order interaction was significant as long as the data are assumed to be distributed quadratically.

On an individual basis, we found that, at 8–9 years of age, the
children's images were very far apart from one another (more than

---

[4]We would like to point out that we also carried out the statistical analysis of the
data using the fifth measurement obtained for each subject instead of the mean of
the five measurements. Absolutely no difference was found between the results of
this analysis and the analyses presented here.

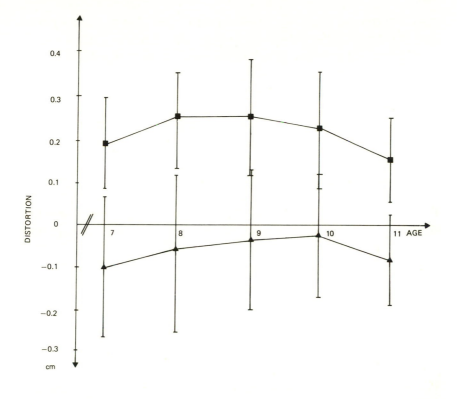

Figure 3. Effect of curvature in relation to age; ■ = concave measurements; ▲ = convex measurements.

3 mm apart) for the convex-concave order and close for the concave-convex order (between 0 and 1.5 mm apart), whereas at ages 10 and 11, there was no difference from this point of view between the two orders. Compared to Figure 4, this graph shows an even greater asymmetry between the order effects, in favor of the concave-convex order.

Effects of Curvature and Order with Respect to Age. The initial measurements (concave or convex) scarcely differentiated the age groups (see Figure 5). Generally speaking, the images defined by the initial measurements were at their most distant for the 9-year-olds and at their closest for the 11-year-olds. The second concave measurements corresponded to the first concave measurements, except that they showed to a greater extent the fact that the 7-year-olds and

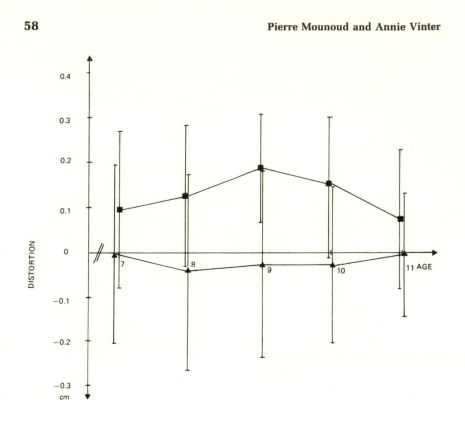

Figure 4. Effect of order in relation to age; ■ = concave-convex order; ▲ = convex-concave order.

the 10- to 11-year-olds distorted themselves less than the 8- and 9-year-olds. Finally, the second convex measurements were clearly different from the first convex measurements and radically differentiated the age groups. If the 7- and 11-year-olds chose minimally distorted images (although on the average they were leaner), the 8- and 9-year-olds chose concave images and thus tended to move toward the image chosen following an initial concave curvature of the mirror. It all seems as if, although influenced by the initial mirror position (of first measurements), the 8- and 9-year-olds sought to establish a relationship between the diverse facial dimensions revealed by the different mirror curvatures in order to arrive at coherent choices. The diverse images selected by the 10- and 11-year-olds in particular

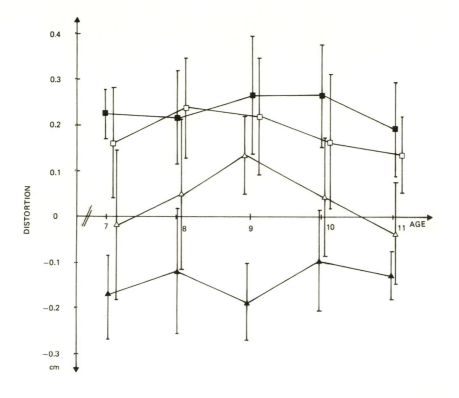

Figure 5. Effect of curvature and order in relation to age; first measurements: ■ = concave; ▲ = convex; second measurements: □ = concave; △ = convex.

converged on a single image, situated within the range of convex distortions.

Compared with the 6-year-olds, the 7-year-old children no longer chose images that were as accurate and relatively independent of the initial mirror position. On the contrary, they appear to have been affected by the changes in the curvature of the mirror, although to a smaller extent than the 4- and 5-year-olds. Above all, the greatest contrast between the 3- to 6-year-olds and the 7- to 11-year olds was that the third-order interaction of age × curvature × order became significant for the latter group. To us, this finding suggests that children between the ages of 7 and 9 are progressively establishing relationships between various images of their face revealed by the mirror, and that they manifest a systematic preference for fatter images. Between ages 10 and 12, on the other hand, children abandon their preference for fatter images, and their choices tend toward similarity. The analyses of repeated measures shows, in accordance with the results, a consistency in the choices of the 10-year-olds and a tendency to incline toward thinner images at age 11. From our point of view, the age of 10 indicates a detachment from the period between 3 and 9 years of age. From age 11 on, children begin to construct new images of themselves.

We have not yet discriminated the data for boys from those for girls, as we found sex not to be a significant factor. Nevertheless, it may be remarked that the girls had a tendency to distort themselves more than the boys, regardless of the initial mirror curvature for the 9- to 10-year old girls, and following an initially concave curvature for the 7- to 8-year old girls.

Discussion

Despite the noticeable differences in the experimental design and the methods used, we will discuss the results obtained for each age group with respect to the results for all the groups together. We will also formulate hypotheses about the kind of effect resulting from these differences with the aim of varifying that the differences in the results obtained from the 3- to 6-year-olds and the 7- to 11-year-olds are not artifacts of methodological differences. However, it should be noted at the outset that neither at ages 3–6 nor at ages 7–11 were there any general effects that held for the whole set of age groups; it thus becomes difficult to attribute the differences to methodology.

In Figure 6, we have plotted the effects of curvature with respect to age for all of the age groups studied. For concave and convex curvatures alike, the children distorted themselves more or less according to age; regardless of the curvature of the mirror, the 4- and 5-year-olds distorted themselves most. These results are in clear contradiction to those of Gottschaldt (1954) who showed that only adolescents choose distorted photographs of themselves. Still, according to their age, the children in our study opted for images that were more or less far apart when the curvature of the mirror was modified.

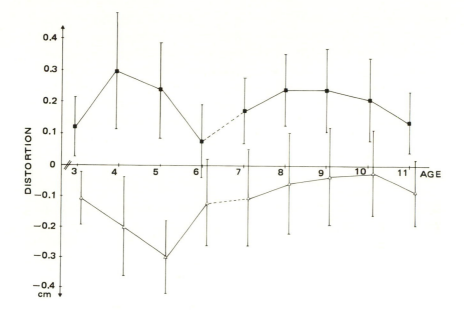

Figure 6. Effect of curvation in relation to age; ■ = concave measurements; △ = convex measurements.

The 4- and 5-year-olds chose images of themselves that differed according to the mirror position or to the order of taking measurements. Thus, they did not seem to possess a unique and accurate image of themselves; instead, they accepted the fact that diverse images might fit them. For us, their choices are to be referred to different internal representations of themselves, each independently constructed with respect to certain particular dimensions of their faces. It is in this sense that we propose the term *multiple identity* to characterize the form of self-identity of these children.

In contrast, compared to the 4- and 5-year-olds, the 3- and 6-year-old children chose images that were similar for the different mirror curvatures. This consistency suggests that they had constructed relatively accurate images of themselves. Six-year-old children have elaborated internal representations of themselves and therefore reflect unified self-definitions, simultaneously encompassing a collection of facial aspects. The form of self-identity of these children may be qualified as *unique*.

The form of identity belonging to the 3-year-old children was related to the unique kind, but the consistency of their choices over the experimental conditions was less marked than that of the 6-year-olds. Thus, 3-year-olds may be placed in an intermediary phase between that phase of complete upheaval in relations with reality, where we have described a kind of syncretic identity (between 18–24 months and 3 years), and a phase of partial reelaboration of this relationship, which synthetizes the multiple form of identity.

The images chosen by children between ages 3 and 6 for the initial concave or convex mirror incurvations were more-or-less symmetrically placed on either side of the objective image. After age 6, and specifically at ages 8, 9, and 10, this no longer held true: the children distorted themselves to an average degree in the concave and hardly at all in the convex curvature (if we consider the means of the convex measures). But above all, the third-order interaction becomes significant, denoting the coherence or consistency introduced into the choices made by these children. They managed to establish relationships between the various facial dimensions revealed by different mirror curvatures and thus were able to opt for images presenting one kind of characteristic. Compared to the 6-year-old children, they seemed to be more affected by the initial mirror curvatures, yet without resembling the 4- to 5-year-olds. The great difference from the latter lies precisely in this peculiarity of the 7-, 8-, and 9-year-old children, that they grouped different images of themselves into one category. We propose to qualify this kind of identity as *typical identity*. The marked preference of these children for fatter images may be a result of their parents' appreciation of "nice chubby cheeks," a sign of good health!

After age 9, we witnessed, on the one hand, a proximity in the images selected by the children for concave-convex curvatures of the mirror and, on the other hand, a loss in the privileged status of the concave distortions compared to the convex. When repeated measurements are taken, we have seen that, at age 10, children maintain a constancy in their choices, a tendency that, at age 11 is accompanied by an incliniation to choose less and less distorted images. We hypothesize that, between ages 10 and 11, children move on to new elaborations, on a higher plane of representations of self (and others). Around ages 10–11, the child acquires new (formal) capacities of representing himself to encode the realities with which he is confronted. The appearance of these new realities provokes a return to a symbiotic, participatory form of relationship with reality, where the child takes account of a large number of dimensions of reality—but in an undifferentiated manner—in his various exchanges with his environment. During this phase of development, the child manifests a fairly accurate, yet intuitive and nondifferentiated, knowledge of himself (his face), hence the proximity of images and the consistency of choices observed for the 10- to 11-year olds. The early imitations of which babies seem to be capable at birth are also evidence of a similarly accurate but intuitive knowledge, which may be ascribed in babies to an automatic functioning of their body schematism (schématisme corporel) (Maratos, 1973; Meltzoff & Moore, 1977).

It seems possible to us to compare the two recognition modes based on a multiple or unique self-identity to those described by Carey and Diamond (1977) following from the research of Levy-Schoen (1964). These authors showed that children under age 10 identified their own faces on the basis of particular and isolated traits, whereas children over age 10 based their recognition judgments on the whole facial configuration. These authors saw the explanation for this new capacity of the child over age 10 to encode configurations of the whole face in maturational changes in the right hemisphere. From our point of view, this opposition of a recognition based on a particularization of traits from a mode based on the global configuration of the face also makes it possible to differentiate between the 3- to 4-month old baby (who distinguishes only certain specific facial traits—Spitz, 1957) and the 8- to 9-month-old baby (who recognizes single faces). There are other differences between the 4- to 5-year-old child and the 6- to 7-year-olds, the 11- to 13-year-old adolescent and the 14- to 15-year-olds. The first of these recognition modes is a result of the partial and fragmentary aspect of the representations possessed by the child, whereas the second is based on total representations of reality.

Now let us see to what extent the differences appearing between 3- to 6-year-old children and 7- to 11-year-olds may be explained by methodological differences. The active method, as opposed to the passive method, may enable the subject to be more precise in his choices of his own image and consequently to select less distorted images. In fact, it was the 6-year-olds with whom the passive method was used, and yet, it was they who showed the greatest accuracy in their choice of image. This hypothesis does not therefore stand up in this form.

The effects introduced by taking repeated measures may be of at least two kinds: they may *favor familiarization* or habituation with respect to the distortions, so that the children would opt for less and less distorted images; they may also serve to *accentuate the contrast* between the concave and the convex distortions, the subject having suffered a certain perceptual anchoring in relation to the kind of distortion to which he became accustomed. From this point of view, one could expect that the second kind of distortion encountered by the child would have less effect on his choices; these choices would be for less distorted images, closer to the first kind of distortion.

Let us examine the first of these hypotheses, which suggests a learning effect, that is, an improvement in performance. If this is indeed the case for certain ages (especially at ages 7 and 11) this tendency is far from being the norm for our results in general. For there to be learning, the subject must be able to extract information from the task in hand and must be able to use this information in the following trials on this task. Thus, the representations used by the child should be neither too rigidly nor too accurately defined, or else the taking of repeated measurements would be translated by a constant performance (at age 10). From this standpoint, a worsening of performance (an increase in distortion) would mean either that the subject has not succeeded in using the information extracted from the first trial by the start of the second, or that he is trying to arrive at a referential image, a subjective standard clearly distinct from the objective standard of the distorted image. To us, it seems more likely that the second alternative would explain the increased distortion found with the 7- to 9-year-olds, and that the first would explain this tendency for the 11-year-olds.

The second hypothesis stipulates that, over repeated measurements, the children would undergo a perceptual anchoring effect with respect to the kind of distortion they are faced with and thus would define their choices, after the change of mirror curvature, in terms of these anchor points. If at first sight this seems to have been the case for the children having the concave-convex order, it was not so for the children passing from convex to concave. Thus, the anchor points can be formed only if they conform to the nature of the subject's representations. Now, if we examine the curve for the convex measures when these came second (Figure 5), we see that the influence of anchor points in the concave condition increased between ages 7 and 9 and then decreased after age 10. This finding means that the anchor effect can really manifest itself only if the subject is capable of establishing relationships between the various images proposed to him.

Thus, these hypotheses, which fit perfectly well into our theoretical framework, permit the rejection of an explanation of the difference based on methodologies.

Conclusions

The genetic evolution shown here between ages 3 and 11 illustrates how the image of his own face elaborated by the child is dependent on his "interpretive frameworks" and their development. This evolution would make no sense if the child came to know his physical image only through "direct" perception, not mentioned by his interpretive frameworks or representations.

In this conclusion, we would like briefly to outline the theoretical conception of child development underlying our research. This theoretical conception has been set out in several articles to which the reader can refer (Mounoud, 1979; Mounoud & Hauert, 1982a,b; Mounoud &Vinter, 1981). We consider the face an object of representational elaborations just like any physical object. Thus, we would not expect results very different from ours if any other object (e.g., an apple) were to be placed in front of the mirror instead of the face.[5]

Temporal *decalages* could obviously occur, but the general genetic evolution would stay the same. The results obtained by Bert-

[5]Similar studies are being planned.

menthal and Fisher (1978) would make this hypothesis quite likely.

Throughout development, the child constructs new representations (models or memories) of objects, of himself and of others.
These representations are conceived as internal structurings or organizations of contents and are elaborated by means of the cognitive
instruments available to the child. They comprise what we have
previously called the subject's *interpretive frameworks*: the set of
the subject's "categories" permitting him to apprehend reality. At
the same time that he is elaborating new representations, the child
constructs new action programs (skills or aptitudes) that organize
his exchanges with his milieu.

From our point of view, the baby possesses, from birth, a set
of representations, of a categorical kind, of both himself and the
external world. It is particularly because of these representations
that the newborn is capable of early imitation and the various inter-
sensorimotor coordinations. But each of these kinds of behavior (imitations or auditory-visual coordinations, for example) disappears,
only to reappear later in development. These "momentary" disap-
pearences signify, to us, that the child is elaborating new representations, by means of new cognitive instruments. The representations
already constituted, which play the role of "support" and from which
new significations may be elaborated, intervene in the construction
of new representations.

It is also necessary, when categorizing the construction of representations, to take into consideration the nature of the child's trans-
lations or encodings of his environment or his own body. We
distinguish four kinds of codes: the sensory code, the perceptual
code, the conceptual code, and the semiotic code. These correspond
to the four successive levels of the construction of representations:
the sensory level, correlative with the perinatal phase: the perceptual
level, reached at around 18 months (perceptual representations); the
conceptual level (conceptual representations), reached at around 9–
10 years of age; and the semiotic level reached at around 16–18 years
of age.

The appearance of these codes (or new coding capacities) is
generated by a maturational process that depends only very indirectly
on the child's interaction with his environment (i.e., the milieu plays
a nonspecific role). The acquisition of new coding capacities constrains
the child to reorganize his exchanges with the environment; these

upheavals define the stages, beginning with a general uniform organization of behaviors, which itself contains the program for ulterior organizations (Mounoud, 1976). The passage from one stage to another takes place, to a certain extent, independently of the degree of completion of the preceding constructions, contrary to Piagetian theory.

Within a given stage, the elaboration of new representations is carried out according to a similar scheme of development. We have tried to characterize, with the development of the self-image, four phases in the construction of representations of the self.

We have distinguished an initial phase, where representations are global and syncretic, where the form of self-identity is qualified as syncretic and undifferentiated. Next comes a phase where new elementary representations are elaborated, in isolation from the others and with no relationship to them. We have made a correspondence between this phase and a "multiple" form of identity. Then, new, total, but rigid and nondecomposable representations are constructed during a third phase because of the coordination and integration of the preceding elementary representations. Here, we have defined a "unique" form of identity. Finally, in a fourth phase, these total representations become decomposable, and the child masters the systems of correspondence or relationship existing between the parts of an object. We have qualified as "typical" the form of identity corresponding to this level.

References

Allport, G. W. *Pattern and growth in personality*. New York: Holt, 1961.

Amsterdam, B. Mirror self-image reactions before age two. *Developmental Psychobiology*, 1972, 5, 297–305.

Bertenthal, B. I. & Fischer, K. W. Development of self-recognition in the infant. *Developmental Psychology*, 1978, 14(1), 44–50.

Carey, S., & Diamond, R. From piecemeal to configurational representation of faces. *Science*, 1977, 195, 312–313.

Erikson, E. H. *Identity, youth and crisis*. New York: Norton, 1968.

Gallup, G. G., Jr., & McClure, M. K. Preference for mirror-image-stimulation in differentially reared rhesus monkeys. *Journal of Comparative and Physiological Psychology*, 1971, 75, 403–407.

Gordon, K. Über den Einfluss unbewegungen respektive Tendenzen zu Bewegungen auf die taktile und optische Raumwahrnehmung. *Klinische Wochenschrift*, 1925, 4, 294.

Gottschaldt, K. Über Persona Phanomeme. *Zeitschrift für Psychologie*, 1954, 157(3–4), 163–198.

Hauert, C. A. Propriétés des objets et propriétés des actions chez l'enfant de 2 à 5 ans. *Archives de Psychologie*, 1980, *48*(185).

Klein, M., Heimann, P., Isaacs, S., & Riviere, J. D. *Développement de la psychoanalyse.* Paris: Presses Universitaires de France, 1966. (Originally published in 1952).

L'Ecuyer, R. *La Gènese du concept de soi: Theorie et recherches.* Sherbrook, Canada: Naaman, 1975.

Levy-Schoen, A. L'image d'autrui chez l'enfant. *Publications de la Faculté des Lettres et Sciences Humaines de Paris* (Paris, Serie "Recherches," Vol. 23). Paris: P.U.F., 1964.

Maratos, O. *The origin and development of imitation in the first months of life.* Unpublished doctoral thesis, University of Geneva, 1973.

Mead, G. *Mind, self and society.* Chicago: Morris, 1934.

Meltzoff, A. N. & Moore, M. K. Imitation of facial and manual gestures by human neonates. *Science*, 1977, *198*(4312), 75–78.

Mounoud, P. Les revolutions psychologiques de l'enfant. *Archives de Psychologie*, 1976, 44 (171), 106–114.

Mounoud, P. La relation mère-enfant de point du vue des theories psychologiques et psychoanalytiques. *La Psychomotricité*, 1977, 1(4), 147–155.

Mounoud, P. Gedachtnis und Intelligenz. In G. Steiner (Ed.), *Die Psychologie des 20. Jahrhunderts* (Vol. 8). Zurich: Kindler Verlag, 1978.

Mounoud, P. Développement cognitif: Construction de structures nouvelles ou construction d'organisations internes. *Bulletin de Psychologie*, 1979, *33*(343), 107–118. (Translation in I. E. Sigel, D. M. Brodzinsky, & R. M. Golinkoff (Eds), *New directions in Piagetian theory and practice*. Hillsdale, N.J.: Erlbaum, 1981 .)

Mounoud, P., & Vinter, A. Representation and sensori-motor development. In G. Butterworth (Ed.), *Infancy and epistemology*. Brighton, Sussex: Harvester Press, 1981.

Mounoud, P., & Hauert, C. A. Sensori-motor and postural behavior: Its relation to cognitive development. In W. W. Hartup (Ed.), *Review of child development research* (Vol. 6). Chicago: University of Chicago Press, 1982. (a)

Mounoud, P., & Hauert, C. A. Development of sensorimotor organization in children: Grasping and lifting objects. In G. Forman (Ed.), *Action and thought: From sensorimotor schemes to symbolic operations*. New York: Academic Press, 1982. (b)

Monoud, P., & Vinter, A. Un point de vue sur l'identité de soi à l'adolescence. *Bulletin de Psychologie*, 1984, *27*(374), 285–292.

Shulman, A. H. & Anderson, J. N. *The effects of early rearing conditions upon the preferences for mirror-image stimulation in domestic chicks.* Paper presented at the meeting of the Southeastern Psychological Association, Atlanta, March 1972.

Spitz, R. A. *La première année de la vie de l'enfant.* Paris: Presses Universitaires de France, 1957.

Symonds, P. M. *The ego and the self.* New York: Appleton-Century-Crofts, 1951.

Wallon, H. Comment se développe chez l'enfant la notion de corps propre. *Enfance* (Special number), 1959, *1–2*, 121–150. (Originally published in *Journal de Psychologie*, 1931).

Widmer-Robert-Tissot, C. *Les modes de communication du bébé: Postures, mouvements et vocalises.* Neuchâtel: Delachaux et Niestlé, 1980.

Zazzo. B. *Psychologie differentielle de l'adolescence* (2nd ed.). Paris: Presses Universitaires de France, 1966.

Zazzo, R. La génese de la conscience de soi. In R. Angelergues, D. Anzieu, E. E.
    Boesch, J. Bres, J. B. Pontalis, & R. Zazzo (Eds.), *Psychologie de la connaissance
    de soi*. Paris: Presses Universitàires de France, 1973.
Zazzo, R. Corps et comportement. In *Actes du XXIème Congres International de
    Psychologie*. Paris: Presses Universitaires de France, 1978.

Introduction to Chapter 4

VALERIE L. SHULMAN

Elsa Schmid-Kitsikis is a clinical psychologist as well as a researcher and theoretician. During the past 15 years, she has endeavored to expand the traditional Piagetian model to include the individual as well as the epistemic subject in order to explicate the dynamics of development in both the cognitive and affective dimensions. While working within the traditional framework, she has introduced basic tenets and vocabulary from Freudian, as well as Kleinian, psychoanalytical theory in order to analyze individual characteristics. Additionally, she has devised a two-phase investigative technique that permits her to elicit multifaceted responses from her subjects, reflecting the dynamics of their mental functioning as well as the role of the primary and secondary processes and their interactions, in creative thinking as reflected in symbolism and phantasmic behavior. The overall theory and model are more fully presented in Chapter 7 of this book.

In this chapter, "Some Epistemological Aspects of Mental Functioning," Schmid-Kitsikis presents an example of how the theories are integrated and the technique is applied. As mentioned earlier, she utilizes an integrated model of cognitive and affective development as her theoretical rationale. Although past attempts have been made to synthesize the two, she has approached the integration from a different perspective. In so doing, she has provided a firm theoretical basis seemingly reflected in Segal's (1964) statement: "The origin of thought lies in this process of testing fantasy against reality; that is, that thought is not only contrasted with fantasy, but is based on it and derived from it" (p. 19).

Three major elements combine to create this holistic theory. First, Schmid-Kitsikis has retained the Piagetian theory virtually in its entirety, using it as the armature for her evolving theory. Accordingly, organization and adaption (assimilation and accommodation) remain key elements, extended to apply equally to the affective as well as the cognitive. In other words, the individual tends to organize both internal and external reality, seeking to order the "chaos" of his world. Equilibration, too, is expanded to the affective level, often in terms of conflicts that derive from the struggle between the pleasure and the reality principles, the former related to the primary processes and thus subjective, the latter to the secondary processes and more objective.

Second, she utilizes the primary and secondary processes as supportive of, rather than subordinate to, the development of cognitive structures. Thus, the emotional elements inherent within primary processes (derived from early ties with the ego and instincts, and related to an array of defense mechanisms) interact with the secondary processes (logical thought akin to Piagetian structures), to produce the undefined, often emotional dimensions of concepts. Accordingly, as the individual develops, these emotional and conceptual processes become more strongly interrelated. This interaction creates one of the ties between imaginary, symbolic, and normative thought. Further, it produces the "breach" from which creativity derives (Arieti, 1976).

Third, in order to provide a deeper understanding of the integrated theory, Schmid-Kitsikis has defined epistemological development in Piagetian terms while describing psychological characteristics in Freudian–Kleinian terms. Using this technique, she has been able to reformulate a neo-Piagetian model which provides a more comprehensive view of the myriad facets of development and the interrelationships between and among them.

In the second part of the chapter, Schmid-Kitsikis presents an example of the emerging theory as applied in a quasi-experimental setting that she describes as neither therapeutic nor fully experimental. However, it is an apt setting for the type of "action" research discussed.

*The method itself is a skillful blend of both Kleinian and Piage-
tian methods. The Kleinian aspect contributes the attention to behavioral details, including posture, facial expression, and body language,
and is particularly evident in the first phase of the method (Klein,
1955). The Piagetian element is best seen in the manner in which
the experimenter "assists" the child, changing his questioning in
response to the child's actions and reframing questions on an ongoing basis. However, the integration of these two components provides
a method that is capable of eliciting multifaceted responses from
the subject and, thus provides insight into the dynamic processes
of development.*

*Thus, in a setting flexibly structured by the investigator to fulfill
the requirements of two divergent situations, Schmid-Kitsikis presents the child first with one problem and then with another. The
following characteristics of the technique should be noted:*

*1. The overall environment apparently remains stable other
than for the materials used by the subject.*

*2. The problem changes from one that requires the child to
organize the problem and determine appropriate solutions from his
repertoire, to one that is guided by the investigator and requires the
child to utilize normative solutions.*

*3. The rules for dealing with the problem change from those
that are more internally determined to those that are more externally
determined, which are posed by the investigator.*

*4. The role of the subject shifts in response to the demands
made on him, from self-directed problem-solving on his own initiative to problem solving that must meet the demands of externally
determined criteria.*

*5. The role of the experimenter shifts from one of passive
observer to one of active controller through the use of rules; additionally, the investigator fulfills the role of facilitator on four levels.*

6. The type of material elicited corresponds to each variation.

*An additional point that should be included concerns the tim-
ing of the experience. Both situations are presented to the child in
rapid succession which provides further insight into the degree of
his mobility and flexibility.*

*The material generated from these situations provides the
investigator with an understanding of the ways in which the child
processes information and organizes the problem and his solutions;
the area(s) of conflict that emerges either from the problem, the*

observer, or the child's solutions; and the degree of spontaneity, originality, and creativity in the child's responses, permitting the investigator to determine the dynamics of individual development. Stated another way, it permits the investigator to determine how, for the individual, "The emotional accompaniment of a cognitive process becomes the propelling drive not only towards action but towards further cognition" (Arieti, 1976, p. 92).

The reader will note that these are the types of data that have been sought by teachers, curriculum developers, school administrators, clinical psychologists, and others who deal with children and young adults professionally on an ongoing basis.

References

Arieti, S. *Creativity: The magic synthesis*. New York: Basic Books, 1976.

Klein, M. The psychoanalytic play technique. *Psychological Review*, 1955, 44, 223–237.

Piaget, J. *Play, dreams and imitation in childhood*. New York: Norton, 1962.

Piaget, J. *The grasp of consciousness: Action and concept in the young child*. Cambridge: Harvard University Press, 1976.

Segal, H. *Introduction to the work of Melanie Klein*. New York: Torchbooks, 1964.

CHAPTER 4

Some Epistemological Aspects of Mental Functioning

ELSA SCHMID-KITSIKIS

Much of our research to date has been related to psychoanalytical and clinical aspects of symbolic and emotional development as related to the rational progress toward knowledge. Although somewhat tangential to the large body of Piagetian research, the concepts of symbolism and imagination are not antithetical, particularly to Piaget's early work. The current study presents some recent clinical experimental research concentrated on the following areas:

1. The problems of the relations between primary and secondary processes
2. The analysis of the factors, movements, and results of the mental process during sublimation
3. The role and significance of these factors in the development of thought and rational activity

Our experimentation and theorizing concerning the stated problems are still going on, and consequently, the ideas presented in this chapter cannot be considered definitive. They should be regarded

ELSA SCHMID-KITSIKIS • Faculty of Psychology and the Educational Sciences, University of Geneva, CH-1211 Geneva 4, Switzerland.

as working hypotheses supported by facts, with promising interpretations.

For the time being, we have chosen a line of thought centered
on the following hypothesis: there is an analogy between, on the one
hand, a child's behavior when faced with a situation in which he
has not been given any directions and which, therefore, remains
chaotic until the child himself tries to render it meaningful and, on
the other hand, a researcher's proceedings when he attempts to find
meaning in the chaotic universe of his momentary incomprehension
and ignorance. We are directly confronted with this problem in what
constitutes the mechanism of development toward knowledge. However, we are dealing here not only with knowledge in finalized situations requiring rational solutions with normative significance,
but particularly with knowledge that maintains a tie that is necessary for communication between the imaginary and the normative
worlds.

We refer to the subject faced with the problem of active search
or creativity: to know and discover himself, the outside world, and
the human and nonhuman objects that occur through rational construction as well as through fantasmic, magical, and identification
processes.

Our methodology is situated at the juncture of the associative
activity found in, for example, daydreaming and psychoanalysis and
activity requiring judgment and a direct confrontation with reality.
The frame of reference for observation is the associative effort made
by a subject in the presence of an experimenter who asks no questions
and makes no demands. It is only his presence that indicates that
an external reality exists and that the individual is expected "to be"
a subject required to "act," in a situation comparable, to a certain
extent, to the researcher's situation. The researcher indirectly confronts the more-or-less anonymous persons or judges who do not
expect anything specific except that he "be" a researcher who "acts"
and produces results. There are differences, however, between the
child researcher and the adult one: the child researcher, in the process of development, can either blend into or isolate himself from the
environment; above all, however, he lives intensely in the present.
The fully developed adult researcher can regress or project himself
into the future while maintaining a dialectical orientation toward

his preoccupations. In the child's case, there is a person present and at his disposal, whose expectations he must try to imagine even though this individual remains silent. In the adult's case, the subject, through his own imagination, confronts a fictitious but very powerful interlocutor who can contradict or possibly resist his work. In both cases, however, the real or fictitious interlocutor plays the role of an indirect judge and represents internal objects of control, irrespective of the genetic level of elaboration.

In our experimental conditions, the experimenter acts as an observer of the child or adolescent subject, who at first finds himself confronted with situations where reality can be dealt with in any way that he wishes. Subsequently, the subject must answer and confront precise demands that he does not know about at the beginning of experimentation. In the same way, at some time during his work, the adult researcher must confront the opinion or the countersuggestions of the person who will have access to his research. The difference between these two situations is that, in the latter case, the researcher is conscious of his predicament before confrontation. However, his desire to create something new and his need for creativity oblige him, to a certain extent, to ignore his predicament.

In our experimentation, the child has access to and can experience two very important stages. The first phase allows for associative work to take place (comparable to daydreaming, play, and the psychotherapeutic setting) in the presence of an observer. The second stage immediately follows the first and places the subject in a situation where he must respond to the experimenter's specific instructions and encouragement and must demonstrate his abilities to take into account different aspects of reality.

The analysis of symbolic work and systems of representation is central to our research insofar as it permits us to grasp how instinctual forces must be worked on to become operational. Without this process, no thought is possible. André Green (1973) writes, "If affection is evidence of unbridled thought which is present and cannot be eliminated even in the most abstract and rational processes, the last refuge of emotion is rationalization." Thus, although neither content nor form distinguishes rationalization from reason, it is nevertheless necessary to stimulate the process once more so that the affect, which created this reason, maintains the challenge.

Creativity and Creation

All of Piaget's work illustrates his central epistemological preoccupation: Why and how does a subject search for newness? Why and how does a child or a scientist—or an artist, we might add—seek to create, and what processes permit him to succeed?

In the Piagetian system, creativity and creation are not distinguishable, at least as far as the child and the scientist are concerned. The different passages from one level of development to another, whether psychological or scientific, and their respective constructions are considered original, although of normative character, the moment they are subject to the laws of universality. Here, of course, we are dealing with creativity and the creation inherent in thought and dependent on reflective abstraction. This process accounts for the increasing wealth of varied structural forms in the course of development: coordinations, the generalization of affirmations followed by that of negations, reversibility, the elaboration of reflexive thought, the systematic search for the "reason" of coordinations, and so on.

Thus, newness due to reflective abstractions finds its justification in equilibrium, the general tendency present in the continuous processes of disequilibration and reequilibration. At different levels of reflection, whatever is new may be summarized as follows: at the sensorimotor level imitation acquires a certain degree of virtuosity, it can function henceforth under deferred and subsequently internalized forms that constitute the beginning of representation, symbolic gestures followed by mental images, strengthened by the acquisition of language. Each new capacity entails the need to be exercised. Consequently, different levels of representation are superimposed on those of actions. Thought, with its newly found powers, can coordinate aims and means, and it becomes possible to give thematic content to operations and to use them as instruments that then acquire status as objects of thought. Thus, the secret of newness lies in the equilibration of differentiations and integrations.

Differentiation is the result of the work of abstraction, which allows for mental separation and transfer of certain characteristics; it entails the need for integration into new totalities, without which assimilation ceases to be possible. Such is the basic principle involved in the formation of newness. To put it in a more general way, the source of novelty lies in the necessity of equilibration between assim- ilation and accommodation because such equilibration causes endog- enous and exogeneous differentiations.

However, a central question still remains: Why is newness cre- ated? In the Piagetian system, the answer lies in the context of dis- equilibria, which are the source of progress in the development of knowledge because they constitute a motivational force. However, it is only when these disequilibria are overcome that they can play a formative role. Thus, it is only when a subject experiences dissat- isfaction and incoherence that he will seek to successfully overcome such disequilibria.

As concerns emotions and their role in the process of the con- struction of newness, Piaget did not discuss them any further. Although they appear to play a major role, they are only postulated in his system without any explanation of their origin. We will return to this important point later, when it becomes necessary to broaden our discussion. For the time being, we must keep in mind that the usual distinction between creativity and creation does not exist in Piagetian theory. Classically, creativity is defined as a predisposition of character and spirit that is cultivated, and creation is defined as the invention, the composition of a work of art or science satisfying two criteria: furnishing novelty, which is doing something never done before, and sooner or later, being recognized as something valuable.

In the Piagetian system, creativity and creation are found in all individuals insofar as these notions can be taken to refer to onto- genetic development and scientific procedure. As such, they imply that the energetic capacities of an individual are in the service of evolution and change, with regard to both his inner and his outer worlds. This conception conveys an idea of vital necessity compa- rable to the biological struggle for self-preservation. With more spe- cific reference to mental evolution, there is a necessity for creation (which makes the process at the same time creative) or for construc- tion insofar as the individual seeks to remove incoherence or the state of disequilibrium, which, if it lasts too long, endangers his status as a thinking subject, that is, one capable of evolution, of creation.

The same idea of the vital necessity of creativity and creation can be found in the work of Winnicott (1971). He stated that if one wanted to specify the place of creativity, the idea of creation must be separated from one referring to works of art. Winnicott's creativity is something universal: "It is inherent to life itself. . . . The creativity which we have seen is one which allows the individual to approach external reality." Thus, it follows an individual's intellectual and emotional development. However, Winnicott pushed his argument further than Piaget, who only mentioned the idea of struggle and danger. Winnicott analyzed the sources of danger by retaining Melanie Klein's fundamental notions of aggressive instincts and fantasies of destruction. These notions appear very early in an individual's life; the fusion of destructive tendencies with erotic instincts enables an individual to experience harmonious development. As far as the problem of creativity is concerned, Melanie Klein's (1955; Segal, 1957, 1964) theory contains the concept of reparation and restitution (also present in the development of symbolism) and, in the background, the fundamental Freudian concept of ambivalence between good and bad, love and hate, in the object relationship. In the same way, one can speak of ambivalence between what is true and what is untrue, assimilated and rejected, in the development of the relationship with the object of knowledge. Consequently, we return once again to the ideas of disequilibrium and conflict as the vectors of creativity, even though the object relationships referred to in the two models are different. In our opinion, however, their connection becomes obvious with reference to the development of mental functions. At the methodological level, one can arrange situations that capture the articulation between the two types of object relationships. On the theoretical level, one can introduce the emotional dimension in the analysis of the progress toward knowledge (Schmid-Kitsikis, 1982, 1985).

The Place of Emotional Activity in the Progress toward Knowledge

As we have already stated, creativity is responsible for the progressive advancement toward knowledge. Such progress implies that the individual possesses the desire to discover and to know. The *desire* referred to here must be distinguished from *need* insofar as the former refers to psychical reality and the latter to a physiological one. Emotions are an integral part of physical reality and, in particular, of instincts dominated by the pleasure–pain principle. Around this duality, other dichotomies gravitate: good and bad, within and without, inner and outer worlds, psychical and extrapsychical realities.

Such dualities play a structural role: In the beginning of a child's life, they participate in the constitution of the ego, originating in the object. During a subsequent phase, they acquire a defensive role permitting the preservation of the object menaced by tensions within the ego.

For Green (1973), these processes are connected by a certain number of concepts: The conjunction is a prearticulated totality escaping an individual's control, a sort of framework comprising the subject's constitution, in the naturalistic sense, the circumstances surrounding his conception and birth, the parents' wishes concerning him, and the biological and social situations he experiences. The conjunction is inscribed in the psychical apparatus. However, even though it constitutes one of the conditions for the elaboration of a structure, in order for this elaboration actually to take place, the mediation of the event and the object is necessary. By *event*, Green means what the English call *experience*, a term difficult to define because it is, in fact, neither experience nor feeling. Thus, the exterior world does not monopolize the event. Likewise, the event is not located totally within the inner world just because it is "experienced." In fact, what we are dealing with here is a breach in the conjunction that causes the event.

In the category of events, one can include the experiences of a want, of the loss of an object, of the revelation of seduction, of castration, and of the primal scene, which all provoke the creation of fantasy, reminiscence, discovery of play, and consciousness.

The reference to the event must be taken in the broadest sense: it maintains relations, on one hand, with the structure that defines the subject as formed by his begetters through the twofold difference of the sexes and the generations (primitive fantasies)—that is, the oedipal structure—and, on the other hand, with the conjunction. These relations are established through a contradiction: without the structure, the event is not intelligible; at the same time, however, the structure does not contain the event, which emerges from the breach sustained by the conjunction. Therefore, the structure is forced to change. For progress to take place, the structure must feed on the event and, in turn, leave its mark on it. This can only take place if there is absorption and profound transformation.

It is at this point that the object intervenes as the consequence of the meeting between the event, originating in the conjunction, and the structure. Freud conceives of the object as divided into invariable and variable fractions. This variability, which is a kind of explosion, can take numerous forms: the object of instinct, the part object, the object of the outer world, the object of desire, the phantasmic object, the narcissistic object, or the object of knowledge. Thus, it becomes obvious that there is a plurality of contexts in which the object appears. However, whatever the context, the object remains tied to the appearance of desire; the construction of the object of knowledge also implies the desire for this object of knowledge. In Piaget's theory, such a desire is attributed to an individual's need for adaptation and evolution. To put it another way, Piaget postulates that the desire for the object is present in any case, and thus, investment has taken place since he takes only successful evolution into consideration.

The individual's inner world is considered an increasingly complex organization of schemes, action schemes, thought schemes, and so on, where there is no room for emptiness, want, and one's own experiences. What is described is the chaos or incoherence of existing elements that the individual seeks to overcome, at all costs, by developing the necessary behavior (compensations, logical operations, and so on). Consequently, there is need for the object in order to succeed in one's interaction with the environment and need for coherence so that evolution toward higher levels of knowledge can take place.

Desire and its fluctuations—because they are tied to the conditions of experience or, to put it in Green's words, "to conditions of appearance of the events" (i.e., the breaches occurring in the conjunction)—were not considered by Piaget. In order to take such considerations into account, Piaget would have had to introduce an additional dimension into his model, on considering instinctual aspects and imagination, both closer to the primary than to the secondary processes. These processes cannot be considered in terms of the notions of total structures and levels of equilibrium. Therefore, we join Freud and Green in stating that the primary characteristics of the object are constituted by desire and identification, which, in the individual, represent both the elements "to be" and "to possess."

One might say, in a way, that Piaget, by insisting on imitative activity, took into consideration only aspects of the identification process.

The conjunction (whatever surrounds and happens to the individual before and after his birth) and the structure (bonds with the begetters entailing the twofold difference of the sexes and the generations) were not considered by Piaget. He affirmed that only what is biological and physiological constitutes the necessary departure points for human evolution, and he dissociated these problems from historical and psychological ones. Thus, in *La Naissance de l'Intelligence* (1952/1954), Piaget wrote:

> The psychological problem begins to play a role as soon as reflexes, posture, etc., are no longer considered in connection with the internal mechanism of a living organism but in their relations with the environment as it appears to a subject's activity.

Consequently, we witness the scotomization that prepares the individual's encounter with the environment, with the exception of the biological and physiological conditions common to all humans. Everything takes place as if one could not speak of the psychological aspect until the "event" originating in the "conjunction" and the "structure,"enters into relation with the environment in such a way that the object can intervene as the consequence of this encounter. It is not surprising, then, that whatever concerns the universal history of the individual and the constitution of primal fantasies is not taken into consideration in the discussions of the individual's progression toward knowledge.

And what can be said about emotions? Emotions can be situated at the point of encounter, resulting from the effects of the tensions originating in the object and the event. It is our belief, however, that emotion is ever present in the unpredictable facets of creativity and therefore must be further explored. As far as the event is concerned, emotion is the support or the apprehension of fantasy, that is, the place where desire appears. With the object, emotion concerns the psychical representation of the search for the satisfaction of a desired goal. Emotion is a force and a subjective experience. It provides the necessary energy for the operations of the psychical apparatus. Freud stated, however, that this energy lies *between* investments. According to Green (1972), emotion has the role of a conjunctive-disjunctive factor; it underlines the signifier. Under the effect of tension, the specificity of emotion is to conceal, to abolish, or to replace representation; that is, the subject conceives of the possibility of a representation but not of the representation of itself. Through this new perspective, it becomes possible to analyze what Piaget told us about the subject's course of action in his search for newness.

There is, first of all, the underlying desire to acquire knowledge. This desire is difficult to analyze if one adheres strictly to Piaget's ideas because he never really distinguished it from the subject's activity itself. Such activity emphasizes a subject's incapacity to become discouraged when faced with failure, which is always momentary and is never likely to provoke his breakdown. Consequently, there is a constant pursuit of higher levels of the organization of knowledge without a breach because of the process of reflective abstraction. Furthermore, Piaget explicitly voiced the idea that the subject will always seek to do away with momentary incoherence in his functioning. However, Piaget's investigations do not clarify whether the subject really experiences this incoherence and, if so, "how." Everything takes place as if incoherence is revealed to be intolerable for the individual, who strives to overcome it by the most powerful defensive means, that is, normative structures and, in particular, logico-mathematical ones. Thus, analyses undertaken by the observer can take into consideration only two or three moments of a subject's course of action:

- One that indicates his failure but, at the same time, places the subject in a disadvantageous position because he lacks certain capacities for success that will appear only when more advanced evolution has taken place
- The second moment, which is intermediary and emphasizes that everything is in place for future success
- The third moment, when success is possible without any danger of failure

Therefore, the source of newness and the explanation for its construction are to be found in the necessity, felt by all individuals, for equilibration between assimilation and accommodation and in the fact that this necessity causes differentiations in the inner and outer worlds. We refer here to progressive differentiations of schemes that become richer and, at the same time, conserve their anterior states, without loss or production of radically new schemes.

We can summarize the preceding by stating that we are dealing here with three aspects of the same emotion (necessity), which implies the idea of a vital need more than the idea of a desire:

- The necessity to remove incoherence
- The necessity for equilibrium between assimilation and accommodation, allowing for differentiations between the environment and the inner world
- The necessity for completeness insofar as nothing must be lost or entirely created

The "need for necessities" represents the subject's search to be in agreement with reality. He seeks such agreement and, at the same time, fears it, for if it is ever attained, the subject would be reduced to stagnation. Therefore, states Piaget, the object of knowledge, which for him represents reality, escapes us. The more we develop the instruments necessary for its possession and think we have succeeded, the more reality, in fact, escapes us. It is true that the subject escapes fusion with reality in this way, but at the same time, this internal pursuit does not permit him to experience his inner self or his own behavior. Concerning the "event," emotion is scotomized; and with reference to the object, we are dealing here only with necessity. Therefore, it is difficult to see how sought-after newness succeeds in enriching itself, as a whole set of experiences, which may cause a subject's behavior to deviate, are ignored. One might also question how such creative activity can cause the abstraction of the other emotions that are inevitably tied to the fact that the goal to be attained, even if limited to research activity itself and the satisfaction that such a pursuit can procure, is never really immediate. All research implies meanderings, which can vary from general orientation without results to diverse trial-and-error procedures, more-or-less efficient in attaining a goal. Furthermore, the representational world of the Piagetian subject seems to be limited only to interalizations concerning the normative world of objects of knowledge. Everything takes place as if the subject were, from the outset, on a path of rational production. Piagetian investigation anticipates such results insofar as the "critical method" is conceived of as a dialectical exchange between the subject and the experimental material. With this method, deviations are rarely permitted.

At this point in our discussion, we would like to return to our initial hypothesis. It concerns the creative-functioning analogy between the child researcher, who is in conditions where the outcome is not finalized by openly formulated demands from the exterior, and the adult researcher, who pursues a work hypothesis without clearly knowing the exterior demands from the outset which would, in fact, greatly diminish the notion of where the research will lead him.

Our own investigations, which we intend to discuss later when dealing with the analysis of symbolism, have brought to light in a most striking manner the fact that even if thought restricts its efforts to the exercise of secondary processes, it remains open to primary processes. These primary processes guarantee the eruption of creative intuition at the very time when rationality is at work. In order for creative results to be attained, the two processes must join forces and must not contradict each other. Thus, daydreaming, or associative activity, must not be blocked by the eruption of thought that is too normative; similarity, intellectual functioning, must not be thwarted by the eruption of unchecked emotions. Green (1972) suggests the concept of a tertiary process, "the process which connects the primary and secondary processes in such a way that the primary processes limit the saturation of the secondary processes and vice-versa." It depends on the notions of libidinal mobility as the "stability of libidinal energy," mobilized to a level that is neither stagnant nor perpetual movement that alternates in variety, diversity, and the spectrum of investments. The transformation of libidinal energy implies the "possibility of converting a primary process into a secondary one and vice-versa." The notion of unstable equilibrium could account for these processes: between "perpetual movement" and what is "permanently set," between "the incessant call from afar" and "the permanent silence of the here and now," between chaos and fixity. Such intraindividual mobility maintained by the dual action of the primary and secondary processes "protects against exclusive tyranny of one over the other."

As stated by Winnicott (1971), in order for such a system to function, a field of illusion is necessary so that the possibility of play, in a sphere where one can make believe, is guaranteed. The subject should not be forced, at least in the beginning of the experiment, to ask himself questions about what is real or unreal, true or untrue. This field of illusion must stay as it is and be delimitated insofar as it constitutes the field of fantasy and recognized as such by the subject.

Children's Symbolic Elaboration: An Example of What Has Just Been Presented

In the context of dual methodology, following both associative and experimental paths, we have been able to delineate, in the same child, a certain number of variations extending from associative elaboration (expressing nonretroactive intentions out of the child's control) to intellectual elaboration (expressing retroactive activities with internal or external goals). Such a study of symbolism is part of a more general analysis concerning relations between primary and secondary processes and their role and meaning in the evaluation of rational thought as well as factors, movement, and issues in the mental process during sublimation with rational character.

We use the term *symbolism* in the broadest sense to include processes expressing:

- Revelations whose symbolic significance escapes the child's conscious and thus can thenceforth take place only when conditions where they do not intervene from the exterior in an overinstrusive manner, in the form of an interpretation of a question.
- Acquisitions whose symbolic significance and a child's awareness of them depend on his use of cognitive schemes in action and in construction. Furthermore, we would like to add that the product of symbolic elaboration is dynamic. It extends to mental combinations that are integrative in character.

Our central hypothesis specifies that a confrontation of symbolic elaboration (of unconscious or conscious signifiers) with that of rational activity (in a more-or-less conflictual confrontation) must be maintained if the latter is to benefit from development, consolidation, and enrichment and is to be of increasingly important thematic specification. Emilio Rodriquez (1956) stated in this regard:

> Symbol-formation and symbolizing are not only indispensable to start intellectual and emotional development, but symbolization is fully active throughout life, underlying the increasingly sophisticated operations of adult thought.

Concerning our study of symbolism, we would like to emphasize the importance of circumscribing and identifying its role in the elaboration of and the differentiation between the external and the internal worlds. Symbolism is, in fact, a juncture for the process of imagination and rationality.

Our Methodology

Our experimentation has two important phases. In the first phase, the child is left relatively "free" to act or not to act, to speak or to be silent, when confronted with certain materials, which can be manipulated with or without verbalization. It is during this moment of relative liberty that we try to grasp the "intentions" of the child through his behavior and activity in situations in which he is authorized to manipulate objects at whatever level of expression he chooses: motor, symbolic, phantasmic, logico-mathematical, and so on. Insofar as nothing in the proposed experimental situations has been chosen by the child, we can seize his attempts to render "significant" what has been purposely left unclarified but, which contains the underlying plan of our investigative "intentions." The experimenter's only interventions are words of encouragement to make the child do what he wishes when and if his inactivity is too prolonged.

During the second phase of experimentation, the investigation procedure is made more specific, through directions that facilitate the appearance of the child's processes of control in his treatment of the proposed situations. It permits us to better define the nature and quality of mental mobility and of the child's mental elaborations through his reactions to directions encouraging differentiated productions; various levels of reality; the need to pass from one type of function to another; and different types of provocations or conflicts introduced within the experimental situation to draw out different ways of coping with the present.

Commentary

It is obvious that the situation that we propose is not comparable to the therapeutic situation. On one hand, the person in the presence of the child has expectations of him and, moreover, makes proposals even if silently. On the other hand, we do not interpret the material produced by the child, and our way of obtaining reactions, reelaborations, and so on has nothing to do with the therapeutic situation. However, it is important to note that the material that we gather is based on what the child projects into the present, within the proposed situations, materials, experimenter, and so on, which are basically game situations or play activities.

Analysis

Our main preoccupation is with content analysis of varied significance. We pay particular attention to the analysis of active configurations, role playing, scenario, and production. As previously stated, we analyze the significance of conscious or unconscious content and diverse types of organization. Furthermore, we are attentive to the analysis of movements that emanate from the bonds between emotions and representation. Through our analysis of the rhythms of unfolding action, of breaches, of disruption of action, or return to calm, or of the child's organization of the experimental universe, we attempt to grasp the relations that hold together the primary and secondary processes when, during the first phase, the child does not receive any outside orientation and, during the second, he could receive directions.

Given this particular methodological situation, which is neither a therapeutic setting nor a purely experimental investigation, our conceptual analysis has to be restructured and reformulated. If a certain analogy with the psychoanalytic as well as the Piagetian conceptual framework exists, it is because these theoretical systems have sufficiently established their solidity concerning the generalizable and universal character of certain psychic and mental mechanisms. Consequently, it is possible by looking for new meanings,

to interpret contents that appear in other contexts outside of, for
example, the transference situation or the critical interview.

In the continual confrontation between primary and secondary
processes kept active by the child himself when the environment
does not oblige him to make a specific choice, one can observe,
through such an investigative procedure, that the child's symbolic
elaboration, at whatever developmental level, has recourse, throughout his evolution, breaches, and regression, to three types of invariants. These are internalized products of an area of historical and
personal experience, which have acquired the status of a mobile
ensemble, but which, during change, do not involve true losses or
true gains linked to varied representations:

- Archaic representations (primary fantasies)
- Conventional representations with cultural and normative
  significance (logico-mathematical, social, and cultural
  invariants)
- Physical, spatial, and temporal representations (the physical,
  spatial, and temporal properties of objects)

Multiple movements among these different representations
inform us, on a synchronic level, about the quality and mobility of
a child's production, both horizontally, in the richness and variety
of the forms of his symbolic elaboration, and vertically, in his passage
from one level of elaboration to another. However, submission to
one or another of these forms of representation leads the child to
any of the following:

- Productions of an archaic character, revealing a certain difficulty in entering into contact with the external world without avoiding a continual eruption of phantasmic acting out.
  Consequently, the child turns inward because an excess of
  assimilation and accommodation takes place only with reference to internal objects.
- Productions of an "operative" nature, a term used by psy-
  chosomaticians to qualify a type of thought in which affects
  do not seem to be able to maintain links with rational thought.
  Reflective abstraction and logico-mathematical thinking pre-
  dominate and bring about a division in thought functioning.
  Everything takes place as if knowledge were formed by a

child's "doing" and "having," by means of acquiring schemas
and logico-mathematical instruments that make activities
possible like putting things together and pulling them apart,
piling them on top of each other, and so on. Structures seem
to function without flaws or disruptions because the child's
intention is to master the universe.

• Productions, especially those of a concrete nature, where the
subject acts on things (the material reality of objects) and
where the associative capacity is absent. Autonomous retroactive procedures, a plan, and orientation toward what is
possible and what is not appears to be difficult and even
impossible. The activity is, above all, empirical and accommodating. There is an incapacity to arrive at relationships
because of the difficulty of maintaining distance with reference to external reality. The elaboration of conscious meanings seems to escape the child.

Our observations of children between the ages of 2 and 10, both
well adjusted and marginal subjects, have permitted us to illustrate
the significance and importance of symbolic elaboration for the
development of rational thought through detailed analyses of associative and normative activity sequences and their relationships.
Analyses of the scenarios, settings, and dramatic games and their
thematic content through the rhythms of productions (as in movements, breaches, and calm periods) and their figurative aspects have
allowed us to identify several processes, some of which follow as
examples. These processes are not mutually exclusive.

Genesis and the Life Cycle. Through a variety of dramatic games,
the child, cautiously and with a certain distance, expresses themes
of archaic character, such as distinctions between the sexes and the
generations, parental ties, life–death seduction, and castration, which
alternate with moments of restitution and reparation and of affective,
social, and normative relations. These activities can be completely
distinguished, in their symbolic meaning, from those that involve
the child in phantasmic imagery in which an elaboration of make-
believe activity fails to appear. The child's participation in the quality of introjections and projections indicates the absence of this type
of activity. However, as concerns our observations, the reference to
these archaic representations, as fantasies acting at a secondary level,

is possible in the forms of invariants that permit the original fantasies to be "played." They permit the symbolic retracing of genesis, of the life cycle with its conflicts, and so on.

Play with Emotions. The child's play indicates affects with contrary meanings: love-hate, pleasure-pain, and so on; everything takes place (as if "he played the ambivalence mechanisms.") For example, in this way, he expresses the desire to venture into what is forbidden, reprehensible, and so on. The appearance of acting out during such play is transitory and is usually followed by a return to what is "normal."

Play with Rules. The child develops symbolic activities with normative and conventional characteristics that can be shared with others and are equivalent, to a certain extent, to a linguistic code. Each representation is fixed and can be decoded in only one manner. However, if submission to the code seems unnecessary to the child, we have observed that make-believe activity moves on to a second stage, where play takes place as if the child wanted to ignore the need to respect certain rules. At this point, he takes the risk of transforming what he has already accepted as a conventional collective symbolism by introducing the impossible, the forbidden, or even the irrational.

At the other extreme, we find certain children who, even in such play conditions, can manipulate symbolism of only a conventional character, which entails certain limitations on thinking activity, that is, stereotyped thought without links to affects, or purely normative thought.

Games with Objects from the Physical Universe. The child develops an activity of a symbolic nature by allowing himself to represent certain physical objects with their well-defined properties as something completely different, while succeeding in maintaining intact the true identity of the object. The substitute objects seem to be necessary for the elaboration of scenarios and projective dramatic games. However, for other children, an object cannot be momentarily transformed. It must always preserve its name and function. In this case, we witness an organization of the universe where everything is identified, realistically manipulated, cataloged, and so on.

The analysis of the movements occurring in the child's associative activities—their interrelations, breaches, and confrontations through creative games and their compromises between submission and opposition—permits us to illustrate to what extent the three types of internalized referent (archaic, normative, and physical) constitute the place and sources of experience. When all three are readily available during the different processes engaged in by the child, they permit him to experience, through his relations with the external world, his relative stability, with his failures, losses, lacks, and incoherences, as well as his possibilities for rebuilding, creating, and innovating. Thus, the child's rational elaboration, which must progressively open itself to possible novelty, paradoxically underlies a frequent recourse to archaic and magic-symbolic referents, which play an important role in trial-and-error behavior, as well as those of surpassing, verification, and new reelaborations.

On the other hand, when the steps chosen—or offered by or to the child—are of a finalized character, rational activity becomes production or reproduction, which satisfies the child, at the symbolic level, with representations whose meanings are those of codes or rules that have limited combinations or are limitable in time and structure because they form a kind of total structure that the child must discover each time.

Thus, even if the work of thought is dedicated to the exercise of secondary processes, it remains open to primary processes that ensure the eruption of creative intuition at the very moment when rationality is at work. In order to achieve a creative end, the two processes must combine forces without becoming conflictive. Associative activity should not be blocked by the eruption of overly normative thought, just as intellectual functioning should not be hindered by the eruption of uncontrollable affects.

References

Freud, S. Formulations on the two principles of functioning. In Complete Psychological Works of Sigmund Freud (Vol. 13). London: Hogarth Press, 1958.

Green, A. Note sur les processes tertiaires. Revue Française de Psychoanalyse, 1972, 3.

Green, A. Le discours vivant. Paris: P.U.F., 1973.

Klein, M. The psychoanalytic play technique. Psychological Review, 1955, 44, 223–237.

Piaget, J. The origins of intelligence in children (M. Cook, trans.). New York: Basic Books, 1954. (Originally published, 1952).

Rodriquez, E. Notes on symbolism. International Journal of Psychoanalysis, 1956, 37, 147–158.

Schmid-Kitsikis, E. *Théorie et clinique de fonctionnement mental*. Liège: Mardaga, 1985.

Schmid-Kitsikis, E., & Nicolaidis, N. *Creativité et/ou symptome*. Paris: Clancier, 1982.

Segal, H. Notes on symbolism formation. *International Journal Of Psychoanalysis*, 1957, *38*, 391–397.

Segal, H. Contribution au symposium sur le fantasie. *Revue Française de Psychoanalyse*, 1964, *28*, 507–513.

Winnicott, D. W. *Playing and reality*. New York: Basic Books, 1971.

Introduction to Chapter 5

VALERIE L. SHULMAN

Willem Doise is a theoretician and researcher concerned with questions that are reminiscent of those posed by Jean Piaget. However,
although his rationale is set within the traditional Piagetian framework, he has elaborated it with additional dimensions, seeking to
generate a theory of cognitive development that is grounded in the
reality of the social milieu. During the past 10 years, Doise has
pursued his research on group relations, social conflict, and social
cognition, as well as on their relations to traditional Piagetian theory—in Geneva, where he is currently a professor of experimental
psychology, as well as in Western Europe. That research has led him
to propose a synthesis of individual and social cognition in the form
of a genetic social psychology (1978, p. 77).

In the chapter "On the Social Development of the Intellect,"
Doise illustrates his approach. He poses the question: How and why
do children of the human species become intelligent? Superficially,
at least, this may appear to be a traditional epistemological question.
However, he makes it quite clear that he is pursuing the question
from a different perspective, that of sociocognitive, or genetic-social,
psychology. In other words, he is concerned with the role of social
interaction in the individual's achievement of Piagetian operations.

It would appear that there are three areas where he has diverged
from the traditional epistemology. First, although his work has relied

on basic tenets of Piagetian "constructivism," it may be more accurately characterized as socioconstructivist. Therefore, although he
may accept the concept that knowledge is constructed and reconstructed by the individual over time through equilibration and the
complementary processes of assimilation and accommodation as
hypothesized by Piaget, for Doise the social milieu creates the necessary context within which those processes occur.

Second, whereas Piaget (1935/1970, 1969; Piaget & Inhelder,
1975) acknowledged the importance of social interaction as a fundamental factor in the development of cognitive structures, it was
accepted as a given in nonspecific form and thus was neither given
much prominence nor investigated independently. Piaget (1973)
commented on the universality of social interaction and its role in
providing information to the individual:

> In every milieu individuals gather information, collaborate, discuss,
> oppose one another, etc., and this constant inter-individual exchange
> intervenes during the whole development according to a socialization
> operation which concerns not only the social life of children among
> themselves, but also the relationships with their elders or with adults
> of any age. (p. 148)

Doise, on the other hand, suggests that it is just those social interactions and interindividual exchanges with peers, as well as with
adults, that create the context within which cognitive structures are
developed. It is the "social operation" with its inherent interactions
that is the encompassing structure that he has studied. In other
words, Doise has selected specific elements of social interaction as
independent variables in order to study their effects on various aspects
of cognitive development. The guiding hypothesis for his work is
that:

> The coordinations of actions between individuals facilitates the coor-
> dination of the same acts by the individual. When several individuals
> have to coordinate their actions with regard to certain objects, they
> should be more inclined to coordinate their own individual actions with
> regulations to these objectives. (1978, p. 77)

A third major point of divergence, and probably the most characteristic of the "neo-Piagetians," is a concern about later applicability of the data. Hypothesizing that social interaction exercises a
causal effect on cognitive development, Doise has designed experimental situations in which cooperative activities are used to foster

individual development. Those formats can be adapted to more general use, as in a school, without the prerequisite quantum leap required by traditional Piagetian experiments.

The research of Doise and his colleagues has provided additional theoretical and empirical support for a variety of "self-help" and "peer-tutoring" programs that are currently popular in the United States. Further, this research may precipitate a reevaluation of the policies and the programs that seek to completely individualize the curriculum, particularly for those students who have been identified as coming from "underprivileged" backgrounds.

References

Doise, W. Groups and individuals: Explanations in social psychology. Cambridge: Cambridge University Press, 1978.

Piaget, J. The science of education and the psychology of the child. New York: Orion Press, 1970. (Originally published in French, 1935.)

Piaget, J. The child and reality: Problems in genetic psychology. New York: Viking Press, 1973.

Piaget, J., & Inheldei, B. The psychology of the child. London: Rutledge and Keegan Paul, 1969.

CHAPTER 5

On the Social Development of the Intellect

WILLEM DOISE

Why and how do children of the human species become intelligent, at least generally, during the first years of their existence? In the first part of this paper, we would like to show how the response to this question has been formulated in terms of social psychology, but without applying social psychological investigative methods to explicate the response. As it were, the social role in cognitive development is frequently accepted as a postulate. In the second part of this chapter, we would like to show that psychological experimentation permits illustrating, if not verifying, some characteristics of the manner in which social factors intervene in cognitive development.

The Social Postulate

Most theories on the development of intelligence, phylogenetic as well as ontogenetic, support the postulate that adaptation to the physical environment is the principal function of the elaboration of

WILLEM DOISE • Faculty of Psychology and the Educational Sciences, University of Geneva, CH-1211 Geneva 4, Switzerland.

99

the cognitive instruments. But is this adaptation developed with respect to that environment? When the development of knowledge is studied in primates, the prototypical environment is often comprised of a bit of food that is unreachable by the subject with a stick, or even with two sticks that fit together, that the individual, becoming intelligent, will use to seize the food. Different theories on cognitive development and on human learning, even those elaborated in Geneva, often assume that the human environment is comprised exclusively of objects, particularly at the level of constructing experimental paradigms.

Fortunately, at the theoretical level, such limitations seem to be outdated. First, we will present the perspective of an ethologist. Humphrey (1976) observed that members of the anthropoid species, and some human tribes, rarely use all of their cognitive capacities to solve problems concerning biological survival in their natural habitat:

> We are thus faced with a conundrum. It has been repeatedly demonstrated in the artificial situations of the psychological laboratory that anthropoid apes possess impressive powers of creative reasoning, yet these feats of intelligence seem simply not to have any parallels in the behavior of the same animals in their natural environment. I have yet to hear of an example from the field in which a chimpanzee (or for that matter a Bushman) uses his full capacity for inferential reasoning in the solution of a biologically relevant practical problem. (p. 307)

Why, then, are higher primates intelligent and, in any case, much more intelligent than other species? Because they are obliged to acquire factual knowledge that they use within the context of the social community, and the principle role of creative intelligence is then to adapt to the social life. In the course of his presentation, Humphrey argued effectively that the more complex cognitive demands made on higher primates are of social origin. It would then be through their adaptation to their social environment, which from the cognitive perspective is much more complex, that higher primates and humans are adapted to their physical environment.

It should be noted that some of Humphrey's points of reasoning are not very different from arguments advanced by a psychologist who has argued in favor of a more social approach to studying cognitive development in children. In effect, Smedslund (1966) also regrets that, in this domain, "actual research uniformly considers cognitive development as an interaction between the child and his non-human environment" (p. 161). Nevertheless,

it is well known that the child's interests (and consequently the majority
of his experiences) are concentrated on the principal aspects of the social
life, notably rules (roles), values, and symbols. Even when the child
plays alone, his play causes roles, symbols, and social products to intervene. For this reason, one must admit that social interaction must be a
major factor in cognitive development. (p. 162)

Then again, "the logico-mathematical tests seem to have relatively
little intrinsic interest for children, and in an instance where interest
intervenes, it seems to reflect a novelty effect of short duration"
(p. 161). Nevertheless, when such problems are embedded in a social
context, and more precisely, when they give way to communication
conflicts between individuals having different concentrations, cognitive progress can be verified in the form of intellectual decentration.

Hypotheses on the social role in cognitive development
advanced by an ethologist and a psychologist can seem to be rea-
sonable. That precisely poses the problem: too many of these
researchers are content to affirm social importance without being
concerned with empirically verifying their hypotheses. In that regard,
we cite Mead and Piaget.

We know that for Mead (1934), social interaction or, more precisely, "gestural communication" occurs at the beginning of cognitive development. "Conversation of gestures" assumes a reciprocal
adaptation:

Just as in fencing the parry is an interpretation of the thrust, so, in the
social act, the adjustive response of one organism to the gesture of another
is the interpretation of that gesture by that organism—it is the meaning
of that gesture. (p. 78)
   "Conversations through gestures" are also based upon the use of vocal
gestures, which are interiorized: the gestures thus internalized are significant symbols because they have the same meanings for all individual
members of the given society or social group, i.e., they respectively
arouse the same attitudes in the individuals making them that they arouse
in the individuals responding to them; otherwise the individual could
not internalize them. (p. 47)

But where in Mead does one find evidence permitting verification
of this thesis?

For Piaget (1967), the epistemologist, there was no doubt that
"human intelligence is developed in the individual as a function of
social interactions that are, in general, greatly neglected" (p. 269).
Elsewhere (Doise, 1978), we have had the opportunity to show how
a certain fluctuation characterizes Piagetian reflections on this
problem. The explicative approach adopted in the book *The Moral*

Judgment of the Child, published in 1932, arises from social psychology; the passage from heteronomy to the autonomy of childlike moral conceptions, the passage from an objective interpretation of the responsibility is explained by the multiple interactions of the cooperation between equals, in which the children participate in their societies. It is not only moral development but also knowledge in general that is thus explained:

> Social life is necessary to permit the individual to become aware of the functioning of the spirit and to transform it in their own norms, the simple functional equilibrium immanent in each mental or even vital activity. (Piaget, 1932, p. 324)

Again, the social is involved as an explicative factor but without being demonstrated in the proper sense.

In *Sociological Studies* (1965), Piaget reexamined "the question, as often debated, of the social or the individual nature of logic" (p. 143). The question is posed with great precision: Can the individual alone attain an operatory idea, this organization of actions that are interiorized, composable, and reversible? Before responding, Piaget first illustrated that there is correspondence between the child's development of cognitive activities and certain forms of social cooperation. The simultaneous changes in the two domains constitute the point of departure of Piagetian reflection:

> To the period properly called the stage of operations (7–11/12 years) corresponds . . . a very clear progress in socialization; the child becomes capable of cooperation, that is to say that he no longer thinks in function only of himself but of the actual or possible coordination of points of view. (Piaget, 1965, p. 157)

The theme is concisely formulated in *Moral Judgment:* "The social life and the individual life are one" (Piaget, 1932, p. 75).

It is, then, shown how, in the case of equilibrium, the relations of intellectual exchange, as well as the exchange of values, manifest a logic identical to what also becomes actualized in individual operations:

> Social relations equilibrated in cooperation will then constitute the "groupings" of the operations, exactly the same as all logical operations exercised by the individual on the external world, and the grouping laws define the form of the ideal equilibrium common to the first as to the second. (Piaget, 1965, p. 159)
>
> . . . between individual operations and cooperation, in the final account, will be fundamental identity, from the perspective of the laws of equilibrium which govern the two. (p. 162)

Can one be truly content with a verification by a correlation, seeing an identity between structures that intervene in physical reality and those that intervene in social interactions, and that no longer pose the problem of eventual social influence?

Evidently, this is not the opinion of authors such as Leontiev, who base their work on dialectical materialism. If that author forcefully called for psychological study as such and combated the falsely interdisciplinary attitude of psychologists who address others with their request "Come into psychology and rule over us," he has nevertheless constantly reverted to the need of studying the human psychism in its social context, affirming that such a study must "put in evidence the category of psychological awareness, and that means understanding the actual passages which connect the concrete individual psychism and social awareness and different forms of the latter" (Leontiev 1976, p. 5).

How did he proceed to attain this objective? We know of his celebrated experiments that illustrate how certain sensory thresholds can be considerably lowered when the sensation becomes more relevant, especially when it is embedded in a system of actions. As human activities are essentially social, we understand that such experiments can illustrate the passages that link individual psychysms to the social group. Other experiments reported by Leontiev (1970–1971) directly studied the effects that different types of social interventions exert on the regulations of cognitive nature. Nevertheless, historical reconstruction seems to be Leontiev's preferred approach to link the psychysm to the social. This approach reflects the thesis of Marx and of Engels, according to which work is the origin of development in human history. Now,

> work carried out under conditions of common collective activity, such that man is at once within this process, not only with nature, but with other men, members of a given society. It is only through this relationship with other men that man finds himself in relation with nature. (Leontiev, 1976, p. 67)

Leontiev (1976, p. 71s) developed the example of "beating up the game" (the big game hunt), a wild-game stalk and kill in which one group of individuals stalks a wild animal that will be chased into an open area, where it will be captured by another group. Apparently for the individual beater (hunter), this is an activity that lacks sense; it acquires meaning only in making a correspondence with the other hunter's activity. In addition, manufacturing a tool, which is specifically a human activity, is basically a social activity. Thus, the tool is a social object, the product of a social practice, a social work experience. Consequently, the generalized reflection of the work object's objective properties are crystallized and also become the product of an individual practice. As a result, the most simple human knowledge is directly carried out in a concrete action of work by a tool. It is not limited to the individual's personal experience; it is carried out on the basis of acquiring the experience of a social praxis (1976, p. 76).

The actual development of intelligence in our children is embedded in social history in the same way through a "process of appropriation from the accumulated experience of humanity throughout social history" (Leontiev, 1976, p. 312). If the child is surrounded by an objective world created by humans, which incorporates the history of their social history, the child does not adopt this heritage by himself alone. For example, this would be an abstract supposition, a Robinson Crusoe story, as in thinking that a child adapts himself to a spoon. In reality, the situation is that the mother feeds the child with a spoon: "The mother helps the child, intervenes in his actions, and in the common action that results, the child develops a skill in using a spoon. Thereafter, he knows how to use the spoon as a *human* object" (1976, p. 314).

Tran Duc Thao (1973) also cited dialectical materialism in order to explain the historical development and the ontogenesis of human intelligence. In a daring manner, he traced a parallel between the steps of the historical and the ontogenetic development of human intelligence, trying to fill our knowledge gaps in each of these developments with what we know, or believe we know, from the other. The pointing gesture would constitute the essential element of intellectual development. It is a social act, an appeal to intervention, as with the child who shows a container of jam to his mother. With the aid of this gesture, Tran Duc Thao reconstructed "the origins of the representational sign in prehuman development," reverting in his way to the story of the hunt, at the point where the hunters have already developed the habit of pointing toward the hunt.

In the child, the adaptation of the sign would be accomplished in an analogous manner:

> The appearance of this new structure of the sign has *without doubt* been
> prepared by the child's social experience, who must have seen on diverse
> occasions people who point a finger at him to indicate an object behind
> a screen which he can not see. (Tran Duc Thao, 1973, p. 124)

It is necessary that we again stress how social intervention is accepted
as a postulate. If that is, perhaps, an indispensable step to the level
of prehistoric reconstruction, one would think that this is not the
case when one studies child development, where experimentation
provides useful support to a thesis as important as the one described
herein.

The six authors mentioned here are evidently not the only ones
who have adhered to the social postulate. One could, for example,
add Berry and Dasen (1974), who attempted to illustrate how different ecological contexts moderate the individual's cognitive functioning, with the intermediary of cultural systems and different
systems of socialization. However, in their research, ecological contexts were the ones that were studied. But seeing the limits of this
account, it is now time to relate how we have tried to study experimentally the links between social interaction and cognitive
development.

Experimental Illustration

Research that indicates that a certain correspondence exists
between cognitive development and the development of the modalities of participation in social interactions is not lacking. Here, we
are content to cite the research completed in Geneva by Piaget (1932),
Nielsen (1951), Moessinger (1975), and Dami (1975), as well as other
research by Flavell and his collaborators (1968), Feffer (1970), Waller
(1971, 1973), and Mikula (1972). Naturally, this enumeration is not
exhaustive. Its only objective is to recall how much research already
exists that effectively shows that the development of social skills
and competence ranks with cognitive development. However, this
body of research also has in common not dealing with the problem
of causality. Thus, the objective for our own research in this domain
was mainly to illustrate how—at least, at certain phases of genetic
development—social interactions can foster the emergence of certain
cognitive operations. Contrary to the research cited, we explicitly

introduce the modalities of social interaction as independent variables at the level of the experimental paradigm in order to study the effect on certain aspects of cognitive development.

To defend the thesis that social interaction plays a causal role in cognitive development is not so much to adhere to the conceptions that would imply that the individual is passively fashioned by the regulations imposed from the outside. Our conception is interactionist and constructionist; in questioning the surrounding environment, the individual elaborates systems of organization from his action on reality. In the majority of cases, it is not only a question of reality; it is precisely in coordinating his own actions with those of others that he elaborates the systems of coordinations of his actions and consequently arrives at reproducing them all alone. The causality that we attribute to social interaction is not unidirectional; it is circular and progresses in a spiral. Interaction permits the individual to master certain coordinations, which then permit him to participate in more elaborate social interactions, which, in their turn, become the source of cognitive development for the individual.

The intention of my co-workers, G. Mugny and A. N. Perret-Clermont, as well as my own, is to undertake the empirical examination of this very question, a domain that has been dropped by the Genevan school. Our basic hypothesis is that social interaction exercises a causal effect on cognitive development. We follow Piaget in considering cognition the coordination of actions, interiorized and reversible. However, we think that these individual coordinations are first made possible by coordination *between* individuals. Interindividual coordinations precede and promote intraindividual coordinations.

Of course, this is a very general thesis that, therefore, is unlikely to be proved in one experiment. In fact, our team has now compiled some 20 experiments (see Doise & Mugny, 1981) on different phenomena, illustrating varied aspects of this general thesis. First, we tried to show that, indeed, interindividual coordinations appear to be earlier developmentally than individual coordinations. More specifically, we tried to show that, at certain ages, children collectively perform more advanced coordinations than they do alone. Second, we are examining the subsequent effects of this participation on the individual in making more advanced coordinations. These experiments illustrate a sentence of Vygotsky (1965): "What children can do together today, they can do alone tomorrow." Third, we are study-ing one important mechanism of social interaction: sociocognitive conflict. In a paper dealing with the social origin of decentration, Smedslund (1966) developed the idea that children can progress when confronted with the centrations of others, even when these centrations are in error. Centrations are here to be understood in the Piagetian sense, as more elementary cognitive schemes that have to be coordinated in more complex cognitive structures in order to give rise to operational thinking. As the rationale of our thesis, we place the role of the sociocognitive conflict at its very core: if a child, all by himself, approaches reality with successive and different centra-tions, these differences are made explicit when two individuals are engaged at the same time in the same problem with opposing cen-trations. Such simultaneity unveils the more urgent necessity of coor-dinating those insufficient centrations. Of course, this coordination can be enhanced by some other factors, for instance, by submitting the child to a systematic questioning, by assigning him a given responsibility in a social interaction, or by facilitating the initial capacity that he is endowed with in approaching the social inter-action. The role of these factors has been examined in various studies, references to which can be found in the appended reference section.

More recently, our research group has begun a fourth series of studies concerned with the correspondence between social relations and cognitive coordinations. When such correspondences material-ize in situations of sociocognitive conflict, they are thought to facil-itate cognitive coordinations.

In the same broad sense, these studies introduce one new per-spective into the classical research on group performance: generally, these studies try to find out which modalities of interaction improve the group efficiency in specific tasks. Our aim, on the other hand, is to examine the effect that those interactions exert on bringing about more elaborated cognitive processes in the individual participating in social interaction. More specifically, when our research deals with an effect of social facilitation, it is not in the sense as Zajonc (1965), who examined primarily the activation of cognitive processes that are already there; specifically, our research goes after the very con-struction of new cognitive capacities in a given social interaction.

Let us now describe some of our main research paradigms, together with the results that they have provided.

The Cooperative Game

This game consists of a motor coordination task. Three activities can be carried out on pulleys attached by strings to a lead pencil target: pulling, releasing, or blocking. A response on one pulley must be coordinated with responses on either one or two other pulleys in order to move the target along a predetermined route; in this sense, the task involves cognitive skills. The scores are obtained by summing across the number of segments in which the target remains correctly in the middle of the "road," and by then subtracting the number of segments where the target leaves the road (errors). (See Figure 1.)

In the first experiments, we (Doise, 1978; Doise & Mugny, 1975) compared the individual performances of younger children (ages 7–8) and older children (ages 9–10), each manipulating pulleys, with the collective performances of pairs in which each member handled only one pulley. As predicted, the younger children performed better in the collective condition. There were no such differences for the older children. Furthermore, developmentally more complex coordinations were observed in interindividual interactions before they were found in individuals acting alone. Similar patterns of findings were obtained when situations were "individualized," either by appointing a leader or by eliminating verbal communication. In both cases, the group performance was contingent to a greater extent on the individual's respective abilities and not on their coordinated efforts. As before, these differences between experimental conditions held for the younger but not for the older children. These results are reminiscent of findings from studies of group problem-solving, where logical tasks are better performed by hierarchical or centralized groups and creative tasks by more homogeneous groups. In our experiment, the older children performed a task that, to them, had acquired logical characteristics, as they mastered the necessary coordinations.

In the fourth experiment (Doise & Mugny, 1981), children of three different ages carried out either individual tasks or collective tasks, interposed between a pretest and a posttest criterion. The same apparatus was used in both conditions. The experimental question was concerned with improvement in the performance on the criterion as a function of performance on the intervening task. For the younger children, only the collective condition had effect, whereas

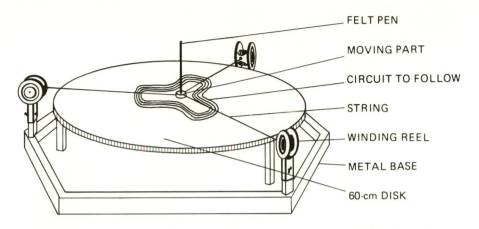

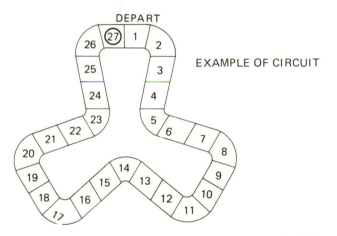

Figure 1. The cooperative game: the instrument and an example of the tracing circuit.

for the older children (who already had some mastery over the necessary coordinations), both conditions had an effect. Thus, again, from the developmental point of view, it was the collective experience that took precedence in efficiency.

The Conservation-of-Liquid Task

These particular experiments were devised by A. N. Perret-Clermont (1979) to study the effects of a social interaction setting on the individual, using the well-known Piagetian tasks as described by Inhelder, Sinclair, and Bovet (1974). On a pretest, the children were categorized as nonconservers, intermediates, or conservers. According to the original and now-famous investigations, the non-conserver is one who, although admitting that two identical glasses equally filled contain the same amount of liquid, judges these amounts to be different when one is transferred to a tall, slender glass and the other to a short and wide glass. On the other hand, the conserver maintains that the two quantities remain the same. To support this inference, conservers usually offer at least one of the following arguments: (a) nothing has been added to or taken from either glass (the identity argument); (b) if the two quantities were poured back into the original glasses, the latter would be found to be equally full again (the reversibility argument); and (c) the liquid is higher in one glass but wider in the other, so that width compensates for height (the compensation argument).

There were two conditions in the present experiment: a control condition with a pretest and a posttest and an experimental condition with an intervening social interaction. A child already defined as nonconserving (or intermediate) was required to serve the same amount of fruit juice to each of two conserving children, where one possessed a tall, slender glass and the other a short and wide one. The would-be donor also had a short and wide glass. The nonconserver was allowed to drink only if the other two children agreed that they had received the same amount of juice. As the two recipients were selected on the basis of being conservers, the nonconserving donor was to some extent forced to act out the role of conservation. Often, the nonconservers were brought to use their own short or wide glass to measure juice for the tall and slender glass. On the posttest, 65% of the subjects in the experimental condition progressed on this task, compared with only about 18% of the control subjects. The authenticity of this progress was marked by the fact that out of the 23 subjects who had progressed, 13 were able, during the posttest, to offer at least one of the three arguments for conservation that had not specifically been voiced during the intervening social interaction. Furthermore, in a replication of this experiment, the subjects who had progressed on the conservation of liquid improved in generalizing as they showed progress on other conservation tasks.

Conservation-of-Length Task

In our research, the role of sociocognitive conflict was first studied in the context of the conservation-of-length task. In all of our experiments on length, we used subjects who were nonconservers, on the conservation of both equality and inequality of length. Conservation of length can be assessed as follows. Two rulers of equal length are laid side by side so that their ends perceptually coincide. They will, of course, be judged to be of equal length. However, if one ruler is displaced to the left or to the right, so that the ends of the two rulers no longer coincide, the nonconserving child fails to compensate for the shift and says that one ruler is now longer than the other. For the conservation of inequality, two wires or chains of different length are first presented in parallel, stretched out. When the longer wire is folded so that its extremities coincide with those of the shorter one, the nonconserving child now says that the two wires are of equal length. When the extremities of the longer wire are brought still closer together, the nonconserving child may actually now consider the shorter wire the longer one. Three conditions were used in our first experiment (Doise, Mugny, & Perret-Clermont, 1976).

Control Condition. Each time, starting with the two rulers in line, four different configurations were obtained by alternatively displacing each ruler in the two opposite directions. After each of these four displacements, the subject was asked whether the rulers were of the same length or not. This was a condition of individual conflict.

Condition of Incorrect Model. Starting with the two rulers in the line and after recognition of their equal length, one ruler was displaced. When the subject claimed that the displaced ruler was longer than the other one, the assistant experimenter pointed to the opposite end of the other ruler and said, "I think this ruler is longer; you see, it goes further there." This judgment was, of course, as incorrect as the subject's own, but it was based on a symetrical concentration. If the subject complied with the assistant, the experimenter reminded him of his previous answer. This was a condition of individual sociocognitive conflict.

Condition of Correct Model. This condition was the same as the previous condition, but the adult assistant performed a correct judgment: "I think both rulers are equal in length; you see, this one goes further here and that one goes further there, so both are the same length." In Piagetian terms the argument given by the assistant was that of compensation.

The results showed that not only the correct-model condition but also the opposed-centration condition led to progress, in about 50% of the subjects, in terms of the generalization of conservation. A second posttest 10 days later, in a double-blind condition with a new experimenter, showed that this progress remained quite stable. These results have been replicated with nonconserving children contradicting each other on the same task (Doise, Giroud, & Mugny, 1978–1979).

A conservation-of-unequal-length task was also used to initiate our studies on the correspondence between social and cognitive relations (Doise, Dionnet, & Mugny, 1979). Two steel chains of unequal length were shown to nonconserving children with the instruction that they could be used as bracelets to wrap around two cylinders of unequal diameter. The longer chain was designed to fit the larger cylinder and the shorter chain to fit the smaller one. There were four presentations of the two chains, and the experimenter systematically folded the extremities of the longer chain until they came closer and closer together, while the subject watched. After each presentation, half the subjects were required to match the bracelets to the cylinders. The subjects often made an error in judging the length or in choosing the bracelet for a cylinder, at which point the experimenter made explicit the conflict between the subject's choice and the preceding judgment or choice. The procedure was similar for the other half of the children, but instead of cylinders, the experimenter's wrist and the child's wrist were used. Of the 17 subjects, 2 progressed in the cylinder condition, and 11 out of 18 progressed in the wrist condition. Again, the stability of this progress was checked by using a new experimenter in a second posttest one week later, as well as by demonstrating generalization in the conservation-of-equal-length task.

The Spatial Transformation Task

Two tables were placed together in such a way that their surfaces formed an angle of 90 degrees. On one, the experimenter formed a village of three differently colored houses, bearing a spatial relation to a fixed marker (e.g., a mountain or a lake) in the upper-left-hand corner. The subject's task was to construct the same village on the other table in such a way that someone coming from the lake or the mountain would find the individual houses in their respective orientations. This is not a difficult task for children 5–6 years of age when the marker on the model table is in the same position on the copy table, relative to the position of the subject (e.g., in the upper-left-hand corner in both cases). The child merely transposes all elements by a body turn of 90 degrees: what is on the left on the model table is also on the left on the copy table, and so on. (See Figure 2.) But when, for example, the marker is in the near right corner of the model table and in the far left corner of the copy table, the perceptual relations present a far more difficult task for the child. In the individual condition of the first experiment, children working alone were required to copy a task of that level of difficulty, twice, each time using three houses. On the average, they placed only 1.3 out of 6 houses in the correct place. On easy items, they placed 4.75 houses correctly. In a collective situation, children working together performed significantly better, placing an average of 3.3 houses in the correct place on difficult items (Doise, 1978).

Three strategies emerged in the task: no compensation, partial compensation, and total compensation. In the first, the children located the houses on the copy table by a 90-degree body shift, regardless of the position of the marker. In the second, the children located the houses correctly on one dimension (e.g., near and far), but not

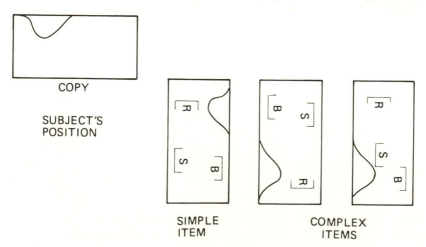

Figure 2. Examples of one simple and two complex items in the spatial transformation task.

on the other (e.g., left and right). In the third, total compensation yielded the correct solution.

In a second experiment (Mugny & Doise, 1978), we required children of different cognitive levels to work together. One important result was that when partially compensating children worked with noncompensating children, both progressed. In other words, the partially compensating children did not need the presence of a correctly responding model in order to improve their performance. The noncompensating children, it must be added, did not improve much when interacting with another noncompensating child, but then again, the same was true when the interaction was with a totally compensating child. In the latter condition, the advanced subject tended to solve the problem alone. In so doing, he ignored the suggestions of the noncompensating child, and no opportunity was provided to coordinate approaches. In the case of two noncompensating subjects, they tended to agree in their errors from the beginning and therefore to show no improvement.

Nevertheless, there is a way of relating two noncompensating children to each other so that their interaction leads to progress. Consider the layout in Figure 3. When one noncompensating subject was in Position X and the other in Y, they gave, by definition, contradictory solutions. In such a situation, 13 out of 21 subjects progressed. This result can be compared with that of an individual condition where the same subject moved from X to Y in order to evaluate his responses from both positions. In this condition, only 6 out of 19 subjects progressed. If we take the results for partially compensating children into account also, it was shown that interindividual conflict leads to significantly more progress than mere intraindividual conflict (Doise & Mugny, 1979).

In another experiment (Carugati & Mugny, 1979), a noncompensating subject was placed in a position from which the situation was viewed as easy and was confronted with another subject from whose position the tasks appeared difficult (see Figure 4). In such a condition, the child for whom the task was easy was not much perturbed by the difficulties encountered by the other. Later, the first child did not show progress (2 out of 12 progressed) on a posttest. However, when the subject was confronted with two others in the difficult position, the sociocognitive conflict was increased, and

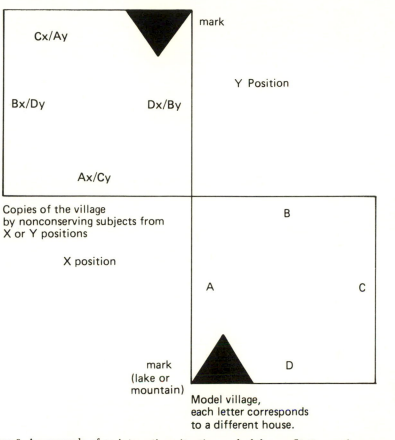

Figure 3. An example of an interaction situation and of the conflicting performances of two nonconserving subjects in different positions. In the interindividual situation, two children, one in the X position and one in the Y position, constructed the copy together; in the intraindividual condition, the child constructed his copy alone in the X or Y position before moving to the other position in order to check his copy.

progress was then shown for 5 out of 7 subjects on a subsequent difficult task.

Usually, in social learning paradigms, children with a wrong answer are confronted with a more correct model in order to progress. In our experiment, the children with a correct answer needed to experience a strong confrontation with incorrect answers in order to make progress on a subsequent task. Similar results have been obtained by Mugny, Levy, and Doise (1978), who have systematically shown

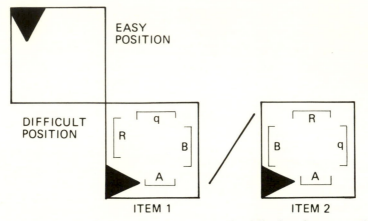

Figure 4. Examples of spatial transformation tasks with a difficult and an easy position.

how the presentation of incorrect models leads to progress when the child is questioned by an adult about his performance in the incorrect model.

Convergence with the Results of Other Research

Before concluding, we will indicate that many other authors have obtained results that corroborate our principal hypothesis on the importance of social interaction in cognitive development. F. B. Murray (1972) published an article reporting that children who had responded by means of consensus to different problems of conservation progressed individually. Silverman and Stone (1972) likewise verified significant progress after an interaction on a test of the conservation of space; Silverman and Geiringer (1973) verified that the social interaction carried on on a given test can give rise to progress on other tests as well. Maitland and Goldman (1974) also obtained improvement at the time of the interaction on problems of moral judgment, and Miller and Brownell (1975) reported on the domain of the conservation of length and weight. Our first experiments, having been initiated without our having known of these research data, thus carried an independent validation.

Many other researchers (Kuhn, 1972; J. P. Murray, 1974; Rosenthal & Zimmerman, 1972; Zimmerman & Lannaro, 1974) have likewise observed progress in the domain of conservation after only observing models. Does that finding mean that an explanation of cognitive development based on the idea of sociocognitive conflict becomes insufficient? We do not think so, because the effect of the model can very well be realized by the conflict that is induced. Kuhn (1972) wrote:

> Thus, the observation of a model performing a task in a manner dis-
> crepant from (but not inferior to) the child's own conceptualization of
> the task may be sufficient to induce in the child an awareness of alter-
> native conceptualizations and will perhaps lead to disequilibrium and
> reorganization. (p. 843)

We are in agreement, providing, however, that the restriction within the parentheses be omitted.

A domain in which our research will soon be developed is the elaboration of formal thought. Laughlin and Jaccard (1975) have like-wise shown that, at this stage of cognitive development, the group prevails over the individual. With a different task, but also causing hypothetico-deductive thinking to intervene, Stalder (1975) verified that the variables modifying social interaction in groups likewise modify the cognitive strategies of their members during this inter-action. It is necessary to examine whether or not it results in effects after the interaction. A vast area still remains to be explored.

Conclusion

A problem with which one can find fault at the end of this account is the apparent lag between the broad span of theoretical considerations reported in the first part of this chapter and the limits of the conclusions that can be drawn from experiments as specific as those described in the second part of the chapter. To be sure, we have seen authors who do not hesitate to open very broad historical perspectives when they are nevertheless reduced to describing ima-ginary situations of specific interactions within the framework of prehistoric reconstructions or in frameworks that are more familiar in the development of the child. Why, then, not study experimentally the concrete interactions that are accessible to us?

However, there is another domain of history as well where there are some other indications that often serve as a daring basis of reconstructions. It is the domain of the "sociocultural handicap" with regard to the institution of the school. It is certainly not our intention to deny the existence of this handicap, nor to argue that there is no difference between life and the social interactions of the dominated and the dominant groups of our society, and that these differences could eventually be reflected in behavior of a cognitive nature in school. We would only like to show how certain indications suggest that perhaps the experimentation is useful in advancing this debate.

This evidence, obtained by A. N. Perret-Clermont (1979) and also by Mugny, Perret-Clermont, and Doise (1981), is as follows: when they reanalyzed the results of the tests on the conservation of liquids and the conservation of number, taking into account the socioeconomic origin of the subjects, they observed that the differences between the children of different backgrounds that existed before the social interaction no longer existed after this interaction. This finding is merely an indication, which must be corroborated by research carried out elsewhere. But if these results are found again, the fact that the interaction between children coming from the same underprivileged environment could be brought up to the same level as the performance of children from a more privileged environment, we would substantiate that the handicap does not bear on cognitive operations. For how it can be considered a serious handicap if it is a difference that the interaction of a few moments is sufficient to erase?

On the other hand, our research seems already to have implied a result that could be of concern in educational practice. It provides a new basic theory to the innovations in this domain that have led teachers to create educational situations in which children are invited to teach each other (Gartner, Kohler, & Riessman, 1971). If these proposed tasks are well chosen, according to our hypotheses, both more advanced and less advanced children must profit equally from these interactions. Thus, Allen and Feldmann (1973) verified that, in response to such experiences of mutual education, the children "teachers" progress considerably in relation to other children who work alone. Certainly, motivational factors intervene in situations such as these and can promote or impede the processes of cognitive order. However, these situations do provide the opportunity for cognitive dynamics to develop according to processes that can be studied experimentally.

References

Allen, V. L., & Feldman, R. S. Learning through tutoring: Low achieving children as tutors. *The Journal of Experimental Education*, 1973, *42*, 1–5.

Berry, J. W., & Dasen, P. R. *Culture and cognition*. London: Methuen, 1974.

Carugati, F., & Mugny, G. Psicologia sociale dello sviluppo cognitivo. *Italian Journal of Psychology*, 1979, *5*, 323–352.

Dami, C. Stratégies cognitives dans les jeux competitifs á deux. *Archives de Psychologie*, 1975.

Doise, W. *Groups and individuals: Explanations in social psychology*. Cambridge, England: Cambridge University Press, 1978.

Doise, W., & Mugny, G. Recherches socio-genétiques sur la coordination d'actions interdépendantes. *Revue Suisse de Pyschologie*, 1975, *34*, 160–174.

Doise, W., & Mugny, G. Individual and collective conflicts of concentrations in cognitive development. *European Journal of Social Psychology*, 1979, *9*, 105–106.

Doise, W., & Mugny, G. *Le développement social de l'intelligence*. Paris: Intereditions, 1981.

Doise, W., Mugny, G., & Perret-Clermont, A. N. Social interaction and cognitive development: Further evidence. *European Journal of Social Psychology*, 1976, *6*, 245–247.

Doise, W., Giroud, J. Ch., & Mugny, G. Conflit de centrations et progrès cognitif. II: Nouvelles confimations expérimentales. *Bulletin de Psychologie*, 1978–1979.

Doise, W., Dionnet, S., & Mugny, G. Conflit socio-cognitif, marguage social et développement cognitif. *Cahiers de Psychologie Cognitif*, 1979.

Durkheim, E., & Mauss, M. De quelques formes primitives de classification. *L'Année Sociologique*, 1903, *6*, 1–72.

Feffer, M. Developmental analysis of interpersonal behavior. *Psychological Review*, 1970, *77*, 197–214.

Flavell, J. H., Botvin, P. T., Fry, C. L., Wright, J. W., & Jarvis, P. E. *The development of role-taking and communication skills in children*. New York: Wiley, 1968.

Gartner, A., Kohler, M. C., & Riessman, F. *Children teach children: Learning by teaching*. New York: Harper & Row, 1971.

Humphrey, N. K. The social function of intellect. In P. P. G. Bateson & R. A. Hinde (Eds.), *Growing points in ethology*. Cambridge, England: Cambridge University Press, 1976.

Inhelder, B., Sinclair, H., & Bovet, M. *Learning and development of cognition*. London: Routledge and Kegan Paul, 1974.

Kuhn, D. Mechanisms of change in the development of cognitive structures. *Child Development*, 1972, *43*, 833–844.

Laughlin, P. R., & Jaccard, J. J. Social facilitation and observational learning of individuals and cooperative pairs. *Journal of Personality and Social Psychology*, 1975, *32*, 873–879.

Leontiev, A. Le mécanisme de la coordination des fonctions motrices interdépendantes réparties entre divers sujets. *Bulletin de Psychologie,* 1970–1971, *24,* 693–696.

Leontiev, A. *Le développement du psychisme.* Paris: Éditions Sociales, 1976.

Maitland, K. A., & Goldman, J. R. Moral judgment as a function of peer group interaction. *Journal of Personality and Social Psychology,* 1974, *30,* 699–704.

Mead, G. H. *Mind, self and society.* Chicago: University of Chicago Press, 1934.

Mikula, G. Die Entwicklung des Gewinnaufteilungsverhaltens bei Kinder und Jugendlichen. *Zeitschrift für Entwicklungspsychologie und pädagogische Psychologie,* 1972, *4,* 151–164.

Miller, S. A., & Brownell, C. A. Peers, persuasion and Piaget: Dyadic Interaction between conservers and nonconservers. *Child Development,* 1975, *46,* 992–997.

Moessinger, P. Developmental study of fair division and property. *European Journal of Social Psychology,* 1975.

Mugny, G., & Doise, W. Socio-cognitive conflict and structure of individual and collective performances. *European Journal of Social Psychology,* 1978, *8,* 181–192.

Mugny, G., Levy, M., & Doise, W. Conflit socio-cognitif et développement cognitif. *Revue Suisse de Psychologie,* 1978, *37,* 22–43.

Mugny, G., Perret-Clermont, A. W., & Doise, W. Interpersonal coordinations and social differences in the construction of the intellect. In G. M. Stephenson & J. M. Davis, *Progress in applied psychology* (Vol. 1). New York: Wiley, 1981.

Murray, F. B. Acquisition of conservation through social interaction. *Developmental Psychology,* 1972, *6,* 1–6.

Murray, J. P. Social learning and cognitive development: Modeling effects on children's understanding of conservation. *British Journal of Psychology,* 1974, *65,* 151–160.

Nielsen, R. *Le développement de la sociabilité chez l'enfant.* Neuchâtel: Delachaux et Niestlé, 1951.

Perret-Clermont, A. N. *Social interaction and cognitive development in children.* London: Academic Press, 1979.

Piaget, J. *Le jugement moral chez l'enfant.* Paris: Presses Universitaires de France, 1932.

Piaget, J. *Études sociologiques.* Geneva: Droz, 1965.

Piaget, J. *Biologie et connaissance.* Paris: Gallimard, 1967.

Rosenthal, T. L., & Zimmerman, B. J. Modeling by exemplification and instruction in training conservation. *Developmental Psychology,* 1972, *6,* 392–401.

Silverman, I. W., & Geiringer, E. Dyadic interaction and conservation induction: A test of Piaget's equilibrium model. *Child Development,* 1973, *44,* 815–820.

Silverman, I. W., & Stone, J. M. Modifying cognitive functioning through participation in a problem-solving group. *Journal of Educational Psychology,* 1972, *63,* 603–608.

Smedslund, J. Les origines sociales de la décentration. In *Psychologie et épistémologie génétique, thèmes Piagétiens.* Paris: Dunod, 1966.

Stalder, J. *Lernen in kleinen Gruppen* (Inauguraldissertation der Philosophisch-Historischen Fakultät Bern). Bern: Kopierservice, 1975.

Tran Duc Thao. *Recherches sur l'origine du langage et de la conscience.* Paris: Éditions Sociales, 1973.

Vygotsky, L. S. *Thought and language.* Cambridge, M.I.T. Press, 1965.

Waller, M. Die Enwicklung der Rollenwahrnehmung: Ihre Beziehung zur allgemeinen kognitiven Entwicklung und sozialstrukturellen Variabelen. *Zeitschift für Sozialpsychologie,* 1971, *2,* 343–357.

Waller, M. Die Stereotypität vs. Personorientiertheit der Verhaltenserwartungen von Kindern in Abhängigkeit von deren Alter und der untersuchten Verhaltensdimension. *Zeitschrift für Entwicklungspsychologie und pädagogische Psychologie,* 1973, *5,* 1–15.

Zajonc, R. B. Social facilitation. *Science,* 1965, *149,* 269–274.

Zimmerman, B. J., & Lanaro, P. Acquiring and retaining conservation of length through modeling and reversibility cues. *Merrill-Palmer Quarterly of Behavior and Development,* 1974, *20,* 145–161.

Introduction to Chapter 6

VALERIE L. SHULMAN

Harold Chipman is a Genevan psycholinguist who may be identified among those scholars endeavoring to maintain the continuity of traditional Piagetian theory while elaborating specific aspects that have been neglected in the past. He is concerned with problems and issues in the areas of psycholinguistics and metalinguistics and, more specifically, in language acquisition. Until recently, those areas were not to be found within the traditional framework.

Traditional Piagetian theory was not concerned either with metalinguistics as the study of the general awareness of the sounds, rules, and ambiguities of language, or with linguistics as the study of language rules, history, and relationships with other languages. Piaget (1971) viewed language as merely one example of the symbolic function within the general development of operational thought; he so aptly stated that

> language is merely one particular instance of the semiotic or symbolic function, and that this function as a whole (imitation with a time lag, system of gestural symbols, symbolic play, mental image, written or drawn pictures, etc.) and not language alone, is what causes sensorimotor behavior to evolve to the level of representation or thought. (p. 46–47)

On another occasion, he did refer to a larger role of language and its development within the context of the elaboration of operational thought:

We are still prepared to admit that some kind of language is essential for the completion of the structures under discussion, i.e., classification, seriation. This is because the operations involve a symbolic, and therefore representative handling of objects, inasmuch as they go beyond what could be done in terms of overt behavior. But the point upon which we would insist is that language alone is not enough. (Piaget, 1964, p. 293)

However, in identifying language as one observable facet of the developmental sequence, illustrating the transitions from phase to phase, he prepared the way for the study of "developmental" psycholinguistics. Within that context, psycholinguistics implied the study of the development of those cognitive structures that support language facility as well as the psychological and social environments in which language is manipulated. Thus, developmental psycholinguistics became a viable area of investigation within the parameters of the traditional Piagetian discipline.

During the past 10 years, Chipman has often collaborated with Hermine Sinclair on the elaboration of psycholinguistic and metalinguistic theory. His research is unique in that he has investigated language acquisition and development both within the general school-aged population as well as in atypical children, specifically the mentally retarded. A majority of his studies have used these populations to generate a comparative or contrastive profile of language acquisition, elaborating a continuum that extends from the "slower" to the more rapid language learners within the range, noting the distinguishing characteristics between and among them. Data derived from those investigations have added a dimension to his hypotheses on the developmental aspects of language acquisition.

In the chapter "Aspects of Language Acquisition: Developmental Strategies," Chipman frames his problem with an apparently traditional epistemological question: When and how are language and cognition related? However, his response is reflective of the neo-Piagetian perspective: he suggests that those links are to be found at the level of general cognitive functioning since: "Metalinguistic ability is a reflected activity that is an aspect of the more general capacity to reflect on problems, situations, and events."

Then, in rapid succession, he asks three more specific questions reflective of the central problem that establish the psycholinguistic position. First, how and why does the child become a good speaker and understander of language so quickly, when by comparison even *the simplest logical thought operations take considerably longer? Second, what does mastering language require the child to develop in terms of a system of competence? And, third, when the child can already speak so fluently, why is it so hard and why does it take him so long to learn the rules of language in school?*

Chipman responds to those questions by illustrating the parallel and inclusive elaboration of strategies that children use from the earliest conceptual words, to early forms of categorization (agent-object), to identifying relationships between words and events (agent-action-object), to the more sophisticated strategies that require combining and reversing elements. He details the changing approaches employed by children along a developmental continuum. Thus, cognitive and linguistic development interact at the point(s) of the evolving structures. Cognitive development is prerequisite to sophisticated language functioning. The unique characteristic of the development of language as a means of representation results from the fact that it is a highly structured system of intricate rules that must be mastered in order to be effectively learned and used as a system.

Chipman has aptly made the transition from the general and epistemological to a developmental pattern specifically directed toward language acquisition strategies. Further, he has sought to identify those characteristics that impede and those that foster development.

References

Inhelder, B., & Piaget, J. *The early growth of logic in the child.* London: Routledge and Keegan Paul, 1964.

Piaget, J. *The language and thought of the child.* New York: Meridian, 1955.

Piaget, J. *Biology and knowledge.* Chicago: University of Chicago Press, 1971.

Sinclair-de Zwart, H. Language acquisition and cognitive development. In V. Lee (Ed.), *Language development.* New York: Wiley, 1979.

Zwingmann, C., Inhelder, B., & Chipman, H. *Piaget and his school.* New York: Springer, 1976.

Aspects of Language Acquisition
Developmental Strategies

HAROLD CHIPMAN

Introductory Remarks

It is usually thought that learning a first language is something "natural" and that it should therefore present no particular difficulty to the young child, save perhaps in its phonetic component. Language is also thought by most adults to be a logically structured and more-or-less simple system for the expression of one's ideas. And since within the first five years of life, children become pretty fluent and sometimes seemingly flawless speakers, it may seem surprising that, when they get to school, they are obliged to spend so much time learning the structure of their language.

The function of school is to make children aware of the rules that are used when speaking—and it is hoped that this awareness will help in the use and understanding of language, in particular with regard to the mastery of creative writing and literature. However, linguistics has shown us that natural language is neither logically structured nor very simple or very clear for either the child or

HAROLD CHIPMAN • Faculty of Psychology and the Educational Sciences, University of Geneva, CH-1211 Geneva 4, Switzerland.

the teacher. Consequently, a number of interesting questions spring to mind. First of all, how and why does the child become a good speaker and understander of language so quickly, particularly when, by comparison, even the simplest logical thought operations take considerably longer to master? Second, what does mastering language require the child to develop in terms of a system of competence? Third, when the child can already speak so fluently, why is it so hard and why does it take so long for him to learn rules of language in school?

A number of answers to these questions lie in the nature of language itself. Language has two facets: automatic know-how and conscious knowledge of the properties and rules of the system, which can be explicitly looked at and defined. All human beings have command of the automatic aspect, but not all have a conscious knowledge of the language's system and properties; indeed, such *conscious* knowledge may not be necessary at all for successful performance as a speaker. However, every speaker does develop an internal grammar that governs language production, and thus he has a competence system, as Noam Chomsky has called it. If nothing else, this system enables the speaker, who may not be aware of all the rules that are part of the internal grammar, to decide whether a particular sentence heard belongs to the grammar of his mother tongue or not. It now becomes clearer why learning language in school is a difficult process: the child is somehow *relearning* language through the discovery of its structure and is thus learning to become not only linguistically but metalinguistically competent, that is, is becoming aware of the internal grammar. A further source of difficulty is that such knowledge about grammar is conveyed by means of language, so that the system is defined by using the system itself. Finally, in contrast to other symbolic systems, language is both arbitrary in nature and conventionally determined. Children must learn that words bear no resemblance to the people, places, or things that they represent, other than for some onomatopoeia, and even these vary from language to language: *bow-wow* in English becomes *vou-vou* in French. They must learn to speak the language of their environment, and even should they so desire, they have no power to change it by themselves.

The Genevan linguist Ferdinand de Saussure stressed the importance of this latter property of language at the beginning of the century, and later, the great psychologist and epistemologist Jean Piaget also pointed to this fundamental difference between language and other symbolic systems. Piaget saw the development of all symbolic systems as starting with the appearance of the "semiotic function" at the end of the sensorimotor period, and he studied the emergence and development of some of these means of symbolization, though not language *per se*, both in his early observations of children (1945) and later in a more experimental way. For instance, imitative behavior appears early in child development, and Piaget saw in the appearance of delayed imitation the first sign of the emergence of the semiotic function. Whereas most forms of external or internal symbolic behavior, such as drawing or mental imagery, develop over a number of years, language mastery seems, by comparison, as we have said, to be acquired much faster suggesting that such mastery is not dependent, in a narrow sense, on cognitive development. Yet, the psycholinguist Dan Slobin (1973) wondered whether Piaget could be taken as "a textbook for psycholinguistics," implying that progress in the cognitive field entailed language acquisition. Experimentation in language development has shown this not to be the case in any direct causal sense. Language and thinking both have their origin in sensorimotor roots but later seem to develop more independently. However, it is not because such a narrow link between language acquisition and cognitive development has not been evidenced that the question must be shelved. On the contrary, although no clear process of dependence has been found between the two, it is a fact that they develop simultaneously, and that, because language competence is a faculty of mind, there should be some kind of link between them. This could be found in the area of metalinguistic development which may well be dependent on the child's progress in reflecting objectively on physical processes, on logical operations, and, consequently, also on linguistic entities. Piaget showed that such objective reflection is linked to the development of the first logical thought operations, and it is therefore no surprise, if this is true, that reflection on language structure is not possible before middle childhood.

In fact, all of these considerations only make it harder for the first of our questions to be answered. Indeed, as language requires an internal creative competence, as it is arbitrary and conventional, and as it is in some general way linked to cognitive development, the early fluency of speech comprehension and production appears all the more mysterious. It suggests an early capacity for actively developing this competence of which evidence is seen in two facts: first, only a comparatively small proportion of the child's speech consists of direct and exact imitations, and second, he makes a number of inferences about the regularities of language. An example of such early inferential activity is seen in his so-called constructive errors: after correctly saying *feet*, he will say *foots*, *feets*, or even *footses* before returning to a systematic use of the correct form, *feet*. A different example comes from the observations of Ramer (1976), where children aged 15–27 months made a number of word order errors in attempting to produce simple sentence constructions such as subject–verb–complement (SVC). These errors were made by a group of fast learners, but hardly ever by a group of slower learners (the target was the point in time when SVC constructions appeared correctly and repeatedly in the children's speech). Ramer regarded the fast learners as showing risk-taking behavior related to speed which also constitutes some form of early constructive experimentation with language. This indeed suggests that the child is actively constructing a language competence system.

Types of Strategies

The construction of language competence constitutes one of the most interesting areas of speculation and investigation for a Genevan developmental psycholinguist. This construction process begins during the first year of life, and between this time and the child's entry into school, a considerable amount of syntax, semantics, and morphology is apparently mastered. Observational studies, such as that of Limber (1973), confirm the rapidity of the process: he found that by age 4, his subjects had produced at least some token utterances of nearly every form of complex syntax. This fact could lead one to think, as has been the case, that the greater part of the language acquisition process is over by age 4; subsequent development represents only a process of refinement in the use of linguistic structures. This idea could be true, however, only if language comprehension develops at the same rate as language production. Yet, a considerable

number of data from experiments on language comprehension suggest that comprehension capacities are only gradually built up by
the child. A first example of this progressive buildup comes from a
study undertaken by Sinclair and Bronckart (1972) on how children
organize the words with which they are familiar into a sentence.
This organization implies assigning to words, in a linear succession,
such roles as agent, action, or patient, which are grammatically
expressed as subject, verb, or direct object. How does a child progressively understand which element in a sentence is the agent or
the patient? Such comprehension is essential for understanding even
the simplest sentence. This was verified experimentally by asking
French-speaking children aged 2.6–7.0 years to act out the meaning
they could read into sequences of three words presented in six different orders. Examples of these sequences are *"fille, garçon, pousser"* ("girl, boy, push") or *"garçon, boite, ouvrir"* ("boy, box, open"),
which were presented in all possible combinations in a list form,
without the usual intonational contour of a sentence. The results can
be summarized as follows. The youngest subjects, aged approximately 2.6–4.0, gave one of the following acting-out patterns: either
they took the boy and the girl and had them go for a walk or jump,
often saying, "Ils se promènent, ils sautent" ("they go for a walk,
they jump"), or they knocked over the boy and the girl themselves.
These responses show that the children did not organize the word
list into a three-part comprehension structure containing agent, action,
and patient. Rather, they used two-part comprehension strategies
that consisted of making either both the boy and the girl agents and
the action intransitive, or of casting themselves as agent, making
both the boy and the girl patients. Between the ages of approximately
4.0 and 6.0, the children attributed different roles to the boy and the
girl, but a close examination of all their acting-out behaviors for the
different sentences showed that the comprehension strategies were
still two-part: the agent was assigned either to the first noun in the
list or to the noun closest to the verb, and the patient role was then
given to the remaining noun. It was only at around 7 years of age
that the children distributed both the agent and the patient role in
terms of one another, considering the word list a sentence unit. This
result clearly indicates that the capacity to distribute roles within a
simple sentence is only *gradually* constructed by the child.

The ways in which the child deals with the word lists have been termed *strategies*, and this term requires definition. A strategy is a stable part of the child's language competence at a particular moment of development. It is a means of organizing a sentence so that it becomes a meaningful entity for the child and, later, for the adult. The stability of the strategy may be seen through its repeated use. Sinclair and Bronckart noted that in the word list "*boite, ouvrir, garçon*" ("box, open, boy"), children between 5 and 7 also applied the strategy consisting of taking the first noun as agent, thus making the box open the boy! This type of solution is antipragmatic; it goes against the child's real-world knowledge of events and possible agents. However, the child applies the strategy so rigidly that, nevertheless, the agent role is attributed to the box. This response shows that the child applies strategies "blindly," obliterating or not considering semantic or pragmatic cues. Strategies can be said to be a mode of understanding created and developed by the child for dealing, in this case, with syntactic problems. The creation of strategies by the child shows the excellent inferential and deductive activity that is applied to the sphere of language; these strategies are not explicitly taught to the child, they do not form an explicit part of adult grammar, and therefore, they represent the child's sophisticated guess at the regularities inherent in the syntax of the mother tongue.

Sinclair and Bronckart's research showed that the child, from an early age, has a strong tendency to make the first noun encountered in a linguistic sequence the agent or grammatical subject of an action. The strategy of *first-noun-as-agent* is applied by the child in under-standing a whole range of syntactic structures. Research undertaken on young children's comprehension of the sentence "The doll is easy to see" (C. Chomsky, 1969) showed that, up to the age of 10, some children still understand that sentence as meaning that the doll can see easily, making the doll the agent. A replication and expansion of Chomsky's work was carried out in French by Cambon and Sinclair (1974). Their results showed a better comprehension for this type of sentence at age 5 than at ages 6 and 7, and a good, though not perfect, comprehension level at age 8. The apparent regression at ages 6 and 7 may be due to the interference of the first-noun-as-agent strategy with the meaning that the child of that age ascribes to the verb *to see*. Indeed, from the justifications that the children were asked to give for their answers, it was clear that the 5-year-olds saw only one possible agent for the verb *to see*, that is, themselves. This may be a manifestation of insufficient cognitive decentration, the capacity to conceive of an action from a point of view other than one's own. After progress in decentration, the child attempts to apply the strategy, and cognitive and linguistic approaches are often in conflict. By age 8, the problem is solved both linguistically and cognitively. Another example of the use that children make of the first-noun-as-agent strategy is seen in their understanding of French (Sinclair & Ferreiro, 1970), English (Sinclair, Sinclair, & de Marcellus, 1971), and Swiss-German (Caprez, Sinclair, & Studer, 1971) passive sentences. The frequent use of this strategy in all three languages was affected by the semantic nature of the verbs and the pragmatic features represented in the sentences. The task sentences were said to be "reversible" or "nonreversible" (Slobin, 1966): a child can use real-world pragmatic knowledge to understand the nonreversible sentence "The stick is broken by the boy" but not the reversible sentence "The boy is pushed by the girl," where pragmatically both boy and girl can be agents or patients. In this last type of sentence, the child is obliged to use syntactic knowledge for comprehension. The verbs used were *casser* ("to break"), *renverser* ("to knock over"), *laver* ("to wash"), *pousser* ("to push"), and *suivre* ("to follow"). The results were comparable for all languages. The nonreversible sentences with *to break* (*casser*) were correctly understood more than 90% of the time by the age of 3. Sentences with the reversible verb *to follow* (*suivre*) were the hardest at all ages; they were correctly understood by 7-year-olds 30% of the time in English and 54% of the time in French. Of intermediate difficulty were sentences with the verb *to wash* (*laver*), which were understood correctly 69% of the time in English at age 4, and 66% of the time in French. By age 7, the scores are above the 90% level for all languages. Of the errors, 80% consisted of an application of the first-noun-as-agent strategy. Interestingly, in the production part of the experiment, the children showed a preference for producing sentences with the agent function expressed in the first noun even though they were induced to produce a passive; for instance, when asked to describe the action *girl washes boy* starting with "the boy," the younger children said things like "The boy is all dirty," "The boy washes the girl," and "The boy gets washed"; only at a later age did they produce a complete form of the passive. Here we may have a reflection of the comprehension strategy in the production data.

The first-noun-as-agent strategy, although not an explicit rule of grammar, is the expression of a correct inference by the child that many sentences that are heard actually do embody it. An example of a strategy constructed by the child that is not at all reflected in adult grammar is that of the "role conservation" strategy that children aged 4–7 apply in comprehending pronominal sentences. This strategy was described in detail by Chipman (1974, 1980). Again, in an acting out a comprehension task, children aged 3–8 were asked to act out sentences containing a third-person pronoun whose antecedent was either the subject agent of the main clause (e.g., "The boy pushes the girl and then he washes the other girl") or the direct object/patient of the main clause (e.g., "The boy washes the girl and then she knocks over the other boy"). Up to age 6, children systematically act out both types of the sentence with the boy performing both actions, that is, conserving the agent role twice despite a clear morphological distinction in the gender of the pronouns. All of the errors showed that they did not apply a minimal distance principle in their search for the antecedent of the pronoun, and that they override a known morphological gender distinction for which they had previously been tested. This is considerable evidence for the strength and the systematic application of the strategy.

The role-conserving strategy was also investigated in relative clause sentences with children aged 4–12. Their comprehension responses evidenced three levels. A first level (ages 4–5) consisted in not acting out the relative clause at all. Thus, in the sentence "The dog that licks the cat pushes the squirrel," the children most often acted out "The dog pushes the squirrel." From ages 5–8, the children systematically applied a role-conserving strategy; sentences like the one above were all correctly understood, but sentences like "The dog licks the monkey that pushes the cat" were not: the errors all consisted of having the dog perform both actions. Sentences like "The bear pushes the cat that the monkey licks" were also correctly understood because the patient role is conserved. Around age 8–9, the systematic use of the role-conserving strategy disappeared, and the third level (ages 8–12) showed the children finding difficulty both with the meaning of the pronoun (they often asked, "What does *that* mean?") and with the center-embedded relative clauses. These results, with regard to the use of the role-conserving strategy, have been confirmed in several languages, specifically, in a comparative study covering English, French, and Spanish (Ferreiro, Othenin-Girard, Chipman, & Sinclair, 1976). At this point, the question arises whether the role conservation strategy is simply another reflection of the first-noun-as-agent strategy in an extended form in these pronominal sentences. Pruner and Solan (1979) tested sentences such as "John was hit by Bill, and then he hit Fred" and children aged 5–8 clearly preferred Bill as the agent for both actions, showing that they were indeed conserving the agent role and not the grammatical subject expressed in the first noun. To summarize what has been said so far, it seems that syntactic strategies such as *first-noun-as-agent* and *role conservation* are indeed developed quite early, are applied systematically in the age period 4–8 (approximately), and can be observed in cases where pragmatic or semantic clauses are not available to the child for use.

Developmental Aspects of Strategies

Two important questions now come to mind. First of all, how extensive is the use of these strategies—that is, for what types of syntactic structures are they used? And second, how and why do they disappear? An attempt to answer the first question in the case of role conversation was undertaken by Chipman and Gerard (1982), who tested French children's comprehension of sentential complement sentences such as "L'ours dit au singe d'aller au lit" ("The bear tells the monkey to go to bed"); "Le renard dit à l'ours qu'il va manger un sandwich" ("The fox tells the bear that he is going to eat a sandwich"); or "Le chat promet à l'ours de sauter la barrière" ("The cat promises the bear to jump over the fence"). For all of these sentences, with or without a pronoun, it is possible for the child to choose as agent, for the sentential complement action, either the agent of speech act verb in the main clause (correct solution for the *promise* sentences) or the indirect object of the main clause (correct solution for the *tell* sentences). The results for children aged 4–8 showed a strong

tendency to use the indirect object of the first clause agent for the
sentential complement, thus apparently giving a solution that goes
in a contrary direction to that imposed by the role conservation
strategy. This result suggests that children of these ages make structural distinctions between groups of sentences and do not indiscrim-
inately apply their syntactic strategies across groupings. In this case,
the children seem to distinguish between pronominal sentences that
are forms of intersentence coordination, on the one hand, and sentential complement sentences involving speech act verbs like *promise, tell,* and *ask,* on the other. In so doing, the children are making
a correct adult linguistic distinction and displaying early syntactic
intuition. Using such an intuition of structural groupings, children
are apparently able to select one of a number of strategies that are
available in their repertoire. It is essential to emphasize that these
strategies are called on to solve a syntactic problem, since explicit
sentences such as "The boy pushes the girl and then the boy knocks
over the truck" are correctly understood even at the youngest age.

The second question is more challenging, as the answers can
be only speculative. We have seen that the period of time during
which the strategies mentioned are predominantly used spans the
ages of approximately 4–8 years. This being so, how do children
solve syntactic complexities before age 4, and why do the strategies
wane and disappear in application after age 8? Before the age of 4,
most of the research to data shows that children apply strategies that
are linked to the comprehension and production of simple sentences
with subject–verb–complement structures: they use simple word-
order strategies (as we have seen) and a number of what Slobin (1973)
has called "operational principles" of the type "Pay attention to the
ends of words," "Pay attention to the order of words and mor-
phemes," "Avoid interruption or rearrangement of linguistic units,"
and also all kinds of contextual or pragmatic knowledge. By age 4,
children can already correctly use both linguistic and nonlinguistic
contextual information. In an experiment verifying young children's
understanding of the possessive pronouns *his* and *hers,* Chipman
(1980) found that, up to age 4½, the subjects consistently applied a
pragmatic strategy. The experimental situation consisted of showing
the children a boy and a girl doll each with its own dog. An example
of the experimental sentences ran as follows: "You see, the boy and
the girl each have a dog; the boy pushes his and then the girl pets

his." The youngest subjects, for all types of sentences with *his* and *hers*, systematically acted out the boy playing with his own dog and the girl with her own. This result can be interpreted as a reflection of some kind of real-life experience that the child brings into the understanding of the sentences, hence giving rise to an *each-on-his-own* acting-out strategy. In a different experiment by Chipman and Gerard (1981), children aged 4–6 were asked to act out a little story in which the last sentence contained a sentential complement of the type described earlier. The story contained a clear indication of the agent of the action represented in the sentential complement, so that a correct understanding of the last sentence involved using the arguments embodied in the linguistic context. The experimental results showed that the children, even the youngest, had no trouble using the linguistic context correctly. This early period in syntax mastery can then be characterized by the child's using a small number of simple syntactic strategies to enable him to deal with the subject–verb–complement units, as well as his using a considerable number of pragmatic or contextual strategies.

One cannot, however, say that with the emergence of *role-con-servation* or *first-noun-as-agent* strategies the child has progressed to a level where attention is paid to syntax. We have already stressed that the strategies are applied "blindly," that is, without a linguistic analysis of the syntactic problem to which they are applied. In other words, the child is not consciously analyzing a passive construction or a pronominal sentence but is intuitively and automatically applying a stable mode of understanding to them. The progress of this period lies more in the fact that the child, with the help of these strategies, is dealing with larger structures: coordinated structures of the type SVO + SVO, in the case of pronominal sentences, and uncanonical word orders, in the case of passive sentences (OVS). The child is either extending the field of application of some of the previous strategies or creating new ones (like role conservation).

The next marked change occurs when the child abandons the systematic use of the strategies. The reason for this abandonment seems to lie in his progress at the metalinguistic level combined with an approach to the syntax of sentences in their surface form. Evidence of this change comes from the study of relative clauses. Around age 8 or 9, when hearing a sentence such as "The squirrel that the cat pushes licks the bear," the children start asking "What does *that*

mean?" This question shows that the child is searching for the meaning of the pronoun *that* and is capable of expressing this reflection
explicitly. But answering this question is hard for the child because
a pronoun is a word that represents not a concept or a thing but
another word, sentence, or entire extralinguistic situation. Before the
age of 8, children do not question the meaning of the pronoun, so it
does not seem to be a problem for them at all. Chipman (1980) tested
sentences in which the relative pronoun was replaced by a nonsense
syllable and found that this substitution did not disturb the children
at all; they acted out the sentences as if they were normal. The
questions posed by children after age 8 show a progression in the
ability to reflect on language. Children at age 8 also have difficulty
with various sentence structures, as is seen in the fact that center-
embedded relative clauses become harder for the child to understand
than the non-center-embedded sentences that do not interrupt normal word order. For instance, the center-embedded sentence "The
cat that pushes the squirrel licks the elephant," which is easy for 5-
year-olds because it is role-conserving, now becomes more difficult
than "The monkey pushes the dog that licks the squirrel," which is
non-center-embedded but role-changing. This change in difficulty
means that that child is now analyzing the sentences syntactically.
Language is approached in an adult way, and the child is ready for
the explicit teaching of language structure. At this point, the child
is able to analyze syntax without the help or the overriding effect of
pragmatic, morphological, and semantic strategies. This represents
a major step forward in language acquisition.

   Strategies can be of pragmatic, semantic, and syntactic nature.
At certain points during language acquisition, the child apparently
calls more on one or the other of these aspects. It has been suggested,
by Lust, Loveland, and Kornet (1980) among others, that the progress
in language development lies in the harmonizing of the three aspects.
The harmonizing process may, in turn, depend on progress at the
metalinguistic level. The development of metalinguistic abilities, as
seen in how children reflect on the concept of *word*, has been studied
by Papandropoulou and Sinclair (1974). In this experiment, 4- to 12-
year-old children were given a number of tasks aimed at investigating
their ideas about the definition of *word*. For instance, the children
were asked whether they could produce examples of small or little
words ("des petits mots"), long words, or difficult words, and they

were asked to invent a word, to count the number of words in utterances such as "Mary has six dolls" and "John doesn't have an apple," or to interpret sentences containing a nonsense word. The final question posed to all the children was "Can you tell me what a word is?" The results showed that, at a first level, around ages 4–5, children do not differentiate words from the objects they represent. Thus, *train* is a long word because "It has a locomotive in front and big carriages"; *eye* is a small word "because it's small"; "Mary has six dolls" contains six words; and "John doesn't have an apple" contains no words. The children cannot interpret the nonsense words at all. At a second stage, around the ages of 5 or 6, they say that a word is "when you speak, when you say something." But the examples given do not respect the idea of the word as a unit; entire sentences, often two or three, are given as examples of words. Thus, for a long word, a child says, "He goes away and then he climbs on the car," and for a short word, "He goes away." The idea of a word is linked to the amount of information conveyed. Around the ages of 6 or 7, a word is defined as "letters" and "part of a sentence." Words have become autonomous through their graphic realization but remain linked to the reality that they represent because only content words are given as examples and articles and other function words are rejected: the article *le* is rejected as a word because "It doesn't have enough letters," but *ape* is accepted "because apes exist." Toward age 7–8, children see a word as a "small bit of a story" and begin to accept articles and functors as words; they also begin to give definitions of words that include both the word-as-letters aspect and the word-as-part-of-story aspect. Finally, it is only at around age 9 or 10 that they are able to give complete adult definitions of words; in particular, they add to their definitions the idea that words have a meaning: "A word is something made with letters and that means something, letters grouped that form a word." Furthermore, at this age, linguistic criteria are invoked: "A word is a noun, an adjective, a verb." From all of this, we can see that the concept of *word* takes a considerable amount of time to develop at the metalinguistic level, and that children of different ages take different properties into consideration: links with reality, graphic realization, insertion into larger entities, and categorization.

     As we have already noted in the study of the acquisition of relative clauses, it is only at around the age of 8 that children begin to wonder about the meaning of the pronoun and begin to analyze sentences in an adult grammatical way. From the above study, it is clear that children begin to ponder about the meaning of functors, such as pronouns, only at the stage where they give them the status of a word at the metalinguistic level. In this sense, metalinguistic knowledge clearly influences the automatic know-how aspect of language comprehension. The following question then arises: Why is metalinguistic activity of the type described here the result of such a long development? A possible answer is that metalinguistic ability is a reflective activity, an aspect of the more general capacity of the child to reflect on problems, situations, and events. Here we can see a general link between cognition and language. Cognitive progress leads from subjective to objective thinking, as Piaget demonstrated so clearly. The preoperational child does not reflect in an objective way about the world, the environment, or actions. Greater objectivity seems to develop hand in hand with more sophisticated reflective powers, and this objectivity enables the child to grasp and understand not only physical events and forms of reasoning but also the definition of linguistic units. Expressing this differently, one can say that, by the time the child comes to reflect and think logically about the world or himself, there is no reason to suppose that he will not apply such thinking to language, or, at least, that he does not become able to apply such thinking to language, if he is solicited to do so.

It is interesting to note that a measure of cognitive ability has always been thought to be a good predictor for linguistic competence and mastery. This is obviously the case when we think about IQ scores, particularly as there is a verbal IQ measure within the intelligence test itself. In considering mental retardation for example, IQ scores below the norm have always been thought of as meaning that the child is both cognitively *and* linguistically subnormal. In other words, we have an explicit hypothesis about the link between language and cognition. However, the link implied is not defined in detail; it does not tell us anything about what aspect of cognition influences language, nor does it answer the important question for a developmental psycholinguist: What aspect of cognition is called on during different periods of the child's linguistic development? An attempt to address this question was made by Sinclair and Ferreiro (1970) in their study of passive sentences. These authors suggested that it is progress in *cognitive decentration* that enables the child to abandon a rigid use of the first-noun-as-agent strategy. Both in language and in thinking, they stated,

> We find a process of decentration and coordination which enable, in case of operativity, the constitution of a quantifiable invariant within a system of transformations, and as in the case of our experiment, the conservation of a semantic invariant—the meaning of the sentence—throughout changes in the sentence deriving from a rearrangement of the constituent task.

If we admit that the meaning is preserved when an active sentence is transformed into a passive sentence, the role of cognitive decentration is to be seen in the fact that the child gradually becomes able, first, to conceptualize the same action from two different points of view (that of the agent and that of the patient), and second, to express this point of view choosing the appropriate syntactic structure. In Sinclair and Ferreiro's study, evidence of such cognitive decentering was seen mainly in the elicited production data, also called the *rearrangement-of-constituents task* when the child was asked to start the sentence using the patient. However, such a hypothesis demands further evidence. Support for it came from a study of the comprehension of passive sentences conducted by Chipman (1977). The comprehension of 10 passive sentences was tested with 21 mentally retarded subjects with IQs ranging from 34 to 80 and chronologically aged 5–15. The results were compared to those obtained by Sinclair and Ferreiro. The mentally retarded subjects showed a significantly higher proportion of errors consisting of taking *both* the boy and the girl as *agents* when asked to act out a sentence such as "The boy is washed by the girl," in other words, having the boy and the girl wash each other. These errors, called *reciprocal* errors, were infrequently noted for normal children, but represented one third of all of the errors made by the mentally retarded. Furthermore, in the case of the mentally retarded, such reciprocal errors were made only by the poorest or by the best performers. What, then, is their importance? First of all, they may well represent some kind of hesitation about who is the correct sentence agent and, consequently, may occur at a moment in time when the child begins to regard the second-mentioned noun (the girl) as being a possible agent rather than a patient. This is because he is becoming decentered enough from the first-noun-as-agent strategy to accept the second noun as agent. Second, and this idea also derives from looking at the data of the mentally retarded, the fact that the more successful performers made such errors suggests that this type of comprehension behavior is a step on the road to correct comprehension. It can be suggested that these reciprocal errors represent the moment of change from one stage to another. Perhaps the point at which normal children change from the systematic application of the first-noun-as-agent strategy is short-lived in time, and that is why Sinclair and Ferreiro found less of that behavior than Chipman since mentally retarded children probably go through developmental stages more slowly than normal children. This highlights the interest of comparative research between normal and mentally retarded children because findings from both types of populations can enrich our knowledge not only of a particular aspect but about the process of language acquisition itself.

Progress in cognitive development can probably be seen as the motor of metalinguistic development, and as the source of a more flexible approach to language problems, which, in turn, leads to an abandoning of rigidly applied comprehension strategies. Without some metalinguistic ability, the child may not be able to construct a creative and complete language-competence system. Without sufficient cognitive progress, children may continue to use language comprehension strategies that are developmentally primitive. Both of these considerations become clearer if one looks at the language development in mentally retarded children, and have been highlighted in a comparative study of the language production of young normal and mentally retarded subjects (Chipman & Pastouriaux, 1982). The mentally retarded subjects, aged 5–7 in this study, showed none of the "creative" errors or "risk-taking behavior" outlined by Ramer (1976) for normal children and produced a curious mixture of correct and incorrect forms, which persisted without progressive elimination of the incorrect forms.

Concluding Remarks

In conclusion, we can only suggest three further questions that are of central interest. First, what is the child's repertoire of available comprehension and production strategies at any one period during language acquisition? Second, what makes a child abandon one strategy for another? And third, what is meant by a child's *linguistic competence?*

The first question can be answered only by further research, in particular in the area of language comprehension, as it is here rather than in language production that strategies have been revealed. Even a tentative repertoire in list form will be of great interest to both psychologists and educators. But an even more precise definition of the term *strategy* is required to answer both the first and the second questions. Chipman and Gerard (1982) suggested that a sentence comprehension strategy has two aspects, one linguistic and one psychological. The linguistic aspect is seen in the fact that these strategies we have discussed appear in language comprehension only. Role conservation strategies, as seen in the pronoun experiments, appear when the child is dealing with a particular type of sentence coordination. In other words, certain types of syntactic structures trigger particular strategies that are not applied outside the language field. The psychological aspect is seen in the extent to which a child systematically or nonsystematically uses a particular strategy, as this phenomenon can be analyzed by analogy with psychological concepts such as *generalization*. So, although a comprehension strategy is developed in order to deal with the language sphere only, the extent to which it is applied is a psychological phenomenon. The very fact that strategies appear and disappear, whereas the language structure to be dealt with remains constant, requires an explanation from the sphere of developmental psychology. Change in the use of strategies can therefore be examined only through changes occurring during cognitive development. Finally, the third question may be answered in part by distinguishing what may be termed *natural language competence* from *underlying grammatical competence.* Chipman and Gerard (1985) noted that whenever semantic or pragmatic clues were available, these were used by the children in their study to the exclusion of a syntactic or a parsing analysis of sentences. Such pragmatic behavior is also typical of adult comprehension and represents what all speakers do naturally when interpreting spoken or written language. This may be termed *natural language competence.* It can be contrasted with grammatical competence, which is required when syntactic structures *have to be* analyzed, as in the case of sentences heard or seen in isolation. All of the experiments that we have described show that grammatical competence develops more slowly than natural language competence. The task of a developmental psycholinguist then becomes twofold: (a) to account for the development of both natural and grammatical language competence and (b) to define the relationship between the two.

It is clear that developmental strategies are a central aspect of language acquisition and constitute a far-from-exhausted topic for theory development and research. Furthermore, they represent a true psycholinguistic issue because they are a meeting point of both linguistics and psychological abilities. Whereas cognitive psychology is the area from which speculations concerning change in the use of strategies derive, linguistics helps us to define its field of application. Comprehension strategies are not only a surface aspect of language acquisition, they are an essential component of the dynamics of the process itself. In speculating about them as well as in researching them, we are indeed close to "the heart of the matter."

References

Cambon, J., & Sinclair, H. Relations between syntax and semantics: Are they easy to see? *British Journal of Psychology*, 1974, 65, 133–140.

Caprez, G., Sinclair, H., & Studer, B. Die Entwicklung der Passivform im Schweizerdeutschen. *Archives de Psychologie*, 1971, 41, 23–52.

Chipman, H. H. *The construction of the pronominal system in English in young children*. Unpublished doctoral thesis, University of Geneva, 1974.

Chipman, H. H. *Children's construction of the English pronominal system*. Bern, Switzerland: Hans Huber, 1980.

Chipman, H. H., & Gerard, J. Le traitement de l'anaphore avec et sans contexte linguistique chez le jeune enfant. *Folia Linguistica*, 1981, 15, 1–2.

Chipman, H. H., & Gerard, J. Anaphore et strategies. In J. P. Bronckart, M. Kail, & G. Noizet (Eds.), *Problèmes de psycholinguitique génétique*. Neuchâtel: Delachaux et Niestlé, 1982.

Chipman, H. H., & Gerard, J. Some evidence for and against a "proximity strategy" in the acquisition of control sentences. In B. Lust (Ed), *Studies in the acquisition of anaphora; Defining the constraints*. New York: Reidel, 1985.

Chipman, H. H., & Pastouriaux, F. La construction de phrases simples chez l'enfant normal et arriéré. In J. Rondal, H. H. Chipman, & J. L. Lambert (Eds.), *Psycholinguistique et arriération mentale*. Bruxelles: Mardaga, 1982.

Chomsky, C. *The acquisition of syntax in children from 5 to 10*. Cambridge: M.I.T. Press, 1969.

Ferreiro, E., Othenin-Girard, C., Chipman, H. H., & Sinclair, H. How do children handle relative clauses? *Archives de Psychologie*, 1976, 45, 230–266.

Limber, J. The genesis of complex sentences. In T. E. Moore (Eds.), *Cognitive development and the acquisition of language*. New York: Academic Press, 1973.

Lust, B., Loveland, K., & Kornet, R. The development of anaphora in first language: Syntactic and pragmatic constraints. *Linguistic Analysis*, 1980, 6(2), 217–249.

Papandropoulou, I., & Sinclair, H. What is a word? *Human Development*, 1974, *17*, 241–258.

Piaget, J. *La formation du symbole*. Neuchâtel: Delachaux et Niestlé, 1945.

Piaget, J., & Inhelder, B. *L'image mentale chez l'infant*. Paris: Presses Universitaires de France, 1966.

Piaget, J., & Inhelder, B. *Memoire et intelligence*. Paris: Presses Universitaires de France, 1968. (Written with the collaboration of H. Sinclair.)

Pruner, A., & Solan, L. *Syntactic relations in children's interpretive strategies.* Paper presented at the New England Child Language Association, Amherst, Mass., March 1979.

Ramer, A. Syntactic styles in emerging language. *Journal of Child Language*, 1976, 3(1), 49–62.

Sinclair, H., & Bronckart, J. P. SVO, a linguistic universal? A study in developmental psycholinguistics. *Journal of Experimental Child Psychology*, 1972, 14(3), 329–348.

Sinclair, H., & Ferreiro, E. Étude génétique sur la comprehension, production, et répétition de phrases au mode passif. *Archives de Psychologie*, 1970, 40, 1–42.

Sinclair, A., Sinclair, H., & de Marcellus, O. Young children's comprehension and production of passive sentences. *Archives de Psychologie*, 1971, 41, 1–22.

Slobin, D. I. Grammatical transformations and sentence comprehension in childhood and adulthood. *Journal of Verbal Learning and Verbal Behavior*, 1966, 5, 219–227.

Slobin, D. I. Cognitive prerequisites for the development of grammar. In C. Ferguson & D. I. Slobin (Eds.), *Studies in child language development*. New York: Holt, Rinehart & Winston, 1973.

Introduction to Chapter 7

VALERIE L. SHULMAN

Elsa Schmid-Kitsikis is a practicing clinical psychologist as well as a researcher and theoretician. She is among those neo-Piagetians currently working in Geneva who have accepted the overall Piagetian model but who have expanded it to include additional dimensions. In this case, she has utilized a unique blend of Freudian, Kleinian, and Piagetian theory in order to explicate the dynamics of development in the individual as well as the epistemic subject in both the affective and the cognitive dimensions.

In this chapter, "Clinical Investigation and Piagetian Experimentation," she discusses the advantages and limitations of using Piagetian theory as the basis for a model that encompasses the cognitive and affective domains and their interactions. In so doing, she has woven a theory based on the interplay of Piagetian, Freudian, and Kleinian concepts, particularly those related to Klein's (1948, 1953) expanded concept of unconscious fantasy. To provide a deeper understanding of the integrated theory, Schmid-Kitsikis defines epistemological development in Piagetian terms while describing individual, or emotional, characteristics in Freudian-Kleinian terms. Using this technique, she has been able to reformulate the Piagetian model by postulating discordant characteristics of individual mental development, thus providing a richer, more comprehensive meaning to the model and the myriad facets of development.

One can see the influences of Klein's later work in the structuring of Schmid-Kitsikis's theory, particularly as she seeks to determine the development of the role of unconscious fantasy in relation to the development of cognitive structures. Accordingly, unconscious fantasy begins virtually at birth in the function of the ego and endures throughout life as a pervasive, active force in all individuals, influencing their perceptions and interpretations of reality, and thus affecting their quality of thought. Although during the earliest period the development of internal reality (unconscious fantasy) is not dissociable from external reality, the child gradually begins to distinguish between the two during the depressive position. One then sees the transition to the Freudian view of the duality of the role of fantasy. The first role, modified by the reality principle, becomes thought, which was studied by Piaget (1962, 1976), in its many facets. The second, which remains under the pleasure principle, Freud called "fantasying." However, both forms and their interactions are important to development and are the nucleus of Schmid-Kitsikis's work.

From this, we observe four major points that distinguish Schmid-Kitsikis's work from that of the traditionalists. The first point involves the subjects. Piaget and his colleagues studied the epistemic subject, seeking to identify the similarities across groups that foster the development of the structures and the functional characteristics of cognitive growth: the universal subject and, hence, the universal aspects of development. However, Schmid-Kitsikis has sought to investigate the individual subject. She has attempted to determine the individual elements of personality that restrict, impede, or foster cognitive and affective development, that is, the individual variations that capture the dynamics of mental functioning.

Second, the traditionalists are concerned with the individual becoming increasingly conscious of the external world through increasingly sophisticated conceptualizations: the interplay between adaptation and cognizance. Needless to say, Schmid-Kitsikis is concerned with the individual's relations with his inner world and the ways in which elements of the unconscious impact on his behavior in the external world.

Third, Piaget directed his research to the investigation of only one form of development, one group of defense mechanisms—the logicomathematical structures—as the structures and functional characteristics of development manifested in normative and/or physical behavior. On the other hand, Schmid-Kitsikis has investigated those mechanisms that affect the individual's adaptation to both inner and outer reality and, hence, the development of the positive and negative aspects of an array of defense mechanisms. She has studied the interactions between and among reality and fantasy and the defense mechanisms of fantasy, anxiety, splitting, projection, and introjection found during the early positions that build a complex inner reality for the child. Further, she contends that these elements are as important to the internal world as to the external and, hence, to the interactions between the two.

Fourth, and characteristic of the majority of the neo-Piagetians, is the method of investigation and its subsequent applications. For the most part, the traditionalists have used a variety of methods of investigation, often derived from the clinical method associated with Piaget. In general, these methods have sought to determine normative behavior, leaving little room for divergence. Schmid-Kitsikis, on the other hand, sought a unique method in order to access the material described herein. She has developed a two-phase model based on elements of both Piagetian and Kleinian technique. Whereas the Kleinian technique (particularly as defined by Segal [1964, 1967]) is a valuable means of dealing with the symbolic, phantasmic inner world and the Piagetian method is appropriate for dealing with the normative, objective information from the external world, Schmid-Kitsikis's method attempts to bridge the gap between the two. Her method is capable of determining the ways in which the internal world specifically affects external functioning by noting the manner in which the subject organizes the problem and determines its solutions.

Together, this method and the underlying theory have vast implications for research and practice in a variety of fields, including education and the social sciences. It should be noted that this form of assessment permits the practitioner to determine the ways in which the subject processes various forms of information, and that it thus suggests the most appropriate means of presentation.

References

Klein, M. The development of a child. In *Contributions to psycho-analysis 1921–1945*. London: Hogarth Press, 1948.

Klein, M. The psychoanalytic play technique. *Psychological Review*, 1955, 44, 223–237.

Piaget, J. *Play, dreams and imitation in childhood*. New York: Norton, 1962.

Piaget, J. *The grasp of consciousness: Action and concept in the young child*. Cambridge: Harvard University Press, 1976.

Segal, H. *Introduction to the work of Melanie Klein*. New York: Torchbooks, 1964.

Segal, H. Melanie Klein's technique. In B. Wolman (Ed.), *Psychoanalytic techniques*. New York: Basic Books, 1967.

CHAPTER 7

Clinical Investigation and Piagetian Experimentation

ELSA SCHMID-KITSIKIS

In this chapter, we shall attempt to bring to light some of the contributions and limitations of Piagetian experimentation as applied to clinical research. The term *clinical* is used here in the broadest sense to include all individual psychological functioning, whether pathological or not. Piagetian experimentation did not have such a purpose; Piaget's study of cognitive development emphasized the epistemological aspects more than the psychological ones.

In 1943, Barbel Inhelder attempted to illustrate the universality of the Piagetian model of cognitive development by studying its applicability to the mentally retarded. She attempted to use Piaget's first discoveries concerning intellectual development with mentally retarded children. Although applied to pathology, her approach kept Piaget's basic epistemological framework by maintaining that a parallel exists between logical and psychological development because of the fundamental unity of operational and mental growth. In her conclusions, Inhelder stated that the retarded child's thinking is coherent and in practice comparable to the egocentric thought of the young normal child. Further, the idiosyncrasies of the retarded child's

ELSA SCHMID-KITSIKIS • Faculty of Psychology and the Educational Sciences, University of Geneva, CH-1211 Geneva 4, Switzerland.

thought processes seem to be exaggerations of the processes found in normal children. Retarded children share the patterns of development common to all rational thought, although partially and in an incomplete manner.

Piagetian experimentation in clinical investigation is a fairly recent phenomenon. It is only since the 1960s that attempts have been made at individual psychological investigation that has moved away from some of the epistemological preoccupations pursued by Inhelder and already present in Piaget's early works on *The Child's Conception of the World* (1926/1960), and *The Moral Judgment of the Child* (1932). The central idea of Piaget and Inhelder was to study intellectual development from the point of view of the subject acquiring knowledge rather than to study psychological development in its affective and cognitive dimensions and individual variations.

However, first attempts to use Piaget's theoretical framework in clinical investigation led to studies that demonstrated the sequential stages of intellectual development and almost systematically neglected an analysis of the dynamics involved in the construction of thought. Thus, a paradoxical situation occurred in which Piagetian dialectical thought was applied at a practical level to the psychological testing situation, where performances were quantified but not always qualitatively analyzed. This point seems paradoxical inasmuch as Piagetian theory centers on the study of the structures and the functional characteristics of cognitive growth.

One of the most likely reasons for the somewhat rigid use of elements of this theory is that, in Piaget's work, epistemological and psychological themes are so tightly interwoven that, for practicing psychologists and researchers, his ideas are difficult to handle in any way other than as general and unalterable terms of reference.

For what reason, then, was Piaget's theoretical framework used in clinical investigation? We believe that there are three fundamental reasons. The first concerns the method of investigation itself. This method, with its relational characteristics of interaction between the subject and the investigator and between the subject and the object of knowledge, and with its dialectical characteristics allowing conflicts and integration, facilitates a psychodynamic approach to the individual. Inhelder's work on mental retardation is an outstanding example of the usefulness of this method of investigation, in spite of its epistemological orientation. She successfully illustrated the importance of certain near-normal forms of behavior while pointing out that mentally retarded children are subject to intellectual growth. Further, she remarked, without sufficient emphasis, on the specificity of mental functioning. The examples she cited make us inclined to think that the method reveals the relations between the subject and the object, as well as the influence that the subject's emotional life may have on his cognitive development. Here, *emotional* is used in the broadest sense of the word, to include conscious and unconscious activity.

The second reason originates directly from Piaget's early works, in which he discussed the importance of imagination, with its affective component, for intellectual growth. This aspect of intellectual development is the least dependent on logico-mathematical structures. When Piaget studied the development of symbolic activity, the child's conception of the world, the moral judgment of the child, and so on, he also emphasized the qualities of the child's individual thought, which, in our opinion, is at this time dependent on the pleasure principle, as is characteristic of primary processes. His studies of the young child's egocentric thought are extremely useful in the analysis of the psychological functioning of the child and of the individual in general. By affirming that each child's mental development passes through the same stages with identical mental structures, irrespective of cultural, biological, or emotional contexts, Piaget attempted to account for the universal aspects of cognitive development. However, his analysis of egocentricity illustrates, in a most outstanding manner, how a child progressively disengages himself from the influences of the pleasure principle to meet the demands of the reality principle. This development is made possible by the gradual construction of logico-mathematical structures. Thus, a close look at Piaget's early work reveals the importance of the influence of emotional factors on cognitive development. Consequently, it becomes clear once again that Piaget's method is extremely useful in individual psychological investigation, even when it concerns the pleasure and reality principles and how an individual deals with them by the elaboration of defense mechanisms, logico-mathematical structures, and so on.

The third and final reason that Piaget's ideas are useful in clinical research concerns the analysis of the fundamental factors of mental development (Schmid-Kitsikis, 1979). These factors, comparable to biological development and common to all levels of cognitive growth, are assimilation, accommodation, and their interaction. We shall discuss later how the discovery of the importance of these mechanisms to clinical investigation opened the way to passing from a simple measurement of intellectual performance to the psychodynamic analysis of affective and cognitive development.

Investigative Procedure: General Considerations

We would like to draw the reader's attention to the fact that our main concern here is with the exploration of mental functioning, as our aim is to discuss the contributions and limitations of Piagetian investigation. Therefore, we will not deal with other aspects of an individual's personality.

One of the characteristics of this type of investigation is the selection of test situations. In view of the long history of clinical experimentation, there exist today a number of tests that can be used to collect information concerning behavior, as this term is used in the broad sense to include physical, emotional, and relational, as well as cognitive acquisition. We are, however, categorically opposed to establishing a battery of tests at the outset of an investigation. The Piagetian approach obliges the clinical investigator to formulate hypotheses during the testing, in an ongoing manner in accordance with the initial results. These hypotheses, in turn, guide him in the further choice of testing material. It is therefore neither the subject's age nor the preliminary information that we may have about him that guide the investigation.

The best test situations are those that permit the subject to engage in continuous activity by actually handling and building with materials, to show his ideas and progression in thinking about the resolution of a particular problem. Furthermore, the subject's initial results should permit him to formulate ideas about what he has already accomplished and what he still has to do. It is therefore our belief that, during the first contact with a subject, the clinician should allow the subject to reveal his capacities for initiative and autonomy in a situation where the investigator and the material to be explored are imposed on him. In this type of investigation, the role of the investigator is to encourage the subject to act and think without necessarily forcing him to give an answer. The subject is left to his own initiative, and it is only when he remains inactive or satisfies himself with easy solutions that the investigator may offer suggestions to guide him in his search for answers. Should the investigator be forced to give the correct answer to a particular problem (if the subject really seems incapable of finding a proper solution), it is imperative to verify what the subject has gained from such help on the cognitive as well as the affective level, for example, better use of his knowledge or greater personal involvement.

In such a way, the clinician becomes both an observer and a participant. He is an observer of all of the subject's activities, of what is said, of attitudes expressed, and so on. He becomes a participant on two different levels: as a guide accompanying the subject's discoveries and as a contradictor, facilitating the presence and the continuity of a dialectical process that permits the subject to reelaborate his ideas and to regress momentarily or permanently in his thoughts. In such a way, the subject will reveal his maximum mental capacities as well as his own individual way of functioning. The investigator should not adopt a teaching attitude, as this type of learning situation normally leads not to new acquisitions, unless they are already in the process of elaboration, but rather to optimum functioning.

The Procedure

In accordance with the ideas already stated, the procedure in this type of investigation has two important phases: the subject is at first left free, without instructions, to do as he likes, to speak or to remain silent for as long as seems acceptable to both parties, with materials that he can handle with or without comments. During this period of relative freedom, the clinical investigator can attempt to understand the significance of the subject's behavior in a situation where he is left to handle material at whatever level of expression he chooses: motor, phantasmic, symbolic, logico-mathematic, and so on. It is interesting to note during this phase how the subject goes about making an experimental situation meaningful, when it has not been chosen by him and has purposely been left undefined.

During this phase, then, we intentionally intervene very little and usually only when the subject is completely inactive for such a long period that tension builds up or when his behavior is so stereotyped that we wish to see if he is capable of expressing himself differently. In the case of any type of intervention and because of the clinical nature of such experimentation, the investigator must have, among other things, ample experience in human relations. A very important aspect of our approach is taking into consideration, for example, the emotional aspects of such an exchange.

During the second phase, however, the investigator gives precise instructions for the purpose of soliciting the subject's maximum functioning possibilities in the handling of the proposed problems. The choice of instructions and their order of presentation depend on the particular problem. However, inasmuch as we wish to capture the dynamics involved in a subject's mental functioning, we are also attentive to individual variations and adapt our instructions so as to bring out the qualitative aspects of a subject's performance. Our interventions usually take place at three successive levels:

- A suggestion is made that the subject assume responsibility for the situation that he has still to explore.
- Verbal or gestural stimulation encourages the subject to consider the objectives of the proposed situation.
- Suggestions are made of solutions that at first are only partial and must be completed by the subject.

If no result is obtained, the investigator can complete the task. In this latter case, however, the subject still has to comprehend the solution and attempt to explain it.

This second phase of our approach elicits the subject's capacities for control and thinking effectiveness. It is at this time that the investigator can observe the nature and the quality of the subject's mental mobility, as seen through his reactions to

- Stimulation to produce varied results
- The realities of the experimental situation
- The requirements of moving from one level of mental functioning to another
- The various challenges and conflicts present in the experimental situation that are capable of causing the subject, among other things, to regress and/or to evolve

Analysis of Results

There are three important aspects to be analyzed: the subject's behavior, his acquisitions, and his mental functioning. We wish to treat these three aspects separately, even though they are closely related; the artificial distinction permits us to grasp each aspect's individual significance.

Behavior

The experimental situation in Piagetian investigation is particularly useful in revealing an individual's behavioral characteristics because it requires the creation of a continuously dynamic relationship between the subject and the proposed problem. Whether the problem is to be solved through handling material or verbal communication, the situation in either case allows for an analysis of the subject's attitudes and postures and his emotions, as well as his ability to establish and maintain distance between various poles of interaction, as with objects or individuals. Accordingly, very close observation is necessary to capture all of these different aspects. The investigator should note in detail how the subject reacts to objects and to the investigator; he should indicate the type of body language, if any, as well as emotional reactions. The investigator should also note how the subject expresses his intellectual activities and his emotions when faced with conflict and how he reacts to stimulation during the session. We are particularly interested in evaluating the individual's characteristics concerning the polarity of dependent-autonomous behavior, for it is those qualities that permit us to formulate hypotheses about mental functioning.

Acquisitions

It is extremely important to discover what stable knowledge an individual has acquired, so that we can establish the extent to which such constancy is part of a frame of reference. The existence of invariants, including relational invariants, continuous and discontinuous quantities, space, time and logical concepts, allows the investigator to evaluate a subject's operational level and to analyze

at a psychological level to what extent such factors have contributed
to the establishment of the subject's identity. In other words, a well-
structured ego requires, among other things, that an individual be
capable of maintaining a certain invariant frame of reference, which,
in turn, gives him the mental mobility to decenter his thinking when
the situation requires it. We believe this point to be particularly
important as it has major psychological implications by contributing
to the evaluation of the organizational level of an individual's personality. It becomes possible, for example, to make inferences, if
certain invariants have not been formed, about the quality of a child's
first relational contacts and, in particular, about the genesis of the
object relationship.

The ideas of Winnicott (1971) on this subject are particularly
enlightening. It seems clear to us that in order to be able to construct
and consolidate the idea of invariance, a child must first be initiated
into experience by way of transitional objects and events. The mother
or her substitute makes such transitional phenomena possible by
adapting to the infant's needs and by allowing him to have the illusion that what he creates really does exist. In such favorable circumstances, the ever-increasing possibilities of the child permit him to
deal with relational and rational conflicts; these, then, will not cause
the disappearance or the momentary or definite substitution of the
desired object. Furthermore, belief in one's own existence and capacity to create is also possible. Although the evaluation of stable acquisitions by means of the constitution of invariants is indispensable,
it is equally important to account for disharmonious elements that
introduce themes of insufficiency, lack, or loss. A certain level of
disharmony is worrisome when originating almost solely from splitting mechanisms or inhibition. Such disharmony, however, seems
necessary for the search and maintenance of knowledge, as it provokes constant exchange among elements situated at different
levels of elaboration, because of the psychological dissatisfaction
created.

It is therefore necessary that Piagetian investigation take into
consideration the dynamic relations maintained by the acquisitions
that form the stable nucleus of the individual's ego and those that
are susceptible to modification by evolution, regression, substitution,
and so on, depending on the type of conflict created by outer or inner
reality.

Mental Functioning

In our opinion, the purpose of Piagetian research should be the psychodynamic analysis of mental activity. Our approach, therefore, must formulate criteria that allow for such analysis; they can be divided into two categories—descriptive and interpretive—based on our theoretical framework, which we propose to discuss point by point.

Our study of mental functioning deals with intellectual procedures developed by the individual as well as with the quality of personal investment in such functioning. In fact, it seemed very important to us that an additional dynamic dimension, in relation to libidinal energy, become part of Piagetian investigation. We believe this to be necessary as soon as an investigator becomes interested in conditions of under- or overinvestment in intellectual activity. Therefore, to the hypothesis concerning basic potential, we had to add one concerning the role played by the pleasure principle in relation to the reality principle.

Careful reading of Piaget's work indicates the importance of the "epistemic" as opposed to the psychological subject, to the extent that the cognitive development described and interpreted is one that takes place under optimal conditions; the subject appears to possess the desire to acquire knowledge, and in his interaction with the world around him, no hampering process can affect his evolution. The individual develops functions that guarantee success in the maximum application of intellectual activity. He takes pleasure in thinking, possesses a narcissistic capacity to face conflict, and believes in the relative organizational role of reality, which, however, does not disturb his phantasmic and symbolic activity. Although all these considerations can be found in Piaget's work, they have not been systematically explicated and should be considered postulates. Thus, the fluctuations in an individual's efforts to control knowledge are only momentary and account for Piaget's explanation of regressive tendencies as being necessary to all new acquisition.

Piaget considered only one single group of defense mechanisms that an individual adopts in his quest to control reality, those that account for the most powerful tools of cognitive activity, that is, the logico-mathematical structures. Defense mechanisms originating in phantasmic or symbolic activity were never touched on, for Piaget considered them too sensitive to various forms of regression.

Our approach attempts to integrate Piagetian investigation with the problem of motivational forces in order to clear up the misunderstanding concerning the distinction between epistemology and psychology that was created by the first users of Piaget's work in applied psychology. In other words, we wish not to interpret mental functioning by referring exclusively to an optimal developmental model, but to reformulate the Piagetian model by postulating the discordant character of mental development.

Therefore, our analysis of the subject's methods and answers emphasizes his reactions, which, in turn, permit us to situate his production at a certain level of development. However, we go beyond these considerations to study the degree and the quality of the meaningfulness of the problem and the conflicts that it causes. Furthermore, we deal with the degree and the quality of the distance that the resolution of the problem necessitates, so as to be able to evaluate mental mobility. In short, we are attentive to the following functional characteristics:

Varied Forms of Regression and Fluctuation. We distinguish forms of regression that do not really jeopardize optimal activity from those that drastically modify an individual's level of functioning and force him to stay at a more elementary level. We also distinguish forms of fluctuation that indicate a subject's difficulties at a decisional level from trial-and-error processes that become progressively integrated into a reversible procedure.

Varied Forms of Contradictions and Discrepancies. With contradictions, a distinction should be made between those that imply a splitting mechanism (indicating difficulty in handling opposed points of view, as when a subject defends an answer and its converse at the same time, as if both solutions were equally possible) and the confrontation of opposed points of view where attempted coordination is not immediately coherent. Discrepancies may also occur when the subject has difficulties in sticking to the problem and digresses constantly in directions that have little to do with it. Discrepancies may also occur when the subject remains within the limits of expected behavior but is not capable of maintaining certain points of reference even over short periods of time; his answers or methods thus become "chaotic."

Different Forms of Initiative. These may extend from, for example, the search for analogies, indicating attempts at identification and generalization at the level of objects, procedures, and imagery, to the creation of completely different situations, signs of avoidance, isolation, substitution, deviation, assimilation, and so on, with regard to the proposed problem.

The Varied Modes of Contact with Objects and Individuals. These enable the investigator to define the distance that the individual maintains between himself and the immediate environment. Thus, it is extremely important to specify the body and verbal language used by the subject, being particularly attentive to

- How he uses information
- How he handles materials
- How he progresses in relation to the discoveries he makes
- How he reacts to the examiner's interventions, and so on

It is important to know, for example, if the individual needs direct and continuous contact with objects, if he needs constant stimulation to continue to function, if he has to be reminded repeatedly that he has a certain amount of available information that could be helpful in his discoveries, if he needs the examiner's approval to feel adequate enough to function, and so on, or if his methods reveal a certain autonomy based on self-evaluation and verification of hypotheses.

The Different Reactions to Conflict and Provocation. The subject's reactions to conflict and provocation introduced by the investigator or originating in the procedure chosen by the subject, allow him to solve or not to solve the problem. We are therefore led to relate types of conflict with the reactions that they provoke. This point has already been made in our discussion of regressions, abandon, fluctuations, deviations, and so on, where we attempted to illustrate the significance of such connections for a certain understanding of mental functioning.

Interpretation of Results:
Theoretical Considerations

Although we are interested in the mental functioning of an individual, either child or adult, well adjusted or marginal, we have found none of the models of development, taken individually, satisfactory in helping us to capture mental dynamics in both its emotional and cognitive aspects. Several attempts have already been made to combine psychoanalytic and Piagetian models. Our approach

uses research and clinical investigation to go beyond a purely theoretical orientation; with clinical material, reformulation or even
rediscovery of a means of integration should be possible. We do not,
at the present time, claim to be able to treat all aspects of such
integration exhaustively, we will discuss only those aspects that
concern our current studies.

The problems of interaction between an individual and the
outer world, as well as the mental relations that exist among the
phantasmic, the symbolic, and the normative aspects of thought, are
at the very center of our type of investigation. The following thus
summarizes the hypotheses originating in our attempts to formulate
functional connections.

1. From the very beginning, the evolution of the subject acquiring knowledge depends on the relation between pleasure and displeasure tendencies. These tendencies rely on two fundamental
mechanisms and their interaction: assimilation and accommodation.

2. Adequate evolution of mental functioning (i.e., the capabil-
ity of responding to the requirements of adaptation) can take place
only if the individual can interact with the outer world by testing
the contents of his emotional life in real situations without giving
them up entirely.

3. Three types of experiences, mental, physical, and normative
(logico-mathematical and social), mutually influencing each other,
permit an individual to apprehend reality.

4. An individual confronted with these types of experience
shows, at the mental level, temporary or durable courses of evolution,
depending on the forms of integration of these experiences.

5. The interplay of assimilation and accommodation, connected to the relations maintained between the pleasure and the
reality principles, has an impact on mental functioning and its modes
of organization.

6. Functioning based exclusively on assimilation leads to a
distorted view of the world. Under such circumstances, phantasmic
activity is all-powerful and does not allow symbolic or normative
thought to develop insofar as outside reality is continually denied
existence and destroyed. There is a suppression of the distinction
of the inner and outer worlds. Mental elaboration, in extreme cases,
takes place without sufficient regard to reality.

7. Functioning based exclusively on accommodation leads to
a constant search for a copy of reality and its normative congruence.

The individual submits to the reality principle at the cost of phantasmic and symbolic activity. Once again, there is suppression of the distinction of the inner and outer worlds. In extreme cases, the individual is aware of reality only through what represents its static aspects (i.e., its rules, laws and norms) and does not succeed in grasping the mobility and significance of all its aspects.

8. The individual who is isolated in one or another of these modes of functioning cannot establish an adequate relationship with the outer world. In order to be able to negate conflicts and disturbing contradictions by using compensatory and substitutive processes that necessarily require confrontation between agreeable and disagreeable situations, the individual introduces splitting mechanisms instead. Such cleavage occurs when the subject systematically functions in only one way (assimilation or accommodation) or only within certain contexts. This prevents the kind of coordinations that allow for the formation of variants and forms of generalization.

9. Phantasmic activity is necessary for mobile mental functioning in cognitive development. However, thought that exclusively serves the pleasure principle cannot reach such levels of knowledge as, for example, the normative one.

10. Logico-mathematical activity is necessary for mental functioning that satisfies the requirements of controlling knowledge. However, thought that exclusively serves the reality principle, normative knowledge, rules, laws of logic, social laws, and so on results in the impoverishment of mental dynamics.

11. In both cases, access to symbolic activity is endangered because of the disturbances present in attempts at differentiation between the ego and the object. In the former case, the predominance of the pleasure principle, as the symbol and the object have not been differentiated, the object itself being used as a symbol. In the latter case, the predominance of the reality principle, symbolic activity, whatever the context of the reality, is limited to the creation of a system of signs, rules, and laws.

It was Jean Piaget, in *Biology and Knowledge* (1967/1971), who emphasized the threat that the outer world (as well as the inner one, we might add) represents for the individual, who is a sort of "open system," continually striving to maintain his entity. He succeeds thanks to the constant flow of exchange with the environment. These exchanges take on contradictory forms: the individual tries to close the system in the face of danger and, at the same time, extends the

environment when it is useful to his development. Therefore, the
search for the closing of the system takes place by a delimitation of
the field in such a way that the probability of exchange is sufficient
for conservation. However, this limit toward which the individual
constantly strives is never really attained inspite of the existence of
powerful mental tools such as logico-mathematical structures.

In the Freudian system, we find a parallel notion of the individual's struggle, starting very early in life, against the tendency to
a return to domination by the pleasure principle, which would constantly seriously endanger his vital integrity. Faced with the ever-
increasing demands of reality, the individual must develop, among
other things, defensive behavior so as to survive as well as to progress
sufficiently. He does not, however, have to abandon all activity that
occasionally allows him to escape the too-stringent requirements of
adaptation.

Therefore, we may conclude that, in both cases, the individual
searches for a closing of the system by developing adequate defense
mechanisms or logico-mathematical structures. Furthermore, in both
cases, the individual fights to attain a level of functioning that allows
him to protect his existence with a minimal investment of energy.
The notion that an individual must fight for adjustment is therefore
common to both the Piagetian and the Freudian theoretical frameworks. However, the type of object relation is different. Psychoanalysis is particularly interested in the conflicts occurring around
the pleasure–displeasure, good-bad poles, whereas Piagetian psychology is centered on the conflicts resulting from the search for a
control of normative knowledge, that is, the true-untrue, coherent-
incoherent poles.

An analysis of the unstable relations between the pleasure and
the reality poles illustrates how an individual, in the psychoanalytic
perspective, never reaches permanent equilibrium. Temporary or
more lasting regressions are always possible at all levels of psychic
functioning because even the most elaborate organization is never
the result of a total and definitive reintegration or a restructuring of
more elementary organization.

On the other hand, in the Piagetian system, only momentary
regressions (which are permanent only in cases of organic damage)
which are the results of temporary conflicts caused by the resistance
of the object of knowledge, may occur. The individual who has

overcome moments of disequilibrium, due to a lack of operational structures, reaches the most elaborate form of thought. For Piaget, cognitive functions constitute a specialized organ of regulation in the individual's exchange with the environment, even though the tools of these functions originate from vital organization in its most general form. Such an exchange takes place between the subject and the object. In Piaget's system, even though there is constant reference to the question of the search for equilibrium in the exchange between subject and object and in the interaction between subject and environment, it is nevertheless clear that knowledge is formed within the individual himself, who structures reality by the progressive coordination of actions.

These exchanges, limited to the subject acquiring knowledge and the object to be discovered, take place mainly in two types of experiences: "physical experience," in which the subject acts on an object to discover its properties, which he abstracts from the object, and "logico-mathematical experience," which also obliges the subject to act on an object to discover its properties, this time not abstracted from the object itself but from the subject's actions. Thus, at a certain level of abstraction, actual experience with objects is no longer necessary. By means of coordinations, the subject is capable of producing another level: symbolic operational activity and deductions. Here we find ourselves in an extreme situation, in which the individual, with logico-mathematical structures acting as instruments of integration, becomes increasingly independent of actual experience. Paradoxically, however, these very same structures also allow the individual to acquire more extensive and intimate knowledge of the environment.

We therefore have, on one side, physical experience, which, because of its weak power of abstraction (if it remains at the level of simple abstraction of the properties of an object, without the support of logico-mathematical structures), entails distortions of reality resembling those produced in the case of excessive projective activity. On the other hand, there exists logico-mathematical or operative experience, which, with its great power of abstraction, allows the individual to escape from both the influence of and a resistance to reality.

In the Piagetian system, then, the object of exterior reality is one to be discovered, with its properties, by an individual seeking objective knowledge. Such a search is possible because of two fundamental mechanisms: assimilation and accommodation, functional invariants that are present at all levels of biological and cognitive development but that we believe to be also present in mental and psychic development.

In fact, psychologically speaking, there is assimilation every time an individual "incorporates" (even at the lowest levels, where there is incorporation and expulsion of bodily impressions that are felt to be agreeable or disagreeable) facts of experience into his personal framework. To assimilate a sensory impression, an object, or an event implies acting on elements of an experience in order to modify its properties or relations; to expel would be an act implying modification in the form of an ejection. The transformatory activity that occurs in the process of assimilation is essential. It is the coordination of all initial acts that constitutes the base or schema or origin, indispensable for all subsequent development of more elaborate structures capable of incorporating new objects or events and of seizing new properties and relations. In such a way, an initial schema, or structure, is formed, which at first simply repeats itself and is only progressively extended in order to acquire the power to discriminate and generalize. Because of the process of assimilation, such a schema is then applied to new experiences. Consequently, assimilation is a mechanism that tends to attribute significance to actions that have instinctual origins: needs and the search for their satisfaction. Piaget accepted this point, but he did not consider its specificity. It is not, however, possible to speak of an assimilatory mechanism without reference to the modifications imposed on an individual's schemas by the demands of the environment. It is at this point that accommodation takes place, and everything happens as if the individual has made a "decision" to modify the schemas of his actions when reality resists them. It is when assimilation cannot take place in the usual manner, because of resistance from the environment, that an individual develops adjustments with accommodatory characteristics. Analysis of the functioning of these two mechanisms appears to indicate that they develop in opposite directions. Paradoxically, however, it is only in the case of their harmonious coordination that an individual can attain well-adjusted behavior with regard to the environment.

In fact, purely assimilatory behavior results in a particularly deformed view of the world; the individual is dominated by subjective influences, comparable to dreams, day-dreaming, phantasmatic activity. Such functioning is evident in two movements which do not exclude each other: on the one hand, projection of internal parts of the individual on outside reality, bringing about systematic distortion of reality as it occurs in the case of projective identification; on the other hand, introjection of certain characteristics or properties of the environment, human, mechanical or physical phenomena, into his inner world and which become substitutes for certain parts of himself.

Functioning which is only "accommodating" appears to be a constant search for a copy of reality, of normative conformity as regards the environment. The individual acts as though all his dynamic possibilities, normally employed to bring about change, were totally subjected to the demands of reality.

Thus, an individual, isolated in one or another of these extreme types of functioning, cannot establish adequate relations with the surrounding world. Consequently, various forms of rupture occur: either between assimilation and accommodation, the individual choosing under which influence he wishes to function, or at the level of experimental content, when the individual does not allow for the construction of invariants and forms of generalization, which are necessary for well-adapted mental development, because such construction necessitates coordination with compensatory elements. In other words, because assimilation does not equilibrate itself with accommodation, it cannot attain conservation and remains deforming.

Clinical Research on Mental Functioning

The hypotheses discussed in this chapter originate from extensive practice of psychodiagnosis. They progressively created the need for verification in clinical research and therapeutic practice.

One of the theoretical problems that, from the beginning, was placed in the center of our investigation concerns the different relations that exist between mental functioning and its phantasmic, symbolic and its normative, logico-mathematical, and social realizations. This theoretical problem is now the subject of systematic experimentation.

As we have already emphasized, Piagetian research undertaken in the field of applied psychology resulted in the illustration of lags between operations and discordancies in various cognitive acquisitions. Our own research emphasized the importance of placing such considerations in a perspective that allows bringing to light, through an individual's development, the positions, the organizational forms, and the significance of such acquisitions with regard to various attempts at adjustment. For the normal individual (who progressively tends toward normative objectivity), phantasmic and symbolic activity, characterizing genetically more precocious functioning, constitutes a type of knowledge that participates in the objectivication process. For the mentally deficient or marginal individual, who does not necessarily ever acquire normative thought, phantasmic and symbolic realizations can be of utmost importance and signify, in certain areas at least, adjustment in the face of individual psychological reality. In the same way, a total commitment to normative thinking, which blocks imaginative and symbolic thought, can signify adaptive functioning on the part of the individual. In fact, studies of the thought processes of individuals who are neurotic, psychotic, mentally deficient, obsessional, and so on cannot be made without seeking to analyze the most individualistic pole of thought, with its double dimension of signifier and signified.

This aspect, whatever the level of intellectual development attained, conserves a certain autonomy that we attempt to capture in situations that we hope are free of constraints imposed by normative activity, as, for example, with associations. Thus, our main goal is to succeed in situating the varied reciprocal relations maintained by and the modes of integration present in imaginative and normative thought. Our objectives require that research take place in both diachronic and synchronic perspectives, so as to permit the description of functioning that creates interaction between these two types of thought, as well as the discovery of the importance, the nature, and the sense of imaginative and normative thought in the personal internal dynamics of an individual.

For this reason, our research takes on a genetic and an individual character, although a detailed account of such work would require a lengthy discussion that would be inappropriate here.

Through experimental and therapeutic situations, our work confronts these two types of thought in their most elementary form and significance, as well as in their most advanced ones.

We are interested in several different aspects of thought processes. Besides transitions to activities with a normative character, we also analyze phantasmic content, as expressed in desires, fears, feelings of omnipotence, and so on, and symbolic content expressed in thought that identifies the world by means of "as if." By illustrating the different types of relations—dependency, passiveness, or control, auxiliary dynamics or antagonism—that the above-mentioned types of thought can present, we hope to demonstrate to what extent the search for adaptation is situated within the vital forces of creation, as well as within the powerful ones of mental control.

References

Inhelder, B. *The diagnosis of reasoning in the mentally retarded child.* New York: John Day, 1968. (Originally published, 1943.)

Piaget, J. *The moral judgement of the child.* New York: Harcourt Brace, 1932.

Piaget, J. *The child's conception of the world.* Totowa, N.J.: Littlefield Adams, 1960. (Originally published, 1926.)

Piaget, J. *Biology and knowledge.* Chicago: University of Chicago Press, 1971. (Originally published, 1967.)

Schmid-Kitsikis, E. Mode de fonctionnement mental et modèles du développement psychologique. *Cahiers de Psychology,* 1979, *22,* 43–58.

Winnicott, D. W. *Playing and reality.* New York: Basic Books, 1971.

Introduction to Chapter 8

LILLIAN C. R. RESTAINO-BAUMANN

During the past decade in cognitive psychology, schema theory has played a critical role in the description of the functioning of the mind. Cognitivists have asserted that schemas act reciprocally, helping to interpret events, while being modified and enriched themselves by these same events. Surely, the debt owed Piaget for the current directions in cognitive psychology must be acknowledged by those involved in its study. Piagetian principles of the organization and the processing of information, as represented by the propositional structures of logico-mathematical intelligence, as well as by the functions of assimilation and accommodation, may be detected in both the research and the theory of cognitive processing and cognitive development. However, although Piaget's theoretical principles have had a profound effect on cognitive psychology, a major weakness in his theory is the manner in which he defined the relationship between cognition and perception, that is, what Piagetian theory terms the relationship between operative intelligence and figurative intelligence. By subordinating perceptual processes, without exception, Piaget seriously underestimated perceptual processes and distorted the nature of their role in cognition.

Elsewhere (Restaino, 1978), I have questioned this general subordination of perceptual processes, particularly in view of the research

and the theoretical questions currently being addressed to determining the nature of perceptual functions. For example, the complex
controversy over perceptual processing between the Gibsonians, who
posit the direct perception of environmental events (Mace, 1974,
1977; Shaw & Bransford, 1977), and the constructivists, who posit
rule-governed mediation (Halwes, 1974; Pribram, 1977), has been
the subject of numerous volumes, culminating in Neisser's attempt
(1976) to integrate both positions in his premise of "anticipatory
schemata." The role of developmental processes in perception has
been studied and described in U.S. cognitive psychology at levels
of sophistication that ought to be acknowledged and represented in
Piagetian theory. Specifically, one might expect to find the work of
Gibson (1969), Wright and Vliestra (1975), Day (1975), and Klahr
and Wallace (1976)—all of whom have attempted to define more
precisely the developmental changes in attention and perceptual
analysis, as these affect cognition—integrated into the current considerations of figurative intelligence.

I am very pleased to acknowledge that the chapter that follows
presents a most significant innovation in Piagetian theory because
it subjects this very question of the relationship between figurative
and operative intelligence to intensive criticism, by the Piagetians
themselves. Of equal interest is the experimental methodology that
the authors used to subject their questions to evaluation.

The authors reveal that they are well acquainted with current
work in perception when they hypothesize that there are more complex forms of interaction between figurative and operative intelligence. They have initiated an ingenious program of experimentation,
appropriate to the seriousness of the questions under examination.
Indeed, by itself, their analysis of the content specificity of tasks,
wherein they define the differentiated role of figurative intelligence
in tasks requiring logico-mathematical and infralogical intelligence,
merits strong praise. There will doubtless be arguments about their
premise that the single object–part relationship demanded of
infralogical tasks is more susceptible to figurative interference than
between-object relationships in tasks requiring logico-mathematical
intelligence (Klahr & Wallace, 1976); nevertheless, their analysis is
thorough and justifiable.

Equally praiseworthy are their hypothesized models of the different intraindividual decalages. Of course, it is the nature of the

research question that has initiated this first of their series of experiments which is the focus of our excitement and anticipation— namely, because infralogical intelligence, although still logical intelligence, is nevertheless more susceptible to figurative resistance, as a consequence of the single-object structure of infralogical tasks, then where figurative intelligence demands are held constant, individual or collective decalages should reflect success on logico-mathematical tasks over infralogical tasks. Clearly, there are many problems to be overcome in establishing a program of research that proposes the examination of such complex variables; these researchers have made an auspicious beginning. As their program of work continues in these procedures of analysis, operationalizing, model building, and experimentation, U.S. cognitive psychologists can look forward to creative sources for collaboration in Geneva in the search for more precise definitions of perceptual processing and development.

References

Day, M. C. Developmental trends in visual scanning. In H. W. Reese (Ed.), *Advances in child development and behavior* (Vol. 10). New York: Academic Press, 1975.

Gibson, E. J. *Principles of perceptual learning and development.* New York: Appleton-Century-Crofts, 1969.

Gibson, E. J. How perception really develops: A view from outside the network. In D. LaBerge & S. J. Samuels (Eds.), *Basic processes in reading: Perception and comprehension.* Hillsdale, N.J.: Erlbaum, 1977.

Halwes, T. Mace-Turvey discussion. In W. B. Weimer & D. S. Palmero (Eds.), *Cognition and the symbolic processes.* Hillsdale, N.J.: Erlbaum, 1974.

Klahr, D. & Wallace, J. G. *Cognitive development: An information processing view.* Hillsdale, N.J.: Erlbaum, 1976.

Mace, W. M. Ecologically stimulating cognitive psychology: Gibsonian perspectives. In W. B. Weimer & D. S. Palmero (Eds.), *Cognition and the symbolic processes.* Hillsdale, N.J.: Erlbaum, 1974.

Mace, W. M. James J. Gibson's strategy for perceiving: Ask not what's inside your head, but what your head's inside of. In R. Shaw & J. Bransford (Eds.), *Perceiving, acting and knowing.* Hillsdale, N.J.: Erlbaum, 1977.

Neisser, U. *Cognition and reality: Principles and implications of cognitive psychology.* San Francisco: W. H. Freeman, 1976.

Pribram, K. Some comments on the nature of the perceived universe. In R. Shaw & J. Bransford (Eds.), *Perceiving, acting, knowing.* Hillsdale, N.J.: Erlbaum, 1977.

Restaino, L. C. R. Individual differences in logical operations: An information processing analysis. In *Monograph of the Seventh Annual Conference on Piaget and the Helping Professions* (Vol. 2). Los Angeles: University of Southern California, 1978.

Shaw, R., & Bransford, J. Introduction: Psychological approaches to the problem of knowledge. In R. Shaw & J. Bransford (Eds.), *Perceiving, acting, knowing*. Hillsdale, N.J.: Erlbaum, 1977.

Wright, J. C., & Vliestra, A. G. The development of selective attention: From perceptual exploration to logical search. In H. W. Reese (Ed.), *Advances in child development and behavior* (Vol. 10). New York: Academic Press, 1975.

CHAPTER 8

Horizontal Decalages and Individual Differences in the Development of Concrete Operations

ANIK DE RIBAUPIERRE, LAURENCE RIEBEN, AND JACQUES LAUTREY

Piagetian theory presents cognitive development as a progressive construction of new structures—*structures d'ensemble*—each of which integrates the preceding one while going beyond it. *Structures d'ensemble* are not content-tied but proceed from general reorganizations that result in a certain synchronism of acquisitions at a given moment of development. The existence of such structures, and of their properties of differentiation and integration, confers a unidimensional trend to development: steps or stages are reached in the

ANIK DE RIBAUPIERRE AND LAURENCE RIEBEN • Faculty of Psychology and the Educational Sciences, University of Geneva, CH-1211 Geneva 4, Switzerland. JACQUES LAUTREY • Laboratory of Differential Psychology, University of Paris V, 75005 Paris, France. The study presented in this chapter results from an international collaboration supported both by a grant from the Fonds National Suisse de la Recherche Scientifique (No. 1.835-0.78) and by a grant from the University of Paris V (Type C). It has also used the usual resources of the Faculty of Psychology and the Educational Sciences and of the Laboratory of Differential Psychology (CNRS-ERA 79, University of Paris V, C.N.A.M., E.P.H.E., Section 3).

same invariant order by all subjects; only the rate at which they are reached can vary. This unidimensional model can be regarded as verified only if the construction of notions acquired during the course of development both is synchronous at each step and follows the same invariant order between the steps. However, the existence of synchronism raises problems.

The fact that children master, at approximately the same average age, various notions pertaining to a same operational structure was regarded by Piaget as a confirmation of the existence of *structures d'ensemble*. For instance, notions of conservation, inclusion, and transitivity, which supposedly all require the same form of reversibility, all generally appear at around age 7 or 8. However, this kind of empirical validation is not sufficient to demonstrate the existence of synchronism because Piaget always studied the various notions using groups of children of different ages. With this approach, it is possible to infer the presence of such structures for a hypothetical, theoretical subject—the so-called epistemic subject—but not for each individual subject. To find out whether the properties of the epistemic subject are also characteristic of real subjects, it is necessary to verify whether the same children have indeed simultaneously acquired notions that are supposedly synchronous. This second approach of empirical validation implies that the same subjects must be examined on the different notions for which synchronism is postulated. This is the only way to find out whether the real subject coincides with the epistemic subject.

When this methodological condition is fulfilled, correlations between acquisitions based on the same general underlying structure prove, in fact, to be rather low. The expected synchronism between operations implied in the construction of number was not found (Dodwell, 1960); neither was the synchronism between conservation and measure of volume, nor the synchronism between conservation and seriation of length (Lunzer, 1960, 1965). The median correlation between operational tasks is about .50 when they all belong to the domain of spatial reasoning (Laurendeau & Pinard, 1968) and only .30 when they require operations that are supposed to be isomorphic across domains (Tuddenham, 1971). In order to explain the rather low correlations, Piaget invoked the presence of "horizontal decalages," which disturb the synchronism of acquisitions. Certain decalages would result, for instance, from the resistances that figurative aspects of the situation offer to the subject's structuring activity; these resistances could vary greatly, and in an unpredictable manner, from one situation to another. Piaget often compared their role to that of friction in physics; the complexity and the number of intervening variables would preclude a general theory in both cases. The disadvantage of such a position is obvious: if the strength of correlations depends on unpredictable factors—for instance, on the rather random choice of experimental material—the hypothesis of the existence of general structures becomes impossible to refute. Whether high or low, correlational values are always attributed to unexpected horizontal decalages, an attribution that implies that they are meaningless.[1] This constitutes a basic obstacle to any study of synchronism of operational development, and it is therefore surprising that researchers concerned with the empirical verification of the presence of general structures have generally avoided dealing with it directly.

This obstacle, however serious, is not necessarily insurmountable; indeed, horizontal decalages cannot result in all forms of asynchronisms. They introduce hierarchical relationships between acquisitions: if, for instance, the resistance due to figurative aspects is more important in Problem B than in Problem A, both problems being isomorphic in their operational structure, certain subjects could solve A while still failing B; others could solve both or fail both, but no subjects could solve B while failing A. Such an asymmetrical relation due to the presence of a horizontal decalage can be tested. In cases where the expected synchronism does not appear between two notions, the hypothesis of a horizontal decalage can be invalidated by subjects whose results do not conform to the asymmetrical relation.

In certain circumstances, asynchronisms between notions implying the same structure do indeed seem to follow the asymmetrical relation. This appears to be particularly the case when the quantity of information to process varies greatly from one situation to the other. Experimental manipulation of the information variable has shown that the expected synchronism can exist, for instance, between multiplication of classes and multiplication of relations

---

[1]Horizontal decalages would not have this impact if the correlations were between continuous variables; however, operational variables are, in fact, usually dichotomous (for instance, conservers/nonconservers) or trichotomous (such as nonconservers/intermediate/conservers). The choice of the experimental material might affect the cutoff positions in the distributions, which might, in turn, affect the correlations greatly. As an example, it is well known that a decalage of approximately two years can be found in the acquisition of inclusion, depending on whether the question is asked about flowers or about animals.

(Toussaint, 1974), or between seriation of weight and seriation of length (Gillieron, 1976). Decalages obeying the asymmetrical relation are coherent with a unidimensional model of development: all subjects go through the stages in the same order (AB, for instance), and they differ only in the rate of their development. Following Longeot (1978), we will use the term *collective* for decalages, whether horizontal or vertical, that are in the same direction for all subjects.

Decalages that are not in the same direction for all subjects (for instance, decalages in the direction AB for some and BA for others) raise a different question; they will be called *individual decalages*. When indications are given in the literature not only on the strength, as is usually the case, but also on the form of the relationships between operational tasks belonging to various groupings or various domains, individual decalages appear to be rather frequent (Jamison, 1977; Tuddenham, 1971). Such decalages are hardly imputable to a greater resistance of figurative aspects in either situation, or to a difference in the quantity of information to process; it is obviously difficult to explain how the same situation could be both a source of resistance for some subjects and a source of facilitation for others. It appears, then, that all subjects do not deal with the same features of a situation, or that, if they do so, they process features differently. In both cases, individual decalages indicate not mere variations in rate, but variations in the form of development itself. They are thus inconsistent with a unidimensional model of development. They allow, moreover, a test of the Piagetian conception of the relationship between operative and figurative aspects of knowledge (e.g., Piaget & Inhelder, 1966).

Theoretical Problems Raised by the Distinction between Figurative and Operative Aspects of Knowledge

The distinction between the operative and the figurative aspects, which was rather important in Piagetian theory, has not been reinvestigated in more recent studies. Nevertheless, the problems that this distinction has raised have not vanished. We have therefore decided in this chapter to focus on this distinction and to try to test its validity.

According to Piaget, the function of the figurative aspects of knowledge—perception, imitation, and mental imagery—is limited to identifying and/or representing static configurations. The figurative aspects can provide valid representations of transformations only if they are controlled by operations that issue from the coordinations of actions. Once operational structures are constructed, the figurative aspects become subordinated to the operative aspects of knowledge.

Currently, we question whether perception, imitation, or mental imagery is simply subordinated to operational structures when identifying or representing transformations. We hypothesize more complex forms of interactions between these two aspects of knowledge and postulate that each can contribute to the structuring of actions. Details on the possible implications of such a hypothesis can be found in a critical paper that one of us wrote on Piaget's model of equilibration (Lautrey, 1981). This theoretical divergence on the respective roles of figurative and operative aspects during development explains why we are interested in the form of decalages between isomorphic notions. An account of asynchronisms through the presence of collective horizontal decalages is consistent with the Piagetian conception of the relationships between the figurative and the operative aspects. Indeed, if figurative aspects on their own allow merely a representation of static configurations, operational structures must first break down these configurations in order to generate representations of transformations. This type of resistance to the subject's structuring activity can result in horizontal decalages in the construction of operational structures, which might increase as the situation accentuates the role of perception and imagery. It should be noted that Piaget sometimes conceded a role of facilitation, and not only resistance, to the figurative aspects. However, figurative aspects, even when facilitating, are always regarded as limited to dealing with static configurations. Therefore, decalages could occur in either direction (although more frequently to the detriment of figurative aspects), but they should always be collective, that is, in the same direction for all subjects.

By contrast, if figurative aspects do not play simply a univocal role of resistance to structuring activity, or of facilitation, but contribute, in fact, to the construction of coordinations of actions, more complex forms of interactions can be expected. Depending on whether a type of cognitive functioning relies more on one aspect or on the other, decalages in either sense could be found and, particularly, individual decalages. According to this conception, it is not impossible that some subjects are more advanced in cognitive domains where figurative aspects are more important, whereas others are more advanced in domains where operative aspects are preponderant. By studying the form, and not only the intensity, of decalages between notions that are isomorphic with respect to underlying cognitive structures, but different in the role played by figurative aspects, two different models concerning the relationships between the figurative and the operative aspects of knowledge can be tested.

The study of decalages between logico-mathematical and infra-logical operations seems to be particularly appropriate for this objective. According to Piaget, these two types of operations are indeed isomorphic and their construction obeys the same process of equilibration. Logico-mathematical operations deal with relations of resemblance or difference *between distinct or individual objects*, whereas infralogical operations, particularly in the spatial and physical domains,[2] bear on relations *between interdependent parts of the same object*. The term *infralogical* refers only to a difference of scale between the two types of operations (between or within objects) and not to a difference in their formal properties, which remain identical. The notion of neighborhood in spatial operations, for instance, is equivalent to that of resemblance in the logic of classes; the inclusion of parts of a same object in the whole corresponds to the inclusion of classes; similarly, differences of order in the placement of parts within the same object are equivalent to the relations of differences existing in the logic of relations. Therefore, the structure of infralogical operations can be described by the same formal properties as that of logico-mathematical operations (Piaget & Inhelder, 1948). These two types of operations are thus isomorphic, but distinct with respect to the domain that they structure: discontinuous in one case (logico-mathematical) and continuous in the other (infralogical).

Strictly speaking, the distinction between logico-mathematical operations and infralogical operations does not fully coincide with the distinction between the operative and the figurative aspects of

[2]Infralogical operations also constitute notions of time or of causality, but only those relative to the physical and the spatial domains are considered here.

knowledge. Figurative aspects exist in the construction of both logico-mathematical and infralogical operations. It is, however, plausible to draw a parallel and, in particular, to think that operations of transformation encounter more resistances because of figurative aspects in the infralogical domain. In the first place, the infralogical "whole" has a tangible reality: it is an existing object that can be directly apprehended through perception or representation. On the contrary, the logico-mathematical "whole"—the class, for instance—has no tangible reality: it cannot be directly apprehended through perception or imagery, although it can, of course, be represented. In the second place, the constitutive parts of the infralogical whole (i.e., of an object) are interdependent and are arranged in definite spatio-temporal configurations. The subject's action, actual or represented, must first break down those configurations in order to introduce other relations between the parts. In the logico-mathematical domain, by contrast, the configuration of elements is not pertinent and is not as stable as the configuration uniting the parts of an object. The inter-dependence between elements in the infralogical domain could create a delay in the elaboration of infralogical operations. Finally, operations on a continuum imply a preliminary act of partition: in order to structure relations between elements that are interdependent, the subject must first be able to isolate those elements. In the logico-mathematical domain, objects are more directly accessible to actual or represented actions because they are distinct and are therefore not interdependent. This is the reason that Piaget invoked to explain, for instance, the delay of measuring operations with respect to isomorphic number operations, or the delay of conservation of continuous quantities with respect to conservation of discrete quantities.

If figurative aspects play mainly a role of resistance in the representation of transformations, asynchronisms in the elaboration of logico-mathematical and infralogical operations should generally appear as collective decalages, to the detriment of infralogical operations, or, less frequently, as collective decalages in favor of infralogical operations. Cases of asynchronisms resulting, on the contrary, from individual decalages (i.e., from the fact that some subjects are more advanced in the infralogical domain than in the logico-mathematical domain, whereas for others the reverse is true) would favor a hypothesis of more complex interactions than a simple relation of subordination between the operative and the figurative aspects of knowledge. It appears, therefore, of prime importance to try to reveal the existence of such individual decalages.

Methodological Problems

At first glance, the problem appears to be simple. It would suffice to determine whether each child has reached the same operational level in the infralogical and in the logico-mathematical domains and, if such is not the case, to compare the form of his intraindividual decalage to those of other subjects. In principle, the structuralist approach should provide the means to proceed with such comparisons between domains.

However, the unpredictable character of certain horizontal decalages raises serious obstacles to between-domain comparisons. If one wants, for instance, to compare the level reached in the construction of notions of inclusion to the level reached in notions of conservation, the results will probably vary greatly, depending both on the material chosen to test inclusion—that is, flowers or animals (Piaget & Inhelder, 1959)—and on the shape and size of the containers used to test conservation (Botson & Deliege, 1979). On no theoretical grounds can one or the other of the above-mentioned materials be considered a better indicator of the "true" operational level of the child. Many uncontrollable factors are likely to produce decalages, in addition to the variation of figurative aspects that we can try to control by systematically comparing logico-mathematical and infralogical tasks. This obstacle precludes any possibility of *directly* comparing operational levels reached by a child in different domains.

It appears possible, however, to get around this obstacle by trying to infer the form of decalages from indirect comparisons based on the study of individual differences. To simplify the presentation of this methodological detour, the different possible forms of decalages between levels reached in logico-mathematical and infralogical tasks are first considered as if the obstacle mentioned above did not exist, that is, in an ideal situation. For each task, development can be symbolized by an oriented vector, and it is temporarily assumed that structural correspondences can be precisely established; that is, it is assumed that Level 1 of the logico-mathematical (LM) task does indeed correspond to Level 1 of the infralogical (IL) task, and so on.

In order to further simplify the presentation, it is also assumed that four levels can be defined for each task, and that the two tasks (LM and IL) have been administered to two subjects, Sa and Sb. Individual differences refer to the subjects' relative positions in each task, that is, the advance of Sa on Sb or the reverse. When two tasks are compared, the existence of decalages between them and the existence of permutations in the subjects' order constitute two independent variables. The combination of these two variables, each of which can be present or absent, leads to the description of four possibilities, represented in Figure 1: (1a) absence of permutation between subjects, absence of decalage; (1b) absence of permutation between subjects, presence of decalage between tasks; (1c) presence of permutation between subjects, absence of decalage between tasks; (1d) presence of permutation between subjects, presence of decalage between tasks.

Case 1a of Figure 1 describes a complete synchronism of development; each subject reaches exactly the same level in both tasks.

Case 1b corresponds to a decalage in the same direction for both subjects (advance of the LM task on the IL task for both subjects). Furthermore, the decalage is of the same intensity for Sa and Sb (i.e., a decalage of two levels). For these reasons, a decalage of this type is called *homogeneous collective decalage*. It respects a less stringent criterion of synchronism than case 1a; the subjects are not at the same level, but they progress concurrently in both tasks: the lead of Sa on Sb in the LM task is conserved in the IL task.

This weakened model of synchronism is violated by the permutation in case 1c. By contrast with a collective decalage, the intraindividual decalages of both subjects are in opposite directions: advance of Sb in the LM task and advance of Sa in the IL task. Decalages of this type are called *individual decalages*.

Case 1d cannot be considered an individual decalage in the sense just defined, even though there is also a permutation of the relative positions of Sa and Sb. The decalage between the levels reached in the two tasks is in the same direction (advance in the LM task for both subjects) but is not of the same intensity (three levels of decalage for Sb and one level for Sa). Decalages of this type are called *heterogeneous collective decalages*, by contrast with the homogeneous collective decalages illustrated by case 1b.

Among the cases that violate a model of synchronism, whether strong or weak, only individual decalages (Figure 1c) can weaken an explanation referring to a univocal role of figurative aspects

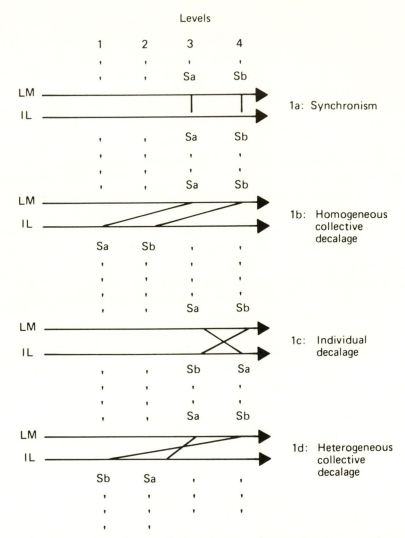

Figure 1. Various types of intraindividual decalages between levels reached by two subjects Sa and Sb in a logico-mathematical (LM) and in an infralogical (IL) task.

(whether of facilitation or of resistance). Within such a conception, the intervention of figurative aspects can hardly be regarded both as making the task more difficult for some subjects and as facilitating it for others. The hypothesis of a univocal role of figurative aspects can, however, be maintained, provided that it is modulated, in the case of heterogeneous collective decalages (Case 1d). If resistance due to the influence of figurative aspects is regarded as varying greatly in intensity from one subject to the other, this variation would be sufficient to explain both the collective decalage and the permutation of subjects. Consequently, the only procedure that can effectively test the hypothesis of the univocal role of figurative aspects consists in trying to reveal the presence of individual decalages. This approach is, in fact, all the more difficult in the real situation of observation, where, unlike in the ideal, artificial situation that was just considered for purposes of demonstration, direct correspondences cannot be easily established between tasks.

In the real situation of observation, the probable intervention of uncontrollable variables resulting in decalages prevents the establishment of exact correspondences between the levels reached in LM and IL tasks. It is as if, for the different cases illustrated in Figure 1, the LM and IL scales were subject to all types of unpredictable shifts, each with regard to the other, that is, as if each scale could be lengthened or shortened like a rubber band. How then can the form of decalages be described under such conditions?

One can try to draw inferences regarding the form of decalages from a study of individual differences, provided that the sources of decalage, even though they prevent direct correspondences between tasks, conserve the order of acquisitions *within* each task. In case 1a, for instance, the advance of Sb on Sa would be conserved whatever the shifts of one scale with respect to the other might be. By relying on the mere properties of order internal to each task, it is possible to decide between the various cases in Figure 1, and in particular between Cases 1a and 1b, on the one hand, and Cases 1c and 1d, on the other. Whenever the subjects' ordering is identical for the two tasks, the hypothesis of synchronism cannot be rejected, although it is not possible to know whether the synchronism is strong (1a) or weak (1b). On the other hand, any permutation in the order of subjects from one task to the other is contradictory to the hypothesis of synchronism, without its being possible to decide whether it is a case of individual decalage (1c) or of heterogeneous collective decalage (1d). The logic underlying such comparisons between pairs of subjects is, in fact, the same as that implied by the computation of the Kendall tau coefficient. When comparing LM and IL tasks, a value of the tau coefficient close to 1 means that there are few permutations in the ordering of subjects; one can therefore assume the existence of either a synchronism of acquisitions or of a homogeneous collective decalage that is compatible with an explanation of asynchronisms in terms of a greater resistance due to the figurative aspects.

By contrast, a low value of the tau coefficient implies that the hypothesis of synchronism is invalidated; the data can then be accounted for either by individual decalages or by heterogeneous collective decalages, without its being directly possible to decide which. In the last case, however, a certain asymmetry should appear between the two tasks that are compared. But heterogeneous collective decalages can be demonstrated only under certain conditions: there has to be a difference of at least one level between the two tasks for the subject whose intraindividual decalage is the smallest (in Case 1d, Level 3 on the LM task and Level 2 on the IL task for Sa); because, by definition, heterogeneous collective decalages introduce permutations between subjects, Sb must present an advance of at least one level on Sa for one task and a delay of at least one level for the other task. The result is an intraindividual decalage for Sb of at least three levels between the two tasks (cf. Sb in Case 1d). Consequently, heterogeneous collective decalages can be demonstrated only when items can be hierarchically ordered in at least four levels, and when a subject is at Level 1 on one task and at Level 4 on the other. Such asymmetrical patterns can indeed result from the exaggeration of collective decalages, for certain subjects; these patterns must, however, all be in the same direction. If they occur as frequently in one direction as in the other, the hypothesis of collective decalages has to be rejected, and only individual decalages can then account for a low tau-coefficient value.

Let us call α and β the two cells of a contingency table that correspond to such asymmetrical patterns (see Table 1): α cell includes subjects who perform at Level 4 on the LM task and at Level 1 on the IL task, whereas cell β corresponds to the opposite pattern. A comparison of α and β should then allow us to determine which type of decalage exists. Table 1b presents such a contingency table for two tasks: the Intersection-of-Classes (LM) and the Unfolding-of-Volumes (IL) tasks, both administered to 154 subjects. A simple inspection of the table shows that α contains more subjects than β: this asymmetry could, however, merely result from unequal marginal frequencies. This effect can be neutralized by relating the observed

Table 1. Contingency Tables of LM and IL Tasks

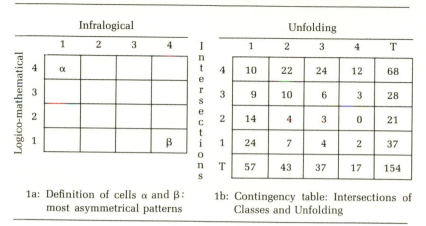

1a: Definition of cells α and β: most asymmetrical patterns

1b: Contingency table: Intersections of Classes and Unfolding

frequencies n to the theoretical frequencies n'; the difference between the two frequencies n and n' must then be weighted by the theoretical frequency. Thus a weighted frequency is computed for each cell: $f = (n - n')n'$.[3] The observed frequencies of cells α and β that correspond to the greatest discrepancy between the two tasks, are generally lower than the theoretical frequencies, as the two tasks present at least some degree of correlation. The weighted frequency $f = (n - n')/n'$ is therefore generally negative and is to be considered an algebraic value. In Table 1b, $f_\alpha = (10 - 25.1)/25.1 = -.60$, and $f_\beta = (2 - 4.08)/4.08 = -.51$; therefore, the weighted frequency f_β is, contrary to appearance, somewhat higher, in terms of algebraic value. In fact, the two frequencies are very close, and it is their relation that is of interest. This can be expressed through an *index of dissymmetry* $(Id = (f_\alpha - f_\beta)/|f_\alpha + f_\beta|)$, which is preferable to a simple ratio f_α/f_β because it varies from -1 to $+1$.[4] Index Id is equal to 0 when $f_\alpha = f_\beta$; it is positive when f_α is greater than f_β, that is, when there are more subjects who perform at Level 4 on the LM task and at Level 1 in the IL task than subjects who present the opposite

[3]The signification of such weighted frequency is close to the contribution of each cell. However, the deviation here is not squared because its direction is important.

[4]It is at least the case when observed frequencies are systematically inferior to theoretical frequencies. The index could, however, be greater than 1 if the theoretical frequencies were higher than the observed frequencies in one cell and lower in the other.

pattern; it is negative when f_α is less than f_β. In Table 1b, $Id = [(-.60) - (-.51)]/|(-.60) + (-.51)| = -.08$; as Id is very close to 0, the hypothesis of heterogeneous collective decalage can be rejected, and asynchronisms between the two tasks can be interpreted as resulting from individual decalages.

To summarize, the aim of the present study is to test the Piagetian view of the relations between the operative and the figurative aspects of knowledge by examining the form of decalages between logico-mathematical and infralogical tasks. This can be done through the methodological approach presented here.

Experimentation

Two tasks requiring logico-mathematical operations and six tasks requiring infralogical operations were administered to the same sample of children.[5,6]

The Sample

One hundred and fifty-four children ranging in age from 6 to 12 (with 22 subjects per age group) were examined on these eight operational tasks. The sample consisted of Genevan children, as representative as possible of the Genevan primary-school age-range population.

The Tasks

It is not possible to give here a detailed description of each task (material, experimental procedures, scoring procedures, and so on). Such a description can be found in Rieben, de Ribaupierre, and

---

[5]For the purpose of this chapter, it would have been preferable to use four LM and four IL tasks. However, this study was also geared toward objectives other than those presented here. A general presentation of the research, in which the present study is inserted, can be found in Lautrey, de Ribaupierre, & Rieben (1981a) and in Rieben, de Ribaupierre, & Lautrey (1983).

[6]Partial results concerning the first half of the sample have been presented elsewhere (Lautrey, de Ribaupierre, & Rieben, 1981b).

Lautrey (1983). The tasks are simply enumerated here, and the reader is referred to the studies of Piaget and his collaborators, from which the tasks have been adapted.

    1. *Logico-mathematical tasks*. Intersections of Classes (Piaget & Inhelder, 1959); Quantification of Probabilities (Piaget & Inhelder, 1951).

    2. *Infralogical tasks*. Physical notions: Conservation of Substance, Weight, and Volume (Piaget & Inhelder, 1941); "Islands" (construction of volume—Piaget, Inhelder, & Szeminska, 1948). Spatial notions: Unfolding of Volumes and Sectioning of Volumes (Piaget & Inhelder, 1948). Mental imagery: Folding of Lines, Folds and Holes (Piaget & Inhelder, 1966).

Results

    The methodological approach for the experiment included three phases. First, it was necessary to verify that each task presented hierarchical levels of success. Scale analyses of the items of each task allowed such a study. A second phase consisted of trying to determine whether the data showed a synchronism, strict or weak, or an asynchronism of development; this determination was made through the computation of Kendall's tau coefficient. Where there was an asychronism, it was then necessary in the third phase to decide between the hypothesis of heterogeneous collective decalage and the hypothesis of individual decalage, through the computation of an index of dissymmetry. The results are presented, following the order of these three phases.

Scale Analyses

    All items need not be hierarchically ordered among themselves. It is sufficient that a strong hierarchy be found between groups of items, without any precise order required within each group. The method of scale analysis developed by Longeot (1969) allows the computation of an index with respect to the relation of order between groups of items, independent of the relations of order existing within each group. This index varies between 1, when the observed patterns are totally coherent with an ordered structure, and 0 when they present a random distribution.

Table 2 shows that the index of hierarchy was approximately .70 for items of the Intersection-of-Classes task and for the spatial tasks, which is not very satisfactory, and close to .90 for the other tasks, which indicates a strong hierarchy. For the three tasks where the items were not strongly hierarchical, the order was strengthened by regarding the subjects who succeeded on *both* of two weakly scaled items as being at a higher level than the subjects who solved one or the other. This distinction was also used to equalize the frequencies of the different levels of success. The 154 subjects were thus distributed among four scaled levels of success on each of the eight tasks.

The Analysis of Relations between the Tasks through Kendall's Tau Coefficient

Table 3 presents the correlations between the eight tasks (the coefficient used here is Kendall's tau B, with corrections for exaequo); all the values are significant at a level of p less than .05, and range from .23 to .50, with a median correlation of .39. As the children's ages range from 6 to 12 years, these correlations are not very high.[7] By taking into consideration all correlations higher than the

Table 2. Indexes of Hierarchy

Logico-mathematical	⎰ Intersections of classes	.71
	⎱ Quantifications of probabilities	.90
Physical Domain	⎰ Conservations	.92
	⎱ Islands	.89
Spatial Domain	⎰ Unfolding of volumes	.75
	⎱ Sectioning of volumes	.63
Mental Imagery	⎰ Folding of lines	.82
	⎱ Holes	.90

[7]The reader used to product–moment correlations has to remember that tau coefficients are usually lower than r coefficients when both can be calculated, in particular with respect to their average values. By computing r on the present data, it was possible to determine that the underestimation of tau was approximately .07. The structure of correlations remained similar for both coefficients, which was not necessarily evident. This provides one more reason to think that the asynchronisms responsible for low correlations in other studies using the r coefficients were probably not due to homogeneous collective decalages.

Table 3. Tau Correlations between Eight Experimental Tasks

	1 Prob	2 Int	3 Cons	4 Isl	5 Lines	6 Unf	7 Holes	8 Sect
1. Probabilities	—	.43	.40	.34	.34	.37	.38	.23
2. Intersections	.43	—	.47	.38	.37	.39	.39	.31
3. Conservations	.40	.47	—	.50	.40	.41	.38	.37
4. Islands	.34	.38	.50	—	.50	.40	.38	.38
5. Lines	.34	.37	.40	.50	—	.44	.40	.39
6. Unfolding	.37	.39	.41	.40	.44	—	.46	.43
7. Holes	.38	.39	.38	.38	.40	.46	—	.35
8. Sectioning	.23	.31	.37	.38	.39	.43	.35	—

median value (i.e., equal to or higher than .40), two main clusters can be found. A first cluster consists of the two LM tasks (Intersections of Classes and Quantification of Probabilities) and the task of Conservation. A second cluster consists of four IL tasks: Conservation, which thus plays a role of junction with the first cluster; Islands; Folding of Lines; and Unfolding of Volumes. The two other IL tasks (i.e., Holes and Sectioning of Volumes) are close to this second cluster, without entirely belonging to it, given the correlations that they present, respectively, with Folding of Lines and Unfolding of Volumes. Generally speaking, such a distinction coincides with that discussed above between IL and LM tasks, with two exceptions: the strong correlation existing between Conservation and the two LM tasks[8] and the low correlation between two IL tasks (i.e., Holes and Sectioning of Volumes).

By looking at the overall ordering of the correlations, the distinction between IL and LM tasks can appear in a different light. The correlations among IL tasks are close to a simplex: they decrease starting from the diagonal, in line as well as in column (here again, the correlation between Holes and Sectioning of Volumes constitutes an exception). This implies that they can be ordered along a common dimension. The two LM tasks cannot be integrated, however, into such a structure: they obey it in column but not in line.

It was discussed above that the comparison between levels of development on the IL and the LM tasks can serve as a way to control

---

[8]In the previous results based on the first half of the sample, it was not the Conservation but the Islands task (i.e., the other physical task) that presented a high correlation with LM tasks; this outcome could, in fact, be more easily interpreted (Lautrey, de Ribaupierre, & Rieben, 1981b).

the between-situation effects of variations in the role of figurative aspects. Correlations tend to be stronger when two LM tasks or two IL tasks are compared to each other than when an LM task is compared to an IL task; this finding is compatible with the hypothesis that variations in the figurative aspects create asynchronisms in the acquisitions. However, an explanation of asynchronisms only through homogeneous collective decalages can be dismissed, as the value of the tau coefficient, which is insensitive to such decalages, is not very high. It is, then, necessary to study whether these asynchronisms result from heterogeneous collective decalages or from individual decalages.

The Analysis of the Indexes of Dissymmetry

Table 4 presents the indexes of dissymmetry between each LM task and each IL task. The corresponding contingency tables can be found in the Appendix.

Certain indices are rather close to 0, and when they diverge from 0, they are as often positive as negative. It is difficult, however, to know whether this is due to random fluctuations around the zero value, or whether some indexes are different enough from 0 so that one can conclude that they reflect heterogeneous collective decalages. This would require that we know the sampling distribution of frequencies in cells α and β well enough to determine the level at which an index differs significantly from 0. This problem cannot be solved for the moment, but it can be partially overcome by the following observation. For three of the IL tasks, the transformations to be represented affect only visible elements: the folding of differently colored lines drawn on tracing paper that is folded along a determined axis (Folding of Lines); the lowering of the faces of a volume,

Table 4. Indexes of Dissymmetry $(f_\alpha - f_\beta)/|f_\alpha + f_\beta|$

LM tasks	IL tasks					
	Lines	Unfold	Cons	Sect	Isl	Holes
Probabilities	−.43	.01	.16	−.18	.37	.43
Intersections	−.08	−.08	−.18	.20	.13	.34

each face being visible when the volume is manipulated (Unfolding of Volumes); the displacement of the parts of the ball of playdough when it is transformed (Conservation).[9] In the three other IL tasks, on the contrary, the transformations to be represented affect only internal parts of the object, which cannot be directly apprehended through perception or imagery: parts situated within a solid object (Sectioning of Volumes, Islands) or hidden by successive foldings (Holes). The sign of the indexes in Table 4 coincides closely with this distinction "surface-interior:" the index is negative or null when the operation deals with surfaces, in five cases out of six, and positive when it deals with the interior of objects, also in five of the six cases. Positive indexes indicate a preponderance of decalages due to a delay in the IL operations over LM acquisitions. Assuming that the value of such positive indexes is high enough for the hypothesis of individual decalages to be rejected, the Piagetian hypothesis of a subordination of figurative aspects to operative aspects can be maintained in such cases; asynchronisms of development responsible for the relatively low tau-coefficient value could then be accounted for through variations in the magnitude of the LM advance for different subjects (heterogeneous collective decalages). But this explanation can be maintained only when the index is positive, that is, when IL operations deal with the interior of objects.

   This demonstrates as well, by contrast, that if the IL operations deal with surfaces, that is, when situations can be directly apprehended through perception or imagery, asynchronisms of development can *not* be explained through collective decalages. In these cases, the indices are either null or negative, which means that at least some subjects are more in advance in IL operations than in LM operations. These data are not easily made compatible with the hypothesis of a subordination of figurative to operative aspects of knowledge.

---

[9]The last case is less clear: the solution of volume items requires, indeed, that subjects also take the interior of the object into consideration (incompressibility); the different status of the conservation-of-volume items with respect to substance and weight is, in fact, not crucial because few children solve the problem, given their age at the time of examination. However, the nonhomogeneity of all Conservation items with respect to the distinction "surface–interior" could help to explain the contradictory results of Conservation with respect to the two LM tasks: the index is positive with Quantification of Probabilities, and it is negative with Intersections.

Discussion

In Piagetian theory, the hypothesis relative to the subordination of figurative to operative aspects of knowledge is linked to the hypothesis of the existence of *structures d'ensemble*. According to this conception, operational structures resulting from the coordination of actions are assumed to constitute a unique source of the organization of cognitive behaviors, controlling all aspects of knowledge. The theory goes as far as to admit that the intervention of figurative aspects can create horizontal decalages between isomorphic notions. Figurative aspects are regarded as constituting a resistance to the subject's structuring activity; variations in the degree of resistance could explain low correlations between acquisitions that are assumed to belong to the same *structure d'ensemble*.

If it is correct to interpret asynchronisms of development in this manner, the decalages that cause them should be in the same direction for all subjects (collective decalages). If not, individual decalages must be hypothesized, which call into question both the notion of *structures d'ensemble* and the hypothesis of a subordination of figurative aspects to operative aspects. An analysis of the form of decalages offers a means of experimentally testing both assertions of Piaget's theory.

However, an approach such as that presented above encounters two main obstacles resulting from the unpredictability of between-situation variations due to the effects of figurative aspects. A theoretical obstacle resides in the difficulty of defining a factor of systematic variation of figurative aspects, which would help to determine the ways in which figurative processes play a more important role in one situation than in another. The distinction between LM and IL domains appears to offer this possibility. A second obstacle is methodological and results from the fact that unpredictable decalages can be created by sources other than those controlled by the LM-IL distinction; such factors prevent the establishment of direct correspondences between levels reached in different domains, and they do not allow an analysis of the form of decalages that could be attributed to a controlled source of variation. It appears possible to get around this second difficulty by analyzing the form of individual differences. The method is based on the following premise: if there is an individual decalage (i.e., a decalage in opposite directions for different subjects), it must result in permutations in the subjects' order on different tasks. The reciprocal is not necessarily true: permutations in the subjects' order can be caused by heterogeneous collective decalages as well.

The comparison between the levels of success on eight operational tasks showed that variations in the frequency of permutations tend to coincide with the theoretical distinction between LM and IL tasks and are thus consistent, although not entirely so, with the variation in the role played by figurative aspects. Through the computation of indices of dissymmetry, it appeared that all permutations cannot be accounted for by collective decalages, even if they are heterogeneous ones, resulting from a systematic delay of the IL operations with respect to LM operations. Although the hypothesis of the heterogeneous collective decalages can be maintained when the subject has to operate on the object's interior, this is not at all the case when the parts of the object that have to be taken into consideration by the subject can be directly apprehended through perception or imagery. In this second case, certain subjects still present an intraindividual decalage to the detriment of IL tasks, where figurative aspects are supposed to be more important; however, other subjects, generally even in a greater number, show evidence of the opposite decalage. These findings are not compatible with the Piagetian hypothesis of a univocal subordination of figurative aspects to operative aspects. They call for consideration of more complex forms of interaction than a subordination, or at least than a univocal relation, between these two aspects of knowledge. Such forms of interaction, in which each aspect could help direct the other while also being directed by it, introduce a greater flexibility in the form of cognitive development than is postulated by the Piagetian theory.

Such an interpretation is consistent with the general outcome of our results, but it cannot yet account for all results. It has been noticed that two correlations did not coincide with the IL-LM distinction (the correlations of Conservation with the two LM tasks), and that two indices of dissymmetry were not congruent with what could be expected from a distinction among IL operations based on whether they deal with visible or nonvisible elements of objects (i.e., Quantification of Probabilities with both Conservation and Sectioning of Volumes). These exceptions cannot yet be satisfactorily and entirely interpreted.

Another shortcoming of the results comes from the lack of clear differences between the correlations on the basis of which clusters can be established (Table 3). It can be hypothesized that the grouping of ages tends to mask a stronger structure that would appear only relatively late in development. The lack of clear differences could also result from the superimposition of different structures existing at different periods of development. To investigate these problems further, it would be necessary to analyze the data for different age groups separately; that is the next step planned in this series of experiments.

References

Botson, C., & Deliege, M. Quelques facteurs intervenant dans la progression des raisonnements élémentaires. *Bulletin de Psychologie*, 1979, *32*, 539–555.

Dodwell, P. C. Children's understanding of number related concepts. *Canadian Journal of Psychology*, 1960, *14*, 191–205.

Gillieron, C. Le rôle de la situation et de l'objet expérimental dans l'interprétation des conduites logiques. *Archives de Psychologie*, 1976, 44 (Monographie No. 3).

Jamison, W. Developmental inter-relationships among concrete operation tasks: An investigation of Piaget's stage concept. *Journal of Experimental Child Psychology*, 1977, *24*, 235–253.

Laurendeau, M., & Pinard, A. *Les premières notions spatiales de l'enfant.* Neuchâtel: Delachaux et Niestlé, 1968.

Lautrey, J. L'équilibration suffit-elle à guider la coordination des actions? *Psychologie Francaise*, 1981, *26*, 259–272.

Lautrey, J., de Ribaupierre, A., & Rieben, L. Le développement opératoire peut-il prendre des formes différentes chez des enfants différents? *Journal de Psychologie*, 1981, *14*, 421–443. (a)

Lautrey, L., de Ribaupierre, A., & Rieben, L. *Lois générales et différences individuelles dans le développement opératoire.* Paper presented at the Colloque International du C.N.R.S.: Les Niveaux d'Explication en Psychologie, 1981. (b)

Longeot, F. *Psychologie différentielle et théorie opératoire.* Paris: Dunod, 1969.

Longeot, F. *Les stades opératoires de Piaget et les facteurs de l'intelligence.* Grenoble: Presses Universitaires de Grenoble, 1978.

Lunzer, E. Some points of Piagetian theory in the light of experimental criticism. *Journal of Child Psychology and Psychiatry*, 1960, *1*, 191–202.

Lunzer, E. Les coordinations et les conservations dans le domaine de la géométrie. In V. Bang & E. Lunzer (Eds.), *Études d'épistémologie génétique* (Vol. 19). Paris: Presses Universitaires de France, 1965.

Piaget, J., & Inhelder, B. *Le developpement des quantités chez l'enfant.* Neuchâtel: Delachaux et Niestlé, 1941.

Piaget, J., & Inhelder, B. *La représentation de l'espace chez l'enfant.* Paris: Presses Universitaires de France, 1948.

Piaget, J., & Inhelder, B. *La genèse de l'idée de hasard chez l'enfant.* Paris: Presses Universitaires de France, 1951.

Piaget, J., & Inhelder, B. *La genèse des structures logiques élémentaires.* Neuchâtel: Delachaux et Niestlé, 1959.

Piaget, J., & Inhelder, B. *L'image mentale chez l'enfant*. Paris: Presses Universitaires de France, 1966.

Piaget, J., Inhelder, B., Szeminska, A. *La géométrie spontanée de l'enfant*. Paris: Presses Universitaires de France, 1948.

Rieben, L., de Ribaupierre, A., & Lautrey, J. *Le développement opératoire de l'enfant entre six et douze ans: Elaboration d'un instrument d'évaluation*. Paris: Editions du C.N.R.S., 1983.

Toussaint, N. A. An analysis of synchrony between concrete operational tasks in terms of structural and performance demands. *Child Development*, 1974, 45, 992–1001.

Tuddenham, R. D. Theoretical regularities and individual idiosyncrasies. In *Measurement and Piaget*. New York: McGraw-Hill, 1971.

Appendix

LINES

INTERSECTIONS

	1	2	3	4	
4	6	9	24	29	68
3	5	6	6	11	28
2	10	4	3	4	21
1	21	6	5	5	37
	42	25	38	49	154

UNFOLDING

	1	2	3	4	
4	10	22	24	12	68
3	9	10	6	3	28
2	14	4	3	0	21
1	24	7	4	2	37
	57	43	37	17	154

CONSERVATIONS

	1	2	3	4	
4	2	18	25	23	68
3	6	6	10	6	28
2	7	12	2	0	21
1	20	11	3	3	37
	35	47	40	32	154

SECTIONING

INTERSECTIONS

	1	2	3	4	
4	9	6	24	29	68
3	7	3	9	9	28
2	6	5	9	4	21
1	14	11	8	4	37
	36	25	47	46	154

ISLANDS

	1	2	3	4	
4	9	28	16	15	68
3	12	8	4	4	28
2	9	10	2	0	21
1	22	11	3	1	37
	52	57	25	20	154

HOLES

	1	2	3	4	
4	14	18	15	21	68
3	14	8	6	0	28
2	12	8	1	0	21
1	22	11	4	0	37
	62	45	26	21	154

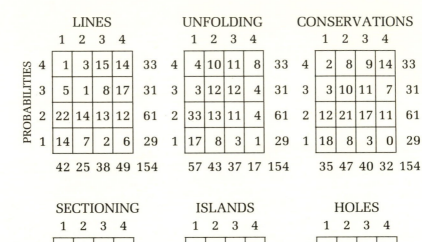

LINES	1	2	3	4	
4	1	3	15	14	33
3	5	1	8	17	31
2	22	14	13	12	61
1	14	7	2	6	29
	42	25	38	49	154

UNFOLDING	1	2	3	4	
4	4	10	11	8	33
3	3	12	12	4	31
2	33	13	11	4	61
1	17	8	3	1	29
	57	43	37	17	154

CONSERVATIONS	1	2	3	4	
4	2	8	9	14	33
3	3	10	11	7	31
2	12	21	17	11	61
1	18	8	3	0	29
	35	47	40	32	154

SECTIONING	1	2	3	4	
4	3	4	13	13	33
3	6	3	11	11	31
2	14	14	16	17	61
1	13	4	7	5	29
	36	25	47	46	154

ISLANDS	1	2	3	4	
4	6	12	7	8	33
3	4	13	7	7	31
2	25	21	10	5	61
1	17	11	1	0	29
	52	57	25	20	154

HOLES	1	2	3	4	
4	8	6	7	12	33
3	6	9	12	4	31
2	29	22	5	5	61
1	19	8	2	0	29
	62	45	26	21	154

The vertical axis of each table is labeled PROBABILITIES.

Introduction to Chapter 9

LORETTA BUTLER

Alberto Munari is currently a full professor in the Department of Applied Genetic Psychology, where his teaching focuses on the implications of Piaget's psychology for educational work—both "inside" and "outside" the school. In regard to the inside aspects, a special concern is directed to institutional and organizational problems; in regard to the outside aspects, he has paid special attention to mass media communication. Munari has also carried out investigations on the psychological development of some basic socioeconomic concepts, such as the child's concepts of money, value, work, and work roles.

Paralleling his academic work, he is engaged as a U.N.E.S.C.O. consultant in program development for school systems throughout Europe and the developing countries in Africa. His research has focused on aspects of the Italian schools, children's perceptions of economic systems, and questions of the structures of experimental knowledge.

Following Piaget's basic epistemological assumption that knowledge is a particular case of the more general adaptation process between an organism and its environment, Munari has been perennially interested in the structure of knowledge. As early as 1971, his doctoral thesis revealed his involvement in the structuring of models of knowledge. The title of his dissertation, "Perception of

*Scholastic Models: An Attempt at Verification of a Probability Model
of Perceptive Mechanisms Proposed by Piaget,"* reveals his interest
in models by which human knowledge can be structured. Consonant
with Piaget's theory and research on models, Munari considers three
additional models—the empirical-experimental model, the hypothetico-deductive model, and the historical-critical model—but he
then pursues new combinations of these models in a more comprehensive or (as he terms it, following Piaget) complete experimental
model.

   In pursuit of the logical components of knowledge, Munari is
cognizant of the contributions of the logician Jean-Blaise Grize of
the University of Neuchâtel, at one time a collaborator of Piaget. He
is also interested in the relationship of the INRC (identity, negation,
reciprocity, and correlation) group at the formal stage of reasoning.
This interest in the logical approach to epistemology is also evident
in the work of Hans Furth (Thinking Goes to School), and aspects
of the various models proposed by Juan Pascual-Leone, the Canadian
scholar. It is important to note that Munari was also familiar with
the work of the Bourbaki group and with the relationship of Piaget's
formal model to the emergence of the "new" mathematics. Thus, it
is evident that the main focus of Munari's research has been the
study and analysis of models of knowledge and the subsequent
applications of these models to pedagogy.

   Other research interests pursued by Munari have to do with
analyses of the stages of development in the child's knowledge of
anatomy and economics and with the implications of formal knowledge for the teaching of science and mathematics. Finally, it could
be anticipated that his future research will be dedicated to the pedagogical implications of the formal models articulated within the
framework of his Piagetian background.

References

Furth, H., & Wachs, H. Thinking goes to school. New York: Oxford University Press,
     1974.
Munari, A. Probability of scholastic models: An attempt at verification of a probability
     model of perceptive mechanisms proposed by Piaget. Geneva: Delachaux et
     Niestlé, 1968.

CHAPTER 9

The Piagetian Approach to the Scientific Method
Implications for Teaching

ALBERTO MUNARI

One cannot really understand the importance of Piagetian psychology, and thus the pedagogical implications of it, if one does not understand its epistemological foundations. Piaget himself said on many occasions that his psychological work was the consequence of epistemological questions that he raised at the beginning of his scientific career. For instance, in 1961 he wrote:

> I decided that for building a biological epistemology it would have been necessary—in the absence of any information on the philogenesis of knowledge and on the prehistorical sociogenesis of men's knowledges— to devote myself to an equivalent of the embriogenetic analysis, and thus to study the growth of the intelligence in the child and the development of the principal intellectual operations. I proposed spending some five years in these preliminary studies, and then returning to general questions. But these preliminary studies occupied me for forty years, and it is from a period of less than ten years that I can approach epistemology from the genetic point of view that I decided to assume. (Beth & Piaget, 1961)

ALBERTO MUNARI • Faculty of Psychology and the Educational Sciences, University of Geneva, CH-1211 Geneva 4, Switzerland.

The years that Piaget devoted to psychological research are probably more important than the ones he consecrated to epistemological reflection. Nevertheless, Piaget is to be considered more an epistemologist than a psychologist. He was a psychologist *because* he was an epistemologist. He studied the development of intelligence in children *because* he was interested in the growth of human knowledge in general. His fundamental assumptions and questions were that knowledge is a particular case of the more general adaptation process between an organism and its environment; thus, what are the mechanisms of this particular adaptation process? Are they the same as for the more general processes? These kinds of questions clearly show the close relationships between biology and psychology in Piaget's theory. But adaptation may have several degrees of success. Thus, how is well-adapted knowledge possible? This question raises the fundamental one: how to explain the fit between formal thinking—as in the sciences—and the empirical world.

Answers to these questions could explain why Piaget's psychology was primarily interested in the development of logico-mathematical thinking, from its more spontaneous and natural appearance, as in the cognitive structures that may be recognized in every knowing subject, to its more formalized aspects, such as those realized in the history of sciences. Thus, genetic psychology and genetic epistemology are two complementary approaches to the same problem:

> Human sciences have to be studied by epistemology as any other kind of knowledge. But on the other hand, what human sciences tell us about man may be useful for understanding the mechanisms of knowledge. Epistemology of the psychologist, of the sociologist, of the linguist, of the economist, etc.; and epistemology of the subject studied by psychology, by sociology, by linguistics, by the economy, etc.: these are the two mainstreams of problems we have to face. (Piaget, 1967)

Jean Piaget's greatest scientific plan was to realize a tight integration between psychology, logic, and epistemology. More precisely, the main objective was to use the experimental results of genetic psychology to provide a better understanding of the epistemological problems of logico-mathematical thinking. These fundamental considerations are particularly relevant when one wishes to grasp the pedagogical implications of Piaget's work. Their misunderstanding leads to erroneous or at least partial interpretations. For example, one of the main pedagogical suggestions that many teachers recognized in Piaget's work is the need to enhance the occasions on which the child may exercise experimental activity. One must allow the child to be generally active, in opposition to assuming the passive attitude usually requested by the traditional school; Dewey, Montessori, Claparède, and Freinet had already formulated this suggestion. Piaget's suggestion refers to a particular kind of activity: *experimental inquiry*—the activity of knowing. This systematic activity of knowing has to be developed not only because it responds to the spontaneous motivations of the child, but moreover because it is the basic character of knowledge, from the early cognitive behavior of the very young child to the sophisticated intellectual work of the scientist, in the development of an individual's cognition as well as in the growth of scientific knowledge. But as Piaget himself pointed out, experimental research does not limit itself to the application of the so-called experimental method alone. It also involves two other fundamental methods of scientific inquiry: the hypothetico-deductive method and the historical-critical method. The traditional approach distinguishes three kinds of scientific methodologies:

1. The empirical-experimental method
2. The hypothetico-deductive method
3. The historical-critical method

Figure 1 summarizes the principal steps of the empirical-experimental method.

Normally, these three methodologies are considered distinct, each belonging to a particular scientific approach:

1. The empirical-experimental method is the method of the natural sciences.
2. The hypothetico-deductive is the method of the axiomatic sciences.
3. The historical-critical is the method generally used by the philosophy of sciences.

In fact, any experimental approach to reality necessarily involves the empirical-experimental *and* the hypothetico-deductive methods, which are strongly correlated. Any systematic observation of reality implies the use of logico-mathematical instruments, and any kind of analysis of experimental data implies some sort of modeling.

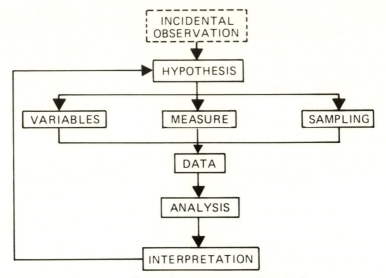

Figure 1. The empirical-experimental method.

Thus, from this point of view, any experimental approach to reality simultaneously raises two kinds of new problems; some relate to new experimental hypotheses, others to new formal hypotheses. The confrontation between these two methods enriches the experimental as well as the deductive approach and leads to progress in scientific knowledge. Figure 2 schematically shows the interrelations of the two methods, thus proposing a first representation of the general process.

The manner in which scientists use these methods, or the conjunction of the two, is not independent of the cultural context of the moment, nor is the manner in which new problems give rise to new experimental or formal hypotheses. These cultural determinants are also responsible for the growth of scientific knowledge. Thus, they raise *epistemological hypotheses* that must be studied and analyzed by the historical-critical method. This brings one to epistemological problems, raising new experimental hypotheses and new formal hypotheses, as well as new epistemological hypotheses. This is the *complete* system of the broad experimental approach to knowledge, as used by Piaget in his work. With Piaget, the "real" experimental method, the "natural" experimental inquiry, is shown in the spontaneous activity of the child, or in the professional work of the scientist. The diagram of the complete experimental method based on Piaget's theory is presented in Figure 3.

The study of the formal and concrete operational reasoning of the child, conducted by Jean Piaget in collaboration with Jean-Blaise Grize, a logician from the University of Neuchâtel, is a particularly good example of this approach, although in its more elaborated form of the scientific inquiry. In studying the reasoning of the child at the formal stage (from about the age of 12), Piaget found that the mental operations of these children are strongly structured and interrelated. These experimental results suggested to him the hypothesis that a formal model may be utilized for describing this level of reasoning. For example, in the search for a *proof* (experimental as well as formal) of an *implication*, the child goes through four distinct operations, which may be formalized as follows:

The implication: $p \rightarrow q$ may be verified by:

1. Repetition (I): $p \rightarrow q$
2. Negation (N): $p \wedge \overline{q}$

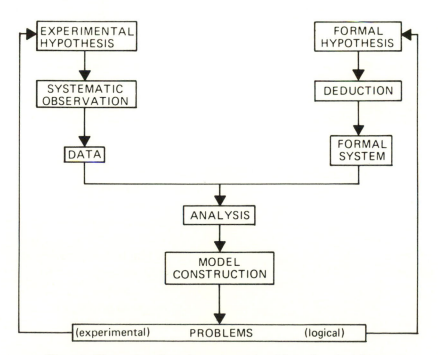

Figure 2. The conjunction of experimental and formal methodologies.

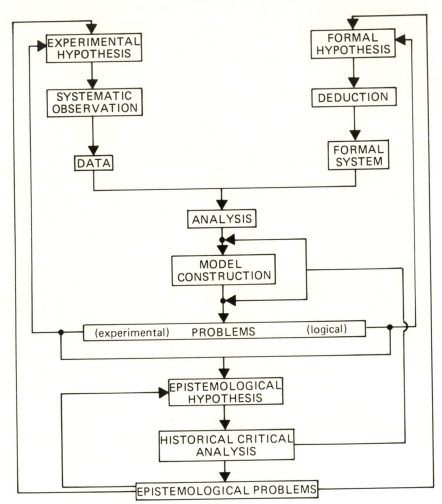

Figure 3. The complete experimental method.

3. Reciprocal (R): $q \rightarrow p$
4. Correlative (C): $q \wedge \overline{p}$

These four operations are constructed in an "Abelian group," as shown by Figure 4:
where:

a. $\forall(x) \; \forall(y)$: $x \; r \; y = y \; r \; x = z \in E$
(Closure and symmetry)

b. $\forall(x)\ \exists(n): x\ r\ n = n\ r\ x = x$
(Neutral)

c. $\forall(x)\ \exists(i): x\ r\ i = i\ r\ x = n$
(Inverse)

d. $\forall(x)\ \forall(y)\ \forall(z): (x\ r\ y)\ r\ z = x\ r\ (y\ r\ z)$
(Associativity)

This analysis, and the resulting model, has been arrived at by combining the empirical-experimental method with the hypothetico-deductive method. But at the end of this work, a new problem arises: What happens with younger children, at the concrete operational stage? "They do not combine the same operations (I, N, R, and C) in the same way as their elders do," said Piaget. "So, what kind of formal structure can be used for modeling this sort of reasoning?" asked Grize. Piaget went further in his experimental research; Grize, in his formal deductions. From their close collaboration, a new model emerged: the *groupement*, a new algebraic structure that is not only for the experimental psychologist, but also for the logician. One can easily see that this dialectic interaction between these two methodologies is full of potential growth of factual as well as formal knowledge. But this interaction and its results are not independent of its own historical and cultural context of the moment in which they appear. The particular attention that Piaget reserved for the formal model is probably not independent of the great interest and subsequent discussions raised at that time by the Bourbaki group

	I	N	R	C
I	I	N	R	C
N	N	I	C	R
R	R	C	I	N
C	C	R	N	I

Figure 4. The four operations of the Abelian group.

and the consequent disputes about "new" mathematics. On a more personal level, the particular kind of psychology and epistemology that Piaget built is not independent of his own history as a biologist, a naturalist, and a man of the beginning of the twentieth century.

The implications of these brief methodological reflections for school practice, with particular reference to science teaching, are easily recognizable. They can be summarized as follows:

1. No type of empirical experimentation can be done without some formal modeling, even if at a very simple level; measuring, for instance, is already modeling, which can be analyzed at many different levels of complexity, depending on the conceptual capabilities of the child.

2. Mathematics and experimental sciences ought to be much more connected and interrelated in school practice, for instance, by active verification of several models of the same set of experimental data.

3. Mathematical concepts do not result only from a formal deductive process but are frequently suggested by empirical experiments; the history of mathematics is rich in examples of this kind.

4. The discoveries of natural sciences, and the systems elaborated by the axiomatic sciences, are not independent of the particular historical moment in which they were formulated.

5. Therefore, *the historical evolution of a concept* must always be pointed out. Transformations, changes, and passages from one concept to another—in the collective as well as in individual knowledge—are much more interesting and informative than the concepts themselves.

6. When studying a particular science, distinguish *but do not dissassociate* its four constitutive domains:

a. The material domain, constituted of the specific objects studied by this science (they may be physical, biological, psychological, mathematical, and so on).

b. The conceptual domain, constituted of the theories elaborated by this specific science on the objects studied (i.e., number theory, mass theory, evolutionary theory, and so on).

c. The internal epistemological domain, constituted of the (meta) theories studying and criticizing the fundamentals of the conceptual domain.

d. The derived epistemological domain, constituted of the (metameta) theories comparing the results of this science with those of other sciences, and thus analyzing how its emergence and its development has been possible in the context of general knowledge.

A final recommendation is never to consider a problem too complicated for a child; there is surely some way to make him understand or at least to perceive some aspects of it. The "metalogues" between Gregory Bateson and his daughter are a good example. Admittedly, this synthesis of models of formal reasoning requires additional exploration. However, the six implications for teaching have immediate relevance to research and also to classroom practice.

References

Beth, E. W., & Piaget, J. *Épistémologie mathématique et psychologie.* Paris: Presses Universitaires de France, 1961.

Piaget, J. *Logique et connaissance scientifique.* Paris: Gallimard, 1967.

Epilogue

LILLIAN C. R. RESTAINO-BAUMANN

Having studied the chapters in this book, the reader is bound to ask: What are the future directions of Piagetian theory, and specifically the theories of the neo-Piagetians? Although we do not presume to predict how the traditional Genevan school will further evolve, we have attempted to provide an insight into how the neo-Piagetians have begun to show a trend toward more individualized endeavors rather than a mere perpetuation of "traditional theory." As we acknowledged earlier, we have viewed our role as that of introducing and presenting these works against the background of what is considered "traditional Piagetian theory."

Until recently, many of the contributors to this book had received limited exposure in the United States. Their work was known through brief references by Piaget, bearing on specific points that supported the parent theories. We acknowledge that, in the past, the research and the researchers represented here had taken their focus from Piaget's evolving, comprehensive theories. That research was generated by and supportive of principles within the master theories. Although we acknowledge the independent significance of the research that they pursued, nevertheless, their work drew its greatest

LILLIAN C. R. RESTAINO-BAUMANN • School of Education, Fordham University, New York, New York 10023.

significance from its relationship to the continuously evolving parent theories.

However, since Piaget's death, these bodies of research have begun to acquire their own significance. In other words, the Genevans have now begun to find the importance of their individual research pursuits within the framework of the evolving theories of specific domains of their own selection, rather than merely within the frame-work of Piaget's evolving theory. They themselves are now the source of the continuing evolution of Piagetian theory, although they are restricted to their own areas of concern; and thus, it is essential that they integrate into that evolution current advances in their chosen domains.

But if the individual Genevans pursue their research as mem-bers of their chosen areas, how then, does the Genevan school func-tion as a school? Although Piagetian theory is no longer evolving from the mind of the Master, nevertheless, the legacy is rich and strong—and its psychological implications are yet to be fully real-ized. Thus, as it is with the individual acquiring new knowledge, viewing it from new perspectives, and developing, so it is with the Genevan school. It will be through the assimilation and accommo-dation of new data in these new domains that the theory—and hence, the school—will continue to evolve.

The reader of this book could not have failed to be struck by the lack of recognition of the work of their own Genevan colleagues reflected in the individual papers. Although they are working in the same institution, with the same theoretical focus and the same men-tor, these authors show little attempt to relate their findings to one another's work. Needless to say, we anticipate that this will change as they strive to maintain a cohesion within the school.

In the first section, these potential relationships are very clear. Bullinger describes the infant's increasing awareness of the workings of his own body, that is, his awareness of his body as the object of his actions. Bullinger even postulates the genesis of this awareness in prenatal development. Mounoud extends the examination of the subject's awareness of his body as object in terms of the develop-mental changes of the subject's construction of his self-image, again subject as object. Clearly, these two neo-Piagetians are constructing fundamental principles of the subject's developing awareness of his actions and image, completely independent of one another. Collaboration between Bullinger and Mounoud would hold great promise for clinicians interested in the emotional aspects of the self, as well as for cognitivists interested in the functioning of the cognitive processes.

In the second section we begin to see the evolution of interactional concerns—that is, interindividual interactions—on both an individual and a group basis. This area is among the most promising as a basis for integrating companion theories, explicating the social and emotional dimensions of development that have been ignored within the parent theory. Schmid-Kitsikis has provided insight into the ways in which the individual responds to and interprets the environment. On a larger plane, Doise demonstrates how the individual child gains additional information from others at a similar level and how he incorporates the information gained from others. To date, Schmid-Kitsikis and Doise have not worked together to investigate those characteristics of the individual that foster or impede interaction and interindividual informational exchange.

Finally, in the third section, we observe that the work of de Ribaupierre, Rieben, and Lautrey provides challenges for Genevan researchers on at least two levels: first, their careful analyses and operationalization of the variables being examined provide an experimental test of the hypotheses of concern that can be more readily understood and accepted by the mainstream of cognitive psychologists; and second, their willingness to subject to further query the relationship between perceptual and operational intelligence can lead to a series of exciting Piagetian-based experiments involving what is termed *depth of processing* in American psychology.

Once again, the relationships between the principles of perception and cognition being examined by de Ribaupierre, Rieben, and Lautrey and those examined by Bullinger and Mounoud are very clear to those of us on the outside. It is our expectation that, once the Genevans begin to implement the principles of their colleagues' work, the relationships between perception and cognition that they construct will provide cognitive psychologists with formidable theoretical principles with which to pursue their own research questions.

It is our belief that the Genevan school has the opportunity to provide means for interaction and integration between the narrow research concerns pursued by perceptual, cognitive, clinical, and social psychologists, so that the comprehensive description of human behavior initiated by the founder of their school may be continued. This narrowness of research is a serious problem in American psychology, which many decry but few try to solve. The Genevan school has a rare opportunity to provide leadership for psychology through the construction of a description of human development that covers the diversity of motivation and emotional, cognitive, and social processes while demonstrating and explaining the elegant relationships between these processes.

Index